Letter from an
Unknown Woman

Rutgers Films in Print

Charles Affron, Mirella Jona Affron, and Robert Lyons, editors

My Darling Clementine, John Ford, director
edited by Robert Lyons

The Last Metro, François Truffaut, director
edited by Mirella Jona Affron and E. Rubinstein

Touch of Evil, Orson Welles, director
edited by Terry Comito

The Marriage of Maria Braun, Rainer Werner Fassbinder, director
edited by Joyce Rheuban

Letters from an Unknown Woman, Max Ophuls, director
edited by Virginia Wright Wexman with Karen Hollinger

Rashomon, Akira Kurosawa, director
edited by Donald Richie

8½, Federico Fellini, director
edited by Charles Affron

La Strada, Federico Fellini, director
edited by Peter Bondanella and Manuela Gieri

Breathless, Jean-Luc Godard, director
edited by Dudley Andrew

Bringing Up Baby, Howard Hawks, director
edited by Gerald Mast

Chimes at Midnight, Orson Welles, director
edited by Bridget Gellert Lyons

L'avventura, Michelangelo Antonioni, director
edited by Seymour Chatman and Guido Fink

Meet John Doe, Frank Capra, director
edited by Charles Wolfe

Invasion of the Body Snatchers, Don Siegel, director
edited by Al LaValley

Memories of Underdevelopment, Tomás Gutiérrez Alea, director
introduction by Michael Chanan

Imitation of Life, Douglas Sirk, director
edited by Lucy Fischer

Letter from an Unknown Woman

Max Ophuls, director

Virginia Wright Wexman

and Karen Hollinger,

editors

Rutgers University Press

New Brunswick, New Jersey

Letter from an Unknown Woman
is volume 5 in the *Rutgers Films
in Print* Series.

**Library of Congress Cataloging-in-
Publication Data**

Main entry under title:

Letter from an unknown woman.

  (Rutgers films in print series; v. 5)

  Filmography: p.

  Bibliography: p.

  1. Letter from an unknown woman (Motion
picture)
I. Ophuls, Max, 1902–1957. II. Wexman,
Virginia Wright. III. Hollinger, Karen.
IV. Letter from an unknown woman (Motion
picture)
PN1997.L4563L49   1986   791.43'72
                        85–27909
ISBN 0–8135–1159–3
ISBN 0–8135–1160–7 (pbk.)

Screenplay courtesy National Telefilm As-
sociates and Richard Rosenfeld Associates.
Still on p. 139 and poster on p. 186 courtesy
British Film Institute. Still on p. 16 courtesy
The Museum of Modern Art/Film Stills Ar-
chive. Frame enlargements courtesy Republic
Pictures Corporation, owner and distributor of
Letter from an Unknown Woman.
"Letter from an Unknown Woman" in *The
Royal Game and Other Stories* by Stefan
Zweig, translated by Jill Sutcliffe, English
translation © 1981 by Atrium Press, Ltd. Used
by permission of Harmony Books, a division of
Crown Publishers, Inc. "Front and Center" by
John Houseman in *Front and Center.* Copy-
right © 1979 by John Houseman. Reprinted by
permission of Simon and Schuster, Inc. "Script
to Screen with Max Ophuls" by Howard Koch
in *Film Comment* (Winter 1970–1971):40–43.
Copyright © 1970 by the Film Comment Pub-
lishing Corp. Reprinted by permission of The
Film Society of Lincoln Center. "Interview
with Max Ophuls" by Jacques Rivette and
François Truffaut in *Cahiers du Cinema* 72
(June 1957): 7–25, translated by Jennifer
Batchelor, in *Ophuls*, edited by Paul Willemen,
1978. Reprinted by permission of the British
Film Institute, London. *New York Times* review
by Bosley Crowther, April 29, 1948. Copyright
© 1948 by the New York Times Company.
Reprinted by permission. *Variety* review by
Baxt. Reprinted by permission of Variety, Inc.
"Max Ophuls" by Andrew Sarris in *The Ameri-
can Cinema* (1968):70–72, reprinted by per-
mission. "The Question Oshima" by Stephan
Heath in *Wide Angle* 2, No. 1 (1978):48–57.
Reprinted by permission of Johns Hopkins
University Press. "Time and Desire in the
Woman's Film" by Tania Modleski in *Cinema
Journal* 23, No. 3 (Spring 1984). Reprinted by
permission of The University of Illinois Press.
"The Ophuls Text: A Thesis" by Paul Wille-
men, originally published in *Ophuls*, edited by
Paul Willemen, 1978. Reprinted by permission
of British Film Institute, London. "Ewig hin
der Liebe Glück" from *Personal Views: Explo-
ration in Film* by Robin Wood (London: The
Gordon Fraser Gallery, 1976):116–132. Reprinted by permission of Robin Wood.

Acknowledgments

Like the film it documents, this book is the product of a collaborative effort. The Ophuls biograph, the transcription of the screenplay, and the notes on the shooting script were done by Karen Hollinger, while Virginia Wright Wexman compiled the bibliography and filmography and wrote the introduction and headnotes, aided by a sabbatical leave granted by the University of Illinois at Chicago. Joyce Drzal at UIC's Office of Instructional Resources was of great help in obtaining prints. The Library of Congress, the Museum of Modern Art, and the British Film Institute were also helpful in arranging for screenings and stills. Joseph Scalafani of Republic pictures generously gave permission for the reproduction of frame enlargements, and John Houseman kindly provided us with a copy of the letter from Max Ophuls we have reprinted. The laborious task of typing the transcribed screenplay was cheerfully and efficiently carried out by Cheryl Baumbach. The series editors, Mirella Affron, Robert Lyons, and E. Rubinstein, offered valuable advice and information; and Leslie Mitchner, the editor at Rutgers, guided our progress at every stage with enthusiasm and understanding.

Contents

viii   **Contents**

Filmography and Bibliography

Introduction

The Transfiguration of History

Ophuls, Vienna, and *Letter from an Unknown Woman*

Virginia Wright Wexman

The masters of our profession, René Clair or Jean Renoir, for example, Jacques Becker in his late work, or John Ford in many of his early films, in their best moments of "in-sight" transcend both dramatic structure and dialogue, and create a new kind of tension which, I believe, has never existed before in any of the other forms of dramatic expression: the tension of pictorial atmosphere and of shifting images. They have the same impetus and produce the same beauty and excitement that can be found in the pure procession of words in the classical theater, where logic is thrown overboard, over the footlights, so that it is the sound and rhythm of the words alone which inspire and maintain the spectators' belief in the action. Just as in the theatre the lighting, the set, faithfulness to nature and other incidentals must play a subordinate role to the word, so in films the words, the technology and the technique and the logic of the visible must be secondary to the image, subordinate to the vision containing untold wonders within it, which, in the cinema, can be the bearer of artistic truth.
—Max Ophuls[1]

1. Max Ophuls, "The Pleasure of Seeing: Thoughts on the Subject Matter of Film," trans. Robin Mann, in *Ophuls*, ed. Paul Willemen (London: British Film Institute, 1978), pp. 33–34.

I adore the past. It is so much more restful than the present. And so much more reliable than the future.
    —the narrator of *La Ronde*

More than most, Max Ophuls's films seem timeless. *Letter from an Unknown Woman* does not seem dated today; it did not seem timely in 1948. Set in a bygone world represented as an elegant fantasy, it addressed no contemporary cultural or political issues and failed to attract the mass audience Hollywood courted. Subsequent critical reaction and Ophuls's own statements about his art reinforce its claim to an a-historical status; it substitutes "the tension of pictorial atmosphere and of shifting images" for social and topical concerns. Yet Ophuls's attachment to the past is in part an attachment to a specific historical moment (the majority of his films are set at the turn of the century) and a particular place (three are set in Vienna). The significance of such settings goes beyond the purely pictorial; they express a vision of the past not as an escape from the restlessness and unreliability of the present and future, but as the origin of these instabilities. Fredric Jameson has observed that "the production of aesthetic or narrative form is to be seen as an ideological act in its own right, with the function of inventing imaginary or formal 'solutions' to unresolvable social contradictions." [2] In Ophuls's work, the extreme formalism which marks the aesthetic solution may be taken as an indication of the highly sensitive nature of the underlying social contradiction.

What did fin-de-siècle Vienna mean to Ophuls? Historically it occupies a special position as "the foremost generator of our current sensibility," as George Steiner has called it. [3] In this world the past and future meet: a rich tradition of architecture and music confronts a new cultural milieu that speaks of the twentieth century, including figures such as Freud, Schoenberg, and Wittgenstein. Ophuls returns repeatedly to this moment. He romanticizes and stylizes it through his formal virtuosity; he is enthralled by the issues it raises.

To understand the meaning of old Vienna in Ophuls's films one must first understand his convoluted depiction of time. Though the issue of temporality provides the focus for much of the critical literature on Ophuls, commentators

2. Fredric Jameson, *The Political Unconscious* (Ithaca: Cornell University Press, 1981), p. 79.
3. Quoted in Malcolm Bradbury and James Macfarlane, "The Name and Nature of Modernism," *Modernism, 1890–1930*, ed. Malcolm Bradbury and James T. Macfarlane (New York: Penguin, 1976), p. 37.

rarely discriminate between various conceptions of time operating within a single Ophuls text.[4] M. M. Bakhtin, however, has categorized a number of ways in which time can be conceived of for the purposes of fictional narration, and he associates each with a characteristic spatial paradigm. Bakhtin calls such spatio-temporal configurations *chronotopes*. Chronotopes are "the organizing centers for the fundamental narrative events in the novel. The Chronotope is the place where the knots of the narrative are tied and untied."[5] Bakhtin traces the evolution of various chronotopes, relating them to the world views of the historical periods in which they were produced. He notes that the increasingly complicated and alienating historical realities of the modern age are reflected in the conflicts among competing temporal modes that characterize modern narratives. *Letter from an Unknown Woman*, the story of a woman's lifelong obsession with a sybaritic musician, is rife with such temporal conflicts, each connected to a particular chronotope.

The most obvious such conflict in the film is associated with the contrast between the modern urban center of Vienna, the home of Stefan Brand, the musician, and the traditional provincial town of Linz, where the mother of Lisa Berndle, the film's heroine, attempts to marry her off to a soldier. In Linz, scenes occur in the public space of the town square, where a sterile militaristic continuity is perpetuated through the socially-acknowledged familial prerogatives exercised by the older generation on the younger. Such prerogatives assure the latter suitable mates and secure careers. Linz even has its own music—characteristically a public music—performed in the square, attuned to the march and to the parade. Ophuls's satiric presentation, which emphasizes awkward formalities set askew by the jarringly ill-matched rhythms of people and objects within the frame, suggests the unsuitability of this rigid temporal mode to the activities of the people it purports to govern. Time in Linz lacks emotional resonance; it is bereft of an accomodating musical flow; it clashes with the private and interior sense which Lisa so cherishes.

Such a responsiveness to the interior life is part of the more modern, urbanized culture represented by Vienna. This is Stefan's world, and it is a world associated with musical harmony. Though the hero of the Stefan Zweig story on which the

4. An exception is Tania Modleski, whose essay "Time and Desire in the Woman's Film," reprinted at the end of this volume, distinguishes between men's time and women's time in somewhat different terms from those employed in the present essay.

5. M. M. Bakhtin, *The Dialogic Imagination*, ed. Michael Holquist, trans. Caryl Emerson and Michael Holquist (Austin: University of Texas Press, 1981), p. 250.

film is based is a writer, the film recreates him as a musician. This vocation, which plays a crucial role in attracting Lisa to him, lies at the heart of the film's theme of romantic love. Stefan represents for Lisa a realm of ineffable intensity. As music historian Robert P. Morgan has observed, music can be thought of as constituting an infinite variety of secret languages that are uniquely designed to speak to the fragmented and interiorized values of the modern age and can penetrate "to the essense of reality and thus express things inaccessible to language." [6] Peter Brooks has pointed to the similar role music plays in the modern melodrama, a role opposed to traditional language and thereby closely akin to muteness: "The emotional drama needs the desemanticized language of music, its evocation of the 'ineffable,' its tones and registers. Style, thematic structuring, modulations of tone and rhythm and voice—musical patterning in a metaphorical sense—are called upon to invest plot with some of the inexorability and necessity that in pre-modern literature derived from the substratum of myth." [7]

Once Lisa has been seduced by the values of modern Viennese culture, she is compelled to return. Yet what she returns to cannot fulfill her desires, for its wholly private nature has no means of acknowledging any meaningful social referent, any law. Like the music he plays and the sexual pleasures he enjoys, Stefan himself exists in an evanescent temporality in which his feeling of the moment is all that exists. When he rediscovers Lisa at the opera, he is passionately moved by his effort to recall her; later, when she comes to his apartment, however, that moment has lost its meaning for him; and his seductive behavior reverts to the vapidly formulaic as he offers her champagne and flattery. Stefan exists in an atmosphere of random temporality, giving up the piano after a concert "like all the others," when he "happened" to look into the mirror and saw that he was no longer young.

Stefan is associated with the chronotope of the street, a multidirectional space where time is governed by chance. There he encounters Lisa as if by accident, telling her shortly afterward: "I almost never get to the place I start out for." Later, on the same street, his sentiments are repeated in an exaggerated form by a drunken soldier, who asks Lisa if he can take her somewhere, "anywhere at all. It makes no difference." This ominous image embodies the schism between the old-fashioned militarism of Linz and the modern anomie of Vienna. Lisa, who

6. Robert P. Morgan, "Secret Languages: The Roots of Musical Modernism," *Critical Inquiry* 10, no. 3 (March 1984): 445.
7. Peter Brooks, *The Melodramatic Imagination: Balzac, Henry James, Melodrama, and the Mode of Excess* (New York: Columbia University Press, 1984), p. 14.

glances up at Stefan's window following this encounter, appears to recognize the relationship of the soldier's aimlessness to the style of casual seduction of Stefan himself.

Lisa's dilemma is especially poignant, for as a woman she is caught between conflicting temporal modes. Her modern sense of a private identity, intimately associated with her sense of her sexuality, emerges in one of the film's earliest scenes. As she listens to Stefan's music while on the backyard swing, she gazes curiously at her hands. Presently she is joined by another young girl, who recounts an experience with a boy who "doesn't keep his hands to himself." Aestheticizing her own similar feelings, Lisa develops a passion for Stefan, whose hands, by contrast, appear in close-up on the piano keys.

Her mother's harsh voice, the harbinger of the older patriarchal order represented by Linz, interrupts Lisa's tentative early indulgences of these incipient feelings: once as the young girl examines the furniture of the building's mysterious new tenant, and again as she watches Stefan from her window. It is the sound of her own name, uttered off-screen in her mother's grating tones, which recalls Lisa to "herself," that is, to her "proper" feminine role. Rejecting the traditional feminine norms her mother espouses, Lisa yearns for a new world of ineffability, represented by Stefan, whose off-screen music invites her acquiescence far more temptingly.

Unlike Stefan's, however, Lisa's sexuality has consequences: pregnancy, marriage, and years that she would "prefer not to remember." For Lisa, time has what Bakhtin would term a biographical dimension, measured by events such as birth and death. As a woman, she balances ephemeral emotions against biological necessity. The resulting feminine aesthetic of masochistic renunciation, as Mary Ann Doane has pointed out, is typical of the woman's film, and is notably expressed by the image of beds.[8] In *Letter from an Unknown Woman* beds are displayed not in conjunction with the sexual invitation suggested by the lovers' tryst, but rather to remind us of its repercussions for Lisa: the shame of childbirth (in the hospital scene), the responsibilities of parenthood (in the scene where young Stefan asks to sleep in his mother's bed), and, ultimately, the death of the child (in the penultimate scene, where the boy's deathbed is shown).

The conflicts inherent in Lisa's emerging sexual identity are associated with two chronotopes: the threshold and the stairway. The threshold represents the

---

8. Mary Ann Doane, "The Woman's Film: Possession and Address," in *Re-Vision: Essays in Feminist Film Criticism*, eds. Mary Ann Doane, Patricia Mellencamp, and Linda Williams (Los Angeles: The American Film Institute, 1984), pp. 67–82.

modality of crisis, in which "one or two moments . . . decide the fate of a [person's] life and determine its entire disposition."[9] For Lisa, these crises involve the assertion of sexual desire. The first of these moments occurs when she initially encounters Stefan at the doorway of the apartment building where they both live. "From this moment on, I was in love with you," she states. Later, a similarly radical crisis occurs at the threshold of the opera, when she decides to leave her husband to devote her "whole life" to the pianist.

Stairways suggest the inescapable consequences of Lisa's sexual assertions. Unlike the street, where Stefan may wander aimlessly, the staircase is directional. Tellingly, the person first glimpsed on the staircase in a sexual context is her mother, whom Lisa sees after her own illicit trespassing in Stefan's apartment. This revelation is announced by an abrupt cut from a medium shot of Stefan's vigilant servant John looking after the escaping Lisa to a point-of-view shot showing Lisa herself gazing down at her disconcerted mother, caught in the act of embracing a suitor. The Oedipal implications of such a depiction are inescapable: Lisa, who has also been unable to "keep her hands to herself" (she has just knocked over a stack of music), is first discovered in her guilty activity by John, then confronted with her mother's prior claim to the possession of sexual power. Frau Berndle further wields this power at the expense of her daughter's sexual desire by asserting her right to take Lisa away from Vienna to join Herr Kastner, her own lover. Yet Frau Berndle's sexuality is expressed in as guilty a manner as her daughter's investigation of Stefan's quarters was and is subsequently legitimated by a "proper" marriage and a secure position in a staid community. In a scene excised from the finished film, she tries to recreate her daughter in this sexually repressed image by having her dressmaker fit Lisa for a dress to wear to her impending wedding, after she herself has been similarly fitted.

The rebellious Lisa, however, wishes to make no such compromises with her mother's version of social conventionality, opting instead to freely express her sexuality. Returning to their former lodging, she again looks down from an upper landing of the stairway, this time only to witness Stefan's assignation with another woman. Later, however, she takes this woman's place when she allows Stefan to bring *her* up the stairs to his apartment, as the camera, in a much admired shot, moves to watch her from the same upper landing as if to emphasize the connection between her role as a witness to sexual pleasure and her participation in it. This drama of sexual self-destruction is later re-enacted at the opera, where the camera follows Lisa up the staircase only to cut back to a shot of Stefan below—

9. Bakhtin, p. 115.

again with another woman. This time it is Lisa's husband who stands in judgment as she gazes down at the object of her sexual longing. Ultimately, Lisa returns to the staircase of her former home to bring the drama full circle. As she is about to mount these stairs to return to Stefan's apartment, Ophuls cuts to a shot of her husband watching her from their carriage. It is at this point that she most willfully asserts her right to sexuality, risking both security and life itself in the service of its expression. The consequences, personified in the figure of her rigidly traditional husband, are again signalled by the directionality of the staircase.

But the disaster brought on by Lisa's Oedipal dilemma ultimately transcends the personal: it grows out of her place in a society that promises women free emotional expression on the one hand while it restricts them to traditional roles on the other. Caught between Linz and Vienna, Lisa thus provides the most dramatic example of the contradiction that lies at the center of Ophuls's vision. Unaware of the implications of her historical position as a woman within the seductive yet unaccommodating culture of modern Vienna, she attempts to idealize her dilemma. Her highly spiritualized sense of her romantic mission is acknowledged by the appearance of a statue of a madonna behind her just as she is about to embark on her first adventure with Stefan and by the harps that are repeatedly associated with him in her vision.[10] Her ignorance of history also leads her to see her life as a series of inevitabilities. "What happened to us had its own reason beyond our poor understanding," she states. As V. F. Perkins has noted, this vision of destiny seeks to avoid social determinants: "A bond sealed, outside society, by Fate, must surely subdue the randomness of appetite and opportunity, uniting Stefan's freedom with the steadfastness of Stauffer."[11] This notion of fate neatly accommodates the temporal modalities of crisis and repercussion—represented by the chronotopes of the threshold and the stairway—that lie at the center of Lisa's sexual dilemma, while denying their historical contingency.

In his Viennese world of evanescent sensation, Stefan is equally bereft of a sense of history. In a romantic idealization similar to that of Lisa, he speaks admiringly of a stone statue of a goddess he has believed could make his life meaningful. Cut off from historical time, Stefan is left without any sense of an existence developed through human endeavor, and thus also lacks any commit-

10. The association of harps with angels is explicitly made in the shooting script, when one of the moving men holds up Stefan's harp and asks Stefan's servant John, "Do I look like one."
11. V. F. Perkins, "*Letter from an Unknown Woman,*" *Movie*, nos. 29–30 (Summer 1982): 71.

ment to the cultivation of his artistry. His world of chance is thus closely related to Lisa's vision of fate. Neither accounts for the workings of the human will that are manifest in history. It is this repression of history, so eloquently alluded to by the film's fin-de-siècle Viennese setting, that creates the atmosphere of tragic inevitability that hangs over the narrative. Beyond human control, the temporal systems that govern the characters' lives remain fixed and unyielding, impervious to manipulation or negotiation.

Where does Ophuls stand in relation to the attitudes expressed in the figures of his hero and heroine? Clearly, he sees more deeply into social processes than they; yet he maintains an attitude as committed to the ephemeral as Stefan's and as rigidly fatalistic as Lisa's. While his ubiquitous tracking shots partake of the aesthetically motivated indulgence that characterizes Stefan and is epitomized by the aimlessness of the drunken soldier who will go "anywhere at all," the conclusion of the film, like that of several of Ophuls's others, features a duel, a privatized ceremony dictated by a rigid and inflexible notion of absolute law.

Ophuls's opposition of chance and fate is most obvious in the bravura crane shot which opens the opera scene. As the camera turns its gaze toward various groups of people in the lobby before "discovering" Lisa and Stauffer in the crowd, Lisa's voice-over (added after shooting began, almost certainly by the director himself) muses: "The course of our lives can be changed by such little things. So many passing by, each intent on his own problems. So many faces that one might easily have been lost . . . I know now that nothing happens by chance. Every moment is measured; every step is counted." This moment is created out of the camera's seductive wandering juxtaposed against the necessity forced upon it by the demands of the narrative. Here "fate" is the fate imposed on the spectator by the narrative presence behind the camera, someone who is counting his actors' every step; in other words, by Ophuls himself.

The story of *Letter from an Unknown Woman* is in one sense about a hero and heroine who are irrevocably trapped in the insubstantiality of their imaginations. While Stefan's urbanized modern world is ultimately formless, Lisa can only reveal the meaning of her experience through the shaping power of her letter, her memory. The wholeness of her life is redeemable only through recollection, and in this she enacts Hans Robert Jauss's characterization of modern art, which requires an act of memory to produce "the telos that perfects the imperfect world and ephemeral experience." [12]

12. Hans Robert Jauss, *Aesthetic Experience and Literary Hermeneutics*, trans. Michael Shaw (Minneapolis: University of Minnesota Press, 1982), p. 12.

Like Lisa, Ophuls too is drawn to recollection: his characteristic flashback structures represent an impulse to recreate wholeness through an examination of the past. This endeavor, displaced as it is from the contemplation of historical process into a preoccupation with doomed romantic passion, conceals a profound despair. For Ophuls's style combines lyrical movements of incandescent emotion with endlessly repetitive patterns that only signify within the private space of memory, never as part of a larger historical reality. The repetitions that are so important to the film's rhetoric must ultimately be associated with this syndrome of obsessive return. While Stefan buys Lisa a single white rose, she later buys him a bouquet of them; while Stefan's promise of "two weeks" at the train station is followed by a long absence, his son's similar, later promise of "two weeks" at the same station is followed by his death. Each sequence involving Lisa on the staircase raises the stakes for the expression of her sexual will. Thus painful memories are invested with increasingly melodramatic intensification in an attempt to exorcise the historically motivated trauma they represent.

This trauma is analogous to Lisa's own; and it can be seen as a response to Oedipal fixation, a fixation that in Ophuls takes the form not of a self-destructive *amour fou* but of artistic creation. In Ophuls's case, one may view this trauma not as personal, but as political, a reaction toward his German fatherland. Here we are again confronted with the film's setting in Vienna, a German-speaking yet quintessentially cosmopolitan culture. Pictured at a moment of grandeur before the First World War, it was shortly afterward to enter a decline, for as George Steiner has observed: "In Vienna the first public programs for the elimination of Jews from the life of Europe were devised and proclaimed." [13] It is this contrast, conceived as a historical contradiction, that calls forth the formal resolution of Ophuls's art.

In considering this connection, it is well to call to mind some of the well-known facts of Ophuls's biography. He altered his German-Jewish name on three different occasions. Having grown up in the Saar, a part of Germany strongly influenced by France, he suffered the opprobrium of being labeled as a "Hun" by the Western allies during the First World War. During the Second, his identity not only as a German but also as a Jew was put at issue. By contrast, his participation in the worldwide culture of film enabled him to work in France, Italy, and the United States. Given this history, he could hardly have avoided being deeply touched by the twentieth century conflict between nationalism and internationalism. In a review of a German film made during the 1930s, he wrote: "The

13. George Steiner, "Dream City," *The New Yorker*, 28 January 1985, p. 92.

literary talents who have emigrated from Germany have long found a place in the world. It is harder for the cinema. With the exception of the Soviet Union, it cannot find a 'publisher.' The international producer anxiously avoids any political avowal. Let us not be unjust; perhaps he is compelled, by censorship, the dangers of diplomatic complications, the requirements for labor permits, to take such a stand." [14]

Letter from an Unknown Woman, shot in the United States shortly after World War II, contains not a single word of German—even *The Magic Flute* is performed in Italian. For the role of the Viennese musician, a Frenchman was sought. Though the film sets the provincial Austrian town of Linz against the more modern international flavor of Vienna, it subverts the implications of its setting by its narrative focus on a woman's romantic obsession. This mechanism of displacement, which distances Ophuls from the film's manifest content, accounts for the predilection he evinced throughout his career for stories of romantic love centered on female protagonists. In *Letter from an Unknown Woman* change is represented through a woman's body: only the modifications in her mode of attire and hairstyle document the passage of time. Thus an impulse originating in history is transformed into one anchored in sexuality, and politics is transformed into style. In this film, as in Ophuls's other work, the mechanisms of denial and displacement function as the inspiration for creative ingenuity and control. The career of the director's son Marcel, whose stylistically unadorned documentaries probe the processes of history, completes the Oedipal trajectory.

It is not simply Ophuls's national identity which is put at issue by the turn-of-the-century setting of *Letter from an Unknown Woman* but his identity as a film-maker as well. The twentieth-century marriage of art and technology, a marriage which gave birth to film, figures prominently here. In this sense, film is the most modern art form, for it offers a broad array of resources for the expression of imaginative fancies, yet requires the use of the most cumbersome modern technology for the realization of these fantasies. Given the disruption of his life which occurred as a result of modern methods of warfare on the one hand and his profession as a filmmaker on the other, Ophuls's acute ambivalence toward technological progress could only have been exacerbated by the then-recent events of World War II. His comments have reflected this ambivalence.

There are plans hanging in our offices which are worked out to the minute— when this, that or the other has to be shot, when this or that actor has to

14. Max Ophuls, *"Der Kampf,"* in *New Theatre and Film, 1934–1937: An Anthology,* ed. Herbert Kline (New York: Harcourt, Brace, Jovanovich, 1985), p. 342.

open his mouth and what time he closes it. The whole thing is a machine which gets in the way of artistic freedom and intuition. . . . People who can only want beautiful goods from film have to be careful that through industrialization, through time and motion, through the race for planning they do not suffocate the spiritual element that believes in the miracle that exists inside the industry. Otherwise it runs the risk of becoming lifeless.[15]

Such suspicions have caused Ophuls, as they have other modern artists, to depict a richly imagined interior life divorced from the material forces required for its realization. Lisa's suggestion to Stefan that he might prefer the Prater in the winter because "you prefer to imagine how it will be in the spring" recalls Ophuls's own confession that he had discovered a novel excuse for never going to the movies: ". . . if the film is by a director I really admire, I can imagine it for myself. When you're familiar with the style of a great director, you can picture the film so clearly that there'd be no point in going to see it."[16]

For Ophuls, as for other modern artists, the imaginative and the mechanical are increasingly estranged from one another, so that art is found lacking on the one hand as overly private and insubstantial and on the other as overly technological and deadening. In the Viennese ambience of *Letter from an Unknown Woman*, technology is imagined as a quaint anachronism rather than an omnipresent leviathan. No automobiles appear, though they exist in Zweig's story. The more traditional artists portrayed in the film by the all-female orchestra and the military band integrate the creative and the quotidian, enjoying an un-alienated creative labor that is seen as too comically naive to retain its credibility.

Produced within the confines of Hollywood realism, *Letter from an Unknown Woman* allows scant opportunity for the inclusion of the self-reflexive devices that characterize most Ophuls films. In the episode of the imaginary train ride, however, we see the director commenting on the filmmaking process. The artificial backdrop of faraway places that forms a background for Lisa's illusions recalls the fanciful depiction of the Vienna skyline that served as a backdrop for the film's credit sequence as well as the moving background Ophuls less conspicuously employs during Lisa's earlier train ride when she "borrows" a program of one of Stefan's concerts from a fellow passenger. In this world of illusion, perpetrated by the director himself, the mechanical and the fanciful are clearly separated: Lisa's imaginative reminiscences occur inside the railway carriage while

15. "Thoughts on Film: An Improvisation by Max Ophuls," in *Ophuls*, ed. and trans. Paul Willemen (London: British Film Institute, 1978), pp. 40, 42.
16. Willemen, p. 29.

the machinery and labor which inspire these fantasies remain outside, for us to see, but unobserved by her.[17]

This scene, where Ophuls seems most present, is marked by Lisa's fantasized vision of the past, a "memory" founded in Oedipal desire. By thus recasting his own impossible desire to change the past of history into the form of a woman's private struggle with sexuality, Ophuls is able to idealize his material and to embellish it with engaging aesthetic flourishes. If he thereby represses history in his films, he compensates by creating a stylistic tour-de-force around this absent center, a tour-de-force that portrays a past suffused with randomness and inevitability in the place of a present and future that could hold out the promise of meaningful change. In Hollywood during the late forties Ophuls existed in an atmosphere which could only have exacerbated his sense of despair, both about his prospects as a German Jew and about the future of technology. Recreating a pivotal moment in turn-of-the-century Vienna allowed him to poeticize that despair if not to master it.

17. This split between Lisa's imaginative fantasies and the mechanical means that trigger them was introduced during shooting, most probaby by Ophuls (who had, in any event, invented the incident to begin with). In the shooting script, the couple merely look out of the window to talk to the ticket-taker.

Max Ophuls

A Biographical Sketch

Karen Hollinger

O n March 6, 1902, Max Ophuls was born Maximilian Oppenheimer to an upper middle-class Jewish family of textile manufacturers in the industrial town of Saarbrücken, Germany, located close to the border between France and the rich coalmining district of Western Germany known as the Saar. Taken from Germany in 1919 and occupied by France under the banner of the League of Nations, the Saar was restored by plebiscite to Germany in 1935. France occupied it again after the Second World War until 1957, when it elected once again by plebiscite to be reunited with Germany. Ophuls thus was a man of mixed nationality. Born a German citizen, his mother tongue German, German the language in which he wrote, he spoke French fluently and adopted French citizenship during the Second World War.

As a young man, he decided not to enter his father's textile business and instead tried his hand at a number of possible occupations. He may have written drama criticism for a local newspaper. Four reviews signed M.O. appeared in the *Saarbrücken Zeitung* in 1920, but Ophuls's authorship has not been firmly established. He also apparently toyed with the idea of becoming a circus or variety performer before he decided to embark on a career as a stage actor. When he made his acting debut in 1919 over his family's objections, he changed his name to Ophuls to avoid embarrassing them. The new name, he claims, was chosen by his mentor, the noted German stage director Fritz Holl, in memory of a stage actress with whom Holl had been hopelessly in love. Ophuls also alleges that Holl agreed to become his mentor in spite of his pupil's very limited acting talents

because he had once been in love with Ophuls's mother. In fact, Ophuls's choice of the acting profession also seems to have been determined for amorous reasons. "Why I wanted to become an actor?—It's simple," he later recalled. "Apart from the fascination of all the classical plays which I regularly watched . . . my imagination was fired by the crowds of young girls waiting at the stage door every night."[1]

Ophuls's career as an actor was not a success, and he spent several years as an extra with only walk-on parts in repertory and opera companies until 1923 when he was given the opportunity to direct a play in Dortmund, Germany. As he describes it: "One night I flopped so terribly in a dramatic part that the next day the manager of the Dortmund theater summoned me to his office. As I was paid for playing both comic and dramatic roles, he told me, I would have to take a fifty

1. Francis Koval, "Interview with Max Ophuls," in *Masterworks of The French Cinema*, ed. John Weightman (New York: Harper and Row, 1974), p. 342.

per cent salary cut. To soothe my indignation he hesitantly suggested an alternative. I could stop playing altogether and become a 'Regisseur,' a director, keeping my original salary. My actor's pride was deeply insulted—but a few days later I accepted." [2]

As a director he was more successful and is said to have directed as many as two hundred plays in Dortmund and several operettas in Elberfeld-Barmen between 1923 and 1925, He also supplemented his income by working in radio, first as a literary reviewer, then by adapting plays and stories, reading poetry, and directing musical shows, sketches, and radio plays. He continued to engage in radio work throughout his career and developed a successful radio talk show format that combined excerpts from literary works of a wide variety of styles with improvisational material, reflections, comments, parodies, sound effects, and musical accompaniment.

In 1926 he was invited to direct at the Vienna Bergtheater—at the age of twenty-three, the youngest man ever to hold this position. There, he met and married Hilde Wall, a well-known dramatic actress of the time. Their son, Marcel Ophuls, who became a filmmaker in his own right, was born in 1927 in Frankfurt where Ophuls served as musical director and then "Oberregisseur" (director-in-chief) at the New Theater. In 1928 he moved to the Municipal Theater in Breslau. During his long career as a stage director, he directed works ranging from classical drama to the more popular plays of his contemporaries. While in Breslau, he also continued writing: a children's play and a popular marching song were products of this period.

In 1930 a radical theater group asked Ophuls to direct at the Lessing Theater in Berlin. While working there, he wrote more songs, contributed material to musical revues, and began to write for theater journals, an activity he would continue to pursue throughout his career. He also began work at this time in the film industry. From an early age, he had been fond of movies and vividly recalled his first memory of them: "I was very young; it was at Worms, during a fair, in a tent. On the screen was a fellow sitting at a desk; he had a headache and seemed quite crazy; he was writing something and smoking nervously. He was in a rage—suddenly he picked up an inkwell and drank the ink; he turned completely blue! This film impressed me enormously because, especially to a child, it was quite unrealistic and just like a fairy story. How can you turn completely blue by

2. Koval, p. 343.

drinking ink? I must admit that, when I got home, I had to try. I drank some ink; only my tongue went blue . . . nothing else happened. And that's the first thing I remember about cinema."[3]

Although Ophuls continued to be drawn to non-naturalistic films and particularly admired the work of Fritz Lang and F. W. Murnau, he had never envisioned film as a form in which to express his own creative ideas. "I didn't want to be in the movies," he claimed. "I didn't think I'd be capable of it, being so much a man of the theater."[4] Future events, however, were to prove him wrong, and he quickly found himself seduced by the cinema. "The camera, this new means of expression which I used for the first time, lured me irresistibly from the word to the image," he later said, "a little as if it were a young mistress luring a married man from his wife. A mistress whom I loved with a passion."[5] His film career began at UFA, the nationally subsidized German film conglomerate. He started as a dialogue director and translator on Anatole Litvak's *Nie Wieder Liebe* (*No More Love*) which was shot simultaneously in German and French.

As a successful stage director with an interest in cinema and a proven ability to handle dialogue, he was asked by UFA to direct a forty minute comedy featurette, *Dann schon lieber Lebertran* (*I'd Rather Take Cod Liver Oil*) in 1930. During the next two years, he directed five films; of these, *Liebelei* is widely regarded as his early masterpiece. Based on a play by Arthur Schnitzler, it is set in turn-of-the-century Vienna and tells the story of a young lieutenant who falls in love with the daughter of a musician. Soon after they have pledged their affection to one another, he is killed in a duel by the husband of his ex-mistress, and the news of his death leads his true love to suicide. The film has been praised for its skillful evocation of Imperial Vienna and for its strongly anti-militaristic sentiments.

With the rise of Nazism in Germany Ophuls and his family were forced to leave for France. Arriving in Paris in 1933, he quickly began work on a French language version of *Liebelei* entitled *Une Histoire d'amour*. At this time, the original version of *Liebelei* was released in Germany and became a great success. Ophuls, however, received little recognition for the film in the Third Reich where the censors saw to it that his name was removed from its credits.

3. Jacques Rivette and François Truffaut, "Interview with Max Ophuls," in *Ophuls*, ed. Paul Willemen (London: British Film Institute, 1978), p. 15.
4. Paul Willemen, "Familmographic Romance," in *Ophuls*, ed. Paul Willemen (London: British Film Institute, 1978), p. 15.
5. Claude Beylie, *Max Ophuls* (Paris: Editions Seghers, 1963), pp. 119–120.

Between 1933 and 1941, Ophuls directed a number of films in France, Italy, Holland, and Switzerland, most notable among them being *La Signora di Tutti* (*Everybody's Lady*, 1934). Filmed in Italy, it deals with the life of a famous film star who is driven to suicide by her love for a young Italian aristocrat and his father. The film is particularly interesting for its use of flashbacks, a technique crucial to the narrative of two of Ophuls's major works, *Letter From an Unknown Woman* and *Lola Montès*. In 1936 the Soviet Union offered him a two-year contract to direct films there if on a visit he liked the country. After a two-month visit, he refused to sign the contract, opting instead for French nationality. In 1938 he became a naturalized French citizen.

In 1939, he was called up into the French army as a private, but with the fall of France in the following year, he was forced to flee with his family to Switzerland where he began work on several stage plays and a film based on Molière's *L'Ecole des Femmes* (*School For Wives*). His work on these projects was terminated, however, when he was denied a work permit by the Swiss government unless he declared himself a deserter from the French army, which he refused to do. He and his family were then forced to leave Switzerland and reenter France (a dangerous undertaking) to arrange passage to the United States.

Arriving in Hollywood in 1941, he spent the next four years unemployed. "America certainly was not as I had imagined it," he later recalled, "and for quite a time I was very depressed. Some people turned my head with easy promises, but for three years or so I was completely idle. I couldn't quite understand the workings of Hollywood machinery, till one day a big-time executive said to me with a friendly pat on the shoulder: 'Our studios are producing a lot of cheaply made money-spinners just now: thrillers, Westerns, and so on. But one day the board of directors may decide to embark on quality production. That is when we shall need you.' His words were true, which meant that waiting for my chance I might well starve."[6] Despite these professional frustrations, Ophuls appears to have retained his good humor. Screen writer Howard Koch describes him during these years as "a baldish Peter Lorre with the same heavy-lidded, wide-set eyes and the same impish sense of humor."[7] Ophuls kept himself busy at this time by writing his autobiography, later published under the title *Spiel im Dasein*[8] (variously translated, it represents a play on the words "play" as in stage play and "existence" or "survival," hence *A Play About Survival*).

6. Koval, pp. 346–347.
7. Howard Koch, "Script to Screen with Max Ophuls," *Film Comment* 6, no. 4 (1970–1971): 41.
8. Ophuls's autobiography was translated into French as *Ophuls par Ophuls* (Paris: Laffont, 1963).

Finally in 1946, the Hollywood writer, director, and producer Preston Sturges discovered *Liebelei* and rediscovered Ophuls. He asked him to direct the film *Vendetta* for Howard Hughes and RKO, but after only a few days Ophuls was removed from the film as a result of severe disagreements with Sturges, who represented Hughes's interests. In 1947, Douglas Fairbanks Jr. asked Ophuls to direct him in a period adventure film, *The Exile*; other directing assignments followed. Ophuls (his name spelled "Opuls" in the credits) ultimately directed three more films in Hollywood, including *Letter from an Unknown Woman* (1948), which is customarily ranked as his best American work. *Caught* (1949), starring Barbara Bel Geddes, Robert Ryan, and James Mason, depicts the disastrous marriage of a young and ambitious woman to a fabulously wealthy but vicious man. *The Reckless Moment* (1949), Ophuls's last American film, stars Mason and Joan Bennett and concerns a mother's attempts to save her family from scandal and blackmail. Both of these last American projects represent Ophuls's struggle to make something stylistically interesting from rather unpromising melodramatic material.

In 1949, Ophuls took his family back to France in hopes of directing a film version of Balzac's *La Duchesse de Langeais* with Greta Garbo and James Mason. When the project fell through, he remained in France and embarked on the final stage of his career, usually considered the high point of his achievement. He directed four major films at this time: *La Ronde* (1950), *Le Plaisir* (1952), *Madame de . . .* (1953), and *Lola Montès* (1955). *La Ronde*, based on Schnitzler's play *Reigen*, presents a series of vignettes depicting love as a merry-go-round of seduction. *Le Plaisir* tells three stories by Guy de Maupassant contrasting the easy attainment of transient pleasure with the difficult pursuit of lasting happiness. *Madame de . . .* portrays the destruction of its eponymous heroine brought about by some earrings given to her by her husband that find their way into the hands of her lover. *Lola Montès*, now usually regarded as a masterpiece, was planned as an expensive, international, CinemaScope production (it cost over 650 million francs) but on its release proved a box office disaster. Reedited by its producers without Ophuls's knowledge, it was rereleased in an altered version over his adamant protests. The film recounts in flashback the liaisons of a notorious courtesan, first with Franz Liszt, then with a shy young student, and finally with the King of Bavaria.

Ophuls left France in 1957 to direct a stage production of Beaumarchais's *Mariage de Figaro* at the Schauspiel Theater in Hamburg. Having long suffered

from a cardiac condition that may have been aggravated by the controversy surrounding the recutting of *Lola Montès*, he was hospitalized in a Hamburg clinic
on the morning of the play's premier performance. Three months later on March
26, 1957, he died: his body was cremated in Hamburg and his ashes buried in the
Père Lachaise cemetery in Paris.

Letter from an
Unknown Woman

Letter from an Unknown Woman

creenwriter Howard Koch based his shooting script for *Letter from an Unknown Woman* on *Brief einer Unbekannten*, a novella by Stefan Zweig. The original version of the screenplay is dated July 25, 1947, but Koch subsequently undertook revisions under the direction of Max Ophuls and John Houseman. Koch's script, now housed in the Wisconsin Center for Theater and Film Research in Madison, includes changes dated from August 18 to September 23, 1947, and an earlier undated description of scene breakdowns can be found in the University of Southern California archives (Universal Studios Collection). Script alterations are apparent from a comparison of these scripts and the continuity script, which has been transcribed here in its entirety from the film as we now know it.

Variant passages are noted at the appropriate points in the continuity script, and earlier versions of each passage are reprinted at the end in the "Notes on the Shooting Script." The notes describe all significant differences, including all additions or deletions of entire scenes. When sections of the shooting script diverge markedly from the continuity script version, they are printed in their entirety.

The continuity script, including both dialogue and visual/aural description, represents the version of *Letter from an Unknown Woman* that opened theatrically in the United States in June, 1948. It had been cut by three minutes from an original version that never found distribution and is no longer extant.

The following abbreviations indicate camera distance:

ECU extreme close-up

CU close-up

MCU medium close-up

MS medium shot

MTS medium two shot

MLS medium long shot

LS long shot

ELS extreme long shot

Credits and Cast

Director
Max Ophuls

Producer
John Houseman

Screenplay
Howard Koch, from the novella *Brief Einer Unbekannten* by Stefan Zweig.

Production Company
A Rampart Production for Universal-International

Director of Photography
Franz Planer

Editor
Ted J. Kent

Art Director
Alexander Golitzen

Costumes
Travis Banton

Music
Daniele Amfitheatrof

Set Designers
Leslie I. Carey and Glenn E. Anderson

Production Coordinator
John Hambleton

Assistant Director
John F. Sherwood

Process
Black and white

Length
Original length 90 minutes; released in an edited version, 3 minutes cut in the U.S. and 4 minutes in Great Britain.

U.S. Release Date
June 1948

Lisa Berndle
Joan Fontaine

Stefan Brand
Louis Jourdan

Frau Berndle
Mady Christians

Johann Stauffer
Marcel Journet

John
Art Smith

Herr Kastner
Howard Freeman

Lt. Leopold von Kaltnegger
John Good

Stefan Junior
Leo B. Pessin

Concierge
Otto Waldis

Porter
Erskine Sanford

Frau Spitzer
Sonja Bryden

Marie
Carol Yorke

Pretty
Audrey Young

Fritz
William Trenk

Officer on street
Fred Nurney

Carriage driver
Torben Meyer

Mother Superior
Hermine Sterler

Col. Steindorf
C. Ramsey Hill

Movers
Will Lee and William Hall

Woman musician
Lotte Stein

Ticket collector
Ilka Gruning

Concierge
Paul E. Burns

Second
Roland Varno

Flower vendor
Celia Lovsky

Critic
Lester Sharpe

Cafe customer
Michael Mark

Woman musician
Lisa Golm

Station attendant
Rex Lease

Carriage driver
Edmund Cobb

Frau Kohner
Betty Blythe

Footman
Arthur Lovejoy

Cafe customer
Guy L. Shaw

Cashier
June Wood

Maid
Jean Ransome

Model
Judith Woodbury

Baron's second
Manuel Paris

Store helper
John McCullum

First officer
Robert W. Brown

Leo Mostovoy

Shimen Ruskin

Lois Austin

Diane Lee Stewart

Vera Stokes

Doretta Johnson

Lorraine Gale

Cy Stevens

Doug Carter

Jack Gargan

The Continuity Script

The credits are shown over a print of Vienna at the turn of the century: an aerial view with parks and trees in the foreground, government buildings in the middle-ground, and church steeples in the distance. An overture, which combines background music used throughout the film, plays on the soundtrack during the title sequence and continues through the fade in to the opening scene.

1. *Fade in to the inscription "Vienna About 1900" superimposed over a long establishing shot of a winding cobblestone street. The scene takes place at night and in continuous rain, and the deserted street is lined by town houses, narrow sidewalks, and lampposts. A horsedrawn carriage, just visible in the distance, turns into the street in the center of the frame. As it pulls toward the camera, a man with an umbrella can be seen running along the sidewalk screen right in the direction of the carriage, his back to the camera. As he runs he moves slightly into the street to avoid a lamppost and nearly collides with the oncoming carriage.*

   The carriage approaches the camera and pulls up next to it, stopping just as the camera, now tracking in slowly, is parallel to the carriage door. The music on the soundtrack stops as the carriage does. Looking through the window, the camera tracks in to a medium shot of the three men inside the carriage. The men, seen in profile and in the shadowy darkness of the carriage, are dressed fashionably in evening clothes.

   The carriage's open window frames the scene as Stefan, sitting screen right, opens the door on the far side of the carriage and descends to the street. Of the two men who remain within the carriage, the one nearest to the camera holds a lighted cigarette in his gloved hand. It is poised in profile in the carriage window dividing the frame between Stefan, who has emerged from the carriage, and his companions, who remain within it. Also dividing the frame between Stefan and the other two men is the rain falling in thin lines from the carriage roof.

FIRST MAN (*nearest to the camera, speaking to Stefan as Stefan leaves the carriage with his back to the camera*): Then you've made up your mind. You're going to go through with it.[1]

The camera tracks in slightly.

STEFAN (*as he closes the carriage door, leans against it, takes his cigarette from his mouth, and looks down*): Why not?
FIRST MAN (*laughing*): For one thing, he's an excellent shot.
STEFAN (*smiling*): So I've heard.
SECOND MAN: At least, try to get some sleep.
FIRST MAN: And if I were you, no more cognac.

Stefan smiles and nods.

FIRST MAN: We'll come for you at five. That gives you three hours.

Stefan looks into the carriage and smiles again.

FIRST MAN: You'll be here?
STEFAN: I don't mind so much being killed . . . (*pauses, looks into the carriage again smiling*) . . . but you know how hard it is for me to get up in the morning.[2]

Stefan smiles and the first man in the carriage laughs.

STEFAN (*turning and walking away toward the rear of the carriage*): Goodnight.
SECOND MAN: Goodnight.

Stefan walks screen left as the carriage pulls out of the frame screen right. The camera pans to follow him from behind in MLS. *As church bells ring off-screen, he walks slowly through puddles of rainwater, looks down, and taps his cane on the pavement.*

2. *When he reaches a large iron gate, cut to frontal* MCU *of the two men in the carriage. Both are smiling.*

SECOND MAN: I'm afraid this time Stefan has picked a fight with the wrong man.

Both laugh.

FIRST MAN: I wonder if he'll be here when we come back?
SECOND MAN (*with casual disregard*): Well![3]

3. *Cut to frontal* MS *of Stefan, a delicately handsome, refined-looking gentleman of about forty, coming through an open glass door. Still smoking a cigarette, he enters a hallway in profile as an off-screen voice calls out.*

CONCIERGE (*off-screen*): Who is it?
STEFAN (*with his cigarette dangling from his mouth*): Brand.
CONCIERGE (*off-screen*): Good Morning, Mr. Brand.

As Stefan walks through the hallway, the camera pans with him. When he reaches a winding staircase, it cranes up to follow his slow ascent in LS. *While on the stairway, he removes his scarf from his neck, and when he reaches the landing at the top, the sound of a door opening can be heard. The landing is then lighted slightly from off-screen left. Stefan, now in low angle* LS *seen through the banister of the staircase, turns and exits the frame screen left.*

4. *Cut to a* MS *of Stefan's manservant John, a grey-haired, older man who looks very solemn as he stands in the doorway of Stefan's apartment holding the door open. Stefan enters the frame screen right and walks with his back to the camera past John and into the apartment.*

STEFAN: Cheer up, John. This is one engagement I have no intention of keeping. (*He removes his hat and hands it with his scarf and cane to John. Then he pats him on the shoulder.*) Honor is a luxury only gentlemen can afford.[4]

Stefan walks slowly down the hallway with the camera tracking him from behind and gradually eliminating John from the frame. Stefan turns in profile to the camera.

STEFAN (*to John as Stefan slowly removes his gloves, smokes his cigarette, and looks down*): Oh, pack my things, whatever you think I'll need for an indefinite stay.

John enters the frame and Stefan hands him his gloves. Stefan then turns, lights a new cigarette, and walks slowly down the hallway with his back to the camera; John follows. John turns and puts Stefan's gloves into a closet to his right. Stefan then turns in profile to the camera and faces John in MS.

STEFAN (*removing his cape*): Oh, and have a cab downstairs in about an hour. I'll go out the back way.

Stefan hands John his cape which John puts into the closet.

STEFAN (*about to enter a doorway to his left, removing his cigarette from his mouth, and laughing*): I'm sorry I won't be here to see their faces.

Stefan has almost left the frame through the doorway when John reaches out and touches his arm. Stefan reemerges from the doorway as John goes to a table in the background and picks up a tray containing an envelope which he offers to Stefan.

STEFAN (*reaching for the envelope*): Oh! (*Taking the letter and turning it over as he looks questioningly at John.*) Did this come during the night?

John, still holding the letter tray, nods.

STEFAN (*again leaving the frame through the doorway*): Oh, would you bring me some coffee?

John nods.

STEFAN (*almost entirely off-screen*): With cognac.

John walks toward the camera.

5. *Cut to* MS *of Stefan in his bedroom again from behind and in profile as he removes his coat. He walks screen right with the camera panning to follow him, turns, still smoking his cigarette, and stands facing the camera next to the footboard of his bed. After taking off his coat, he throws it on the bed, looks at the letter, and also throws it on the bed. He removes his cigarette from his mouth, rubs his eyes, and drops his arms in exhaustion. Then he picks up the letter again and walks with his back to the camera toward another doorway in the background.*

6. *Cut to* MS *of Stefan as he enters the bathroom. He turns and begins to open the envelope while he stands in profile at a small washstand upon which are placed a china bowl and pitcher. In the background, a small*

window can be seen with rain beating against it, a bathtub under it. Stefan puts the letter down on the washstand next to the bowl, removes his cigarette from his mouth, bends down, and splashes his face with water. He then looks back at the letter as he rubs his hands together over the bowl. Suddenly, he stops and rises to his full height.

7. *As he reaches for the letter, cut to* ECU *of its opening lines which read: By the time you read this letter, I may be dead . . .*[5] *Also visible on the letterhead is a cross circled by the name St. Catherine's Hospital. With the cut to* ECU, *background music begins on the soundtrack.*

8–9. *A series of* CUS *follows: Stefan frowning as he looks down at the letter, Stefan's hand as he picks it up, and finally a pan to a medium close-up of Stefan as he dries his face with a towel. He then turns and walks to the door with the camera panning to follow him.*

10. *Cut to a* MCU *through the doorway of the study as Stefan walks into the room. The camera pans to follow him in profile as he goes to his desk upon which in* MS *he places the letter. He then stands behind the desk, lights with one hand a small lamp just next to the letter, and leans over to read. Behind him can be seen a bookcase filled with books and with parcels of sheet music. Lisa's voice is heard in voice-over as Stefan begins to read the letter.*

VOICE-OVER: By the time you read this letter, I may be dead. I have so much to tell you and perhaps very little time. Will I ever send it? I don't know.

Stefan reaches into a cigarette box, removes a cigarette, and lights it as he continues to read.

VOICE-OVER: I must find strength to write now before it's too late, and as I write it may become clear that what happened to us had its own reason beyond our poor understanding. If this reaches you, you will know how I became yours when you didn't know who I was or even that I existed.

As Stefan reads, the camera slowly tracks in to MCU *of his face. The focus blurs and fades out.*

11. *Fade in to blurred* MCU *of a man seen from behind as he enters the frame and picks up a large object. During the fade, the background music changes to a hurdy-gurdy tune.*

   VOICE-OVER (*during the fade*): I think everyone has two birthdays, the day of his physical birth and the beginning of his conscious life.

The focus becomes clearer, and the man, who is lifting a large antique lyre, turns to the camera, which rises slightly to follow his movements. The camera then pans with him as he turns and passes what appears to be a window to his right. Lisa, an adolescent schoolgirl who is watching with open-mouthed fascination, is framed in the window.

   VOICE-OVER: Nothing is vivid or real in my memory before that day in Spring when I came home from school and found a moving van in front of our building.[6]

The camera tracks back as the man moves forward. It then pans right to show him removing the lyre from a truck. Lisa is standing on the street peering in through a window-like opening in the truck's side. After panning through the side of the truck, the camera rests on Lisa in MLS *as she watches the lyre being handed to another man on the street. He then passes before her in the foreground with the lyre.*

After watching him pass, she begins to walk toward the camera, which pans and tracks back with her. As she walks, she stares ahead with fascination at something just off-screen. A man carrying an ornately decorated mirror then enters the frame in the foreground and passes in front of Lisa with his back to the camera. After he passes, Lisa moves to her right in MS *with the camera panning and tracking out to follow her. She then walks over to a pile of furniture and statuary and begins to examine it.[7]*

   VOICE-OVER: I wondered about our new neighbor who owned such beautiful things.[8]

LISA'S MOTHER (*off-screen, calling crossly*): Lisa! Come in, Lisa, come in this minute, you hear?

As Lisa looks up, the camera tilts up the building behind her to reveal her mother calling from an upper story window. Lisa moves away from the pile of furniture, and the camera pans with her in MLS as she returns to the window-like opening in the truck's side.

LISA'S MOTHER (*off-screen*): Lisa!

Startled, Lisa turns abruptly and begins to walk toward the building with her back to the camera. As she walks, she throws the sweater she is carrying up in the air and over her shoulder.

LISA (*sounding disappointed and unwilling to obey*): Yes, mother!

With the camera tracking in slightly to follow her, Lisa approaches the gateway to the building just as a man carrying a large box emerges from it.

12. *Cut to MS of Lisa as she enters a hallway where a fat, mustached concierge with a cigar in his hand is seen walking in the foreground. The camera pans to follow them as they both move into the hallway with Lisa examining furniture piled in the background.*

CONCIERGE (*pointing off-screen left with his cigar*): Who is going to clean that up? Me, I suppose.

A moving man enters the frame screen left in the extreme foreground, walks in front of the concierge and exits screen right.

MOVING MAN (*passing the concierge*): Ya.
CONCIERGE (*exasperated*): I haven't enough work to do!

The concierge exits screen left, and Lisa begins to walk toward the camera.[9] She looks interestedly before her and avoids several moving men in her path.

FIRST MOVING MAN (*off-screen*): I told you we couldn't tie it to the last one. You better get another rope.

SECOND MOVING MAN (*off*): What?

FIRST MOVING MAN (*off, shouting*): You better get another rope!

SECOND MOVING MAN (*off*): Alright! (*Shouting.*) Hans, get another rope for the wagon!

As Lisa walks to the winding staircase at the end of the hall, the camera pans to follow her. The hallway appears to be the same one that Stefan entered in the opening sequence.

The camera cranes up to follow Lisa in MLS *as she climbs the stairs. She continues to look ahead interestedly and ignores two moving men who are standing on the staircase. They are struggling with a pulley that is lifting a piano in the extreme foreground.*

FIRST MOVING MAN: This is the last time I move a musician.

SECOND MOVING MAN: Why does he have to play the piano; why not the piccolo?

As the camera reaches the top of the stairs, Stefan's servant, John, comes into the frame screen left. He stands in MLS *on the landing at the top of the stairs, writing in a ledger and supervising the moving. Lisa in the background watches as a moving man with books piled up to his chin and a cigarette dangling from his mouth comes up the stairs.*

MOVING MAN (*to John*): Where do these go?

John, who is mute, tries to reply, but makes no sound.

MOVING MAN: What?

John takes out a small piece of paper and writes his answer, which he then shows to the moving man.

MOVING MAN: Uh-huh, in the study.

As he walks off screen left, sounds of the moving men shouting in the background can be heard.

FIRST MOVING MAN (*off*): Hey Paul, where's that rope? We are waiting.
SECOND MOVING MAN (*off*): I'm coming.

John turns and notices Lisa who smiles shyly at him and backs away. As she moves, she drops her sweater, which he retrieves for her.

13. *Cut to a* MS *from over Lisa's shoulder of John smiling and handing Lisa her sweater.*

LISA: Thank you.

14. *Reverse shot of Lisa who is also smiling.*

LISA'S MOTHER (*off*): Lisa, what are you doing out there? Come inside!

Lisa looks over her shoulder, then back at John, and backs away toward a door directly behind her. After she opens the door, she turns again to smile shyly at John. Closing the door very slowly, she continues to look out through the crack.

The camera holds briefly on the closed door.[10]

15. *Dissolve to a* CU *of a piano keyboard with Stefan's fingers gliding across the keys. With the dissolve, the music on the soundtrack changes to a piano étude by Franz Liszt (No. 3 in D flat major).*

VOICE-OVER (*during the dissolve*): I didn't see you that day or for many days thereafter, but I could listen to your playing.[11]

16. *Dissolve to low angle* MLS *of a shuttered garden window. Under it is a window box filled with flowers and hanging above are tree branches and leaves. The camera pans and cranes down to a garden below the window and finally comes to rest in* MLS *on Lisa, who is swinging on a swing and*

listening dreamily to the music. The sound of the swing creaking can be heard above the music. Lisa is framed in profile through the fork of a tree trunk, and the camera swings slightly as she does.[12]

17–19. *A series of shots follow which juxtapose Lisa on the swing with the garden window and Stefan playing:*[13] *cut to* MCU *of Lisa as she swings and looks up in the direction of the window, cut to low angle* MS *of the window as Lisa would be seeing it with the camera swinging slightly as she is, cut to frontal* MCU *of Lisa as she swings and stares at her hands. When she looks at each hand, she slowly removes it from the rope of the swing. Then she looks back up in the direction of the window.*

20–21. *Cut to* MS *from under the lid of Stefan's grand piano with Stefan sitting at the keyboard playing and then back to the previous* MLS *of Lisa on the swing framed by the two forks of the tree trunk. From screen left, a girl*

Lisa's age enters in the foreground, leans against the tree, and looks at Lisa. Then she moves in to rest against the pole supporting the swing.

GIRL: I wish he'd stop that noise.
LISA: It's not noise.

The girl walks around Lisa to the far side of the swing where she leans on the other pole of the swing and begins to eat a piece of cake. The camera pans left and then right to follow her movements. When she stops, it slowly tracks in as she and Lisa talk.

GIRL: Don't bite my head off.
LISA: It's Mr. Brand playing.
GIRL: If you call that playing.
LISA (*waving her hand at the girl*): Shhh!

22–23. *Cut to the previous shot of Stefan as he plays and then back to* MS *of Lisa and the girl talking. The camera again swings slightly with Lisa.*

GIRL: How old is he?
LISA (*again looking at her hands as she rhythmically removes them and then replaces them on the ropes of the swing*): Who?
GIRL (*looking behind her in the direction of the window*): Him.
LISA (*looking in the direction of the window and then down*): Oh, I don't know, quite old, I guess.

Lisa stops swinging and then looks down at the ground.

GIRL: Oh, you know the boy I was talking to outside the school? The bony one with the yellow hair and the long nose . . .

Lisa leans dreamily against one rope of the swing and ignores the girl.

GIRL: . . . the one that lives next to the grocery. I'm going to have to do something about him if he doesn't keep his hands to himself. The things he does and right out in the street.

Lisa stares up in the direction of the window.

24–27. *Several shots follow in quick succession: cut to* MS *of Stefan at the piano, then to* CU *of his hands on the keys, back to* MS *of him at the piano, and finally to* MS *of Lisa and the girl. Suddenly, the music stops, and the sound of Stefan banging the cover down on the keys of the piano can be heard. Lisa responds by abruptly standing up and looking in the direction of the window.*

28–29. *Cut to previous* MS *of Stefan as he slams the cover down over the keys and puts his hands on the top of the piano in frustration. Then cut back to* MS *of Lisa as she turns, walks behind the swing, stops briefly to look in the direction of the window, and then runs with her back to the camera into the background toward a door. As Lisa runs through the door, a gardener with a large box of tools enters screen left and the girl walks to the center of the frame. She stands with her back to the camera watching after Lisa.*

30. *Cut to* MS *of Lisa running through a courtyard with the camera panning quickly to follow her. She stops before a glass door and peers in with her back to the camera. As she moves back to the side of the door, waits in* MS, *and then goes back to look in again, the camera pans to follow her movements.*

31. *Cut to* MCU *through the glass door of Lisa who looks in anxiously as Stefan's voice is heard.*

STEFAN (*off-screen*): Thank you, John. I'll be home late. You needn't wait up for me.

32. *Cut to* MLS *looking through the glass door from over Lisa's shoulder as Stefan, looking very young and handsome, dressed in a suit, and carrying a briefcase under his arm, comes down the stairway and walks toward the camera. When he reaches the door, Lisa opens it for him and remains standing behind the open door, looking frightened. He stops in* MS *as he comes through the doorway and looks at her.*

33. STEFAN (MCU, *smiling*): Thank you.

34. *Cut to* MS *of Lisa and Stefan facing each other in profile. As she looks down, he turns and walks away with the camera panning to follow him.*

    STEFAN (*turning to look at her again*): Good morning.

    He turns once more in MLS *and looks back at Lisa when he reaches the gate to the street.*

35. *Cut to Lisa in* MLS *as she stands seemingly paralyzed with fright behind the door.*

36. *Cut back to Stefan in* MLS *as he turns and walks through the gateway into the street. As he enters the street, a boy with a dog enters in the background screen right and a man on a bicycle enters screen left.*

37. *Cut to previous* MLS *of Lisa as she stands behind the door.*

> GIRL (*off-screen*): Why, Lisa! (*She enters the frame in the foreground, climbs up on a step, and holds onto a banister which separates her from Lisa.*) You're all red in the face. You're blushing!

> *Lisa turns, pushes the girl off the step, and then runs off-screen right with the girl running after her.*[14]

> GIRL: I'll get you for that.

> *The camera pans with them as background music begins on the soundtrack. The two girls run through a gateway to the garden and out of the frame, the camera holding on the gateway as the voice-over begins again.*

> VOICE-OVER: Yes, I was blushing, and hard as it may be for you to realize, from that moment on I was in love with you. Quite consciously, I began to prepare myself for you. I kept my clothes neater so you wouldn't be ashamed of me.[15]

38. *Dissolve to* MLS *through a doorway of Lisa as she irons a dress. As she irons, she slowly circles the ironing board.*

39. *Dissolve to another* MLS *of Lisa at a dancing lesson. Music appropriate for dancing instruction replaces the background music on the soundtrack, and the dancing master is heard repeating, "Bow, two, three, four. One, two, three, four." The frame is dominated by a partition in the middleground behind which boys and girls can be seen dancing. In the foreground separated from the other dancers by the partition, Lisa in a white party dress is dancing by herself with very little expertise.*[16] *The dancing master stands in the middleground screen right waving his baton.*

> VOICE-OVER: I went to dancing school. I wanted to become more graceful and learn good manners for you.

Lisa, after practicing before the partition, finally goes shyly in to join the other dancers.

40. *Dissolve to* MS *of Lisa in a library as she climbs a bookcase to replace one book and take down another.*[17] *The bookcase is marked with the sign "Musik" and each shelf has the name of an individual composer on it. The music on the soundtrack changes with the dissolve to a violin piece.*

    VOICE-OVER (*beginning during the dissolve*): And so I would know more about you and your world, I . . . I went to the library and studied the lives of the great musicians of the past.

    Having found a book, Lisa takes it to a table. As she approaches the table, a man sitting in the background looks disapprovingly at her. She sits down, looks over her shoulder at the man, and then begins to read.

41. *Dissolve to* MS *at night of people riding on a streetcar. The camera looks through the windows of the car as the music changes on the soundtrack.*

    VOICE-OVER (*during the dissolve*): Though I was not able to go to your concerts, I found ways of sharing in your success.

    The streetcar moves out of the frame screen left, and Lisa, who is standing on the rear platform of the car, enters in MS *screen right just as she is reaching into the side pocket of a man's coat.*[18] *Absorbed in his conversation with another passenger, the man fails to notice Lisa picking his pocket. She opens the program she has taken and begins to read it.*

42. *Cut to* CU *of a program from one of Stefan's concerts. A photograph of him sitting at a piano is on the cover and beneath it is printed his name Stefan Brand. The program is held in Lisa's gloved hands.*

43. *Cut to previous* MS *of Lisa as she replaces the program in the man's coat pocket.*[19] *When she has finished, he turns to look at her and feels his pocket. She stands up very straight to avoid suspicion as the streetcar begins to move out of frame screen left.*

44. *Dissolve to extreme high angle* LS *through a window on a rainy night. Two men dressed in evening clothes escort elegantly dressed women from their carriages and run into the building below the window.*[20] *The background music stops on the soundtrack and is replaced by the laughter of the women.*

> VOICE-OVER (*beginning during the dissolve*): And as the months went by, I began to know your friends.

The camera tracks back to reveal Lisa from behind and in profile as she sits in the window seat and looks out of the window.

> VOICE-OVER: Many of them were women, most of them.[21]
> FRAU BERNDLE (*off-screen, calling*): Lisa!

45. *Cut to* MLS *from within the room looking toward the door as Lisa's mother enters with a bowl in her hands. The room is a combined parlor and dining area.*

> FRAU BERNDLE: Lisa, where are you, Lisa?

The camera pans to follow her as she walks into the kitchen where Lisa is sitting at the window.

> FRAU BERNDLE (*reaching the table*): Aren't you going to finish your dinner?

Lisa leaves the window seat, walks to the table, and sits down.

> LISA (*looking down*): I'm sorry, mother.

She begins to pick at her food as her mother remains standing at the table with her back to the camera.

46. *Dissolve to* MLS *of Lisa as she lies in bed at night. During the dissolve, the Liszt's étude begins on the soundtrack.*

VOICE-OVER (*beginning during the dissolve*): What I really lived for were those evenings when you were alone and I pretended you were playing just for me.

Lisa in her nightgown gets up and sits on the edge of the bed. She walks to the door and stands there briefly, listening to the music. Then she backs up until she is again seated on the edge of the bed, dreamily cradling the bedpost. The camera pans to follow her movements.

VOICE-OVER: And though you didn't know it, you were giving me some of the happiest hours of my life.

Still sitting on the edge of the bed, enraptured by the music, Lisa suddenly rises, walks to the door, opens it quietly, and goes into the hall.

47. *As she walks through the doorway, cut to* MLS *from the hall of Lisa walking toward the camera. She sneaks past a glass doorway through which her mother can be seen in profile. Frau Berndle sits at a small table in the background playing solitaire and does not notice her daughter sneaking past the door.[22] With the camera panning to follow her, Lisa passes a stairway in the background and looks down it momentarily, then quickly moves screen right to a closed door. Climbing up to open a small transom, she stands listening to the music while leaning against the door frame.[23]*

48. *Dissolve to the camera tracking back from blurred* ECU *to* MLS *of Lisa beating a large rug which is now seen to be hanging on a clothesline.[24] During the dissolve, the Liszt étude is replaced on the soundtrack by the sound of people talking and working.*

VOICE-OVER (*during the dissolve*): Then came a great day for me. In the building where we lived, Thursday was rug-beating day.

When Lisa has finished with the rug, she pulls it from the line and wipes her mouth with the back of her hand. Behind the rug the rest of the garden is revealed, and it is filled with other residents working on their rugs. Lisa runs into the background and in LS *tries to help John lift a large rolled carpet. Failing in her attempt, she runs to get her girlfriend's help. The camera pans to follow her to the foreground screen right where she finds her friend (the girl from the previous garden scene) beating a small rug.*

LISA: Come on, let's help him.
GIRL: Oh, I've got to do my own rug.

Lisa pulls her reluctant friend away from her rug-beating.

LISA: I'll do it for you afterwards. Come on!

49. *Cut to* MLS *of Lisa and the girl as they help John pick up the carpet. They drop it and then change positions at John's directions with the girls now at the front of the carpet and John behind.*

GIRL (*as they carry the carpet*): Remember what you promised.
LISA: I will.

The camera pans to follow them as they move toward the stairway, and then it cranes up as they mount the stairs.

LISA (*on the stairway, to the girl*): It's a beautiful rug. (*After receiving no response.*) It's a beautiful rug, isn't it?
GIRL: Oh, it's just a rug.
LISA: Oh, you wouldn't know.

The girls wait at the top of the stairs as John indicates that he wants to come around to carry the front of the rug into the apartment.

GIRL: Say, what are we doing this for?
LISA: Shhh, he'll hear you.

John picks up the front of the carpet, enters the door at the top of the stairs with it, and leaves the frame.

GIRL: Ah, he can't talk.

LISA (*pulling on the carpet to help get it through the door*): Well, he can hear, can't he?[25]

The girl stands looking on as Lisa pulls and pushes on the carpet to get it through the door.

LISA (*to the girl*): Come on!

The girl does not help, but Lisa still manages to get the rug into the door. John then looks out from the doorway, nods his thanks to Lisa, pats her on the cheek, and goes back in.

LISA (*to John*): You're welcome.

The girl starts down the steps, but Lisa runs to the door and catches it before it is completely closed. She stands there holding the door and looking in.

GIRL: Come on, Lisa!
LISA (*not moving*): I'll be right down.
GIRL: What are you going to do?
LISA (*waving her off*): Go away. I'll be right down.
GIRL (*again*): What are you going to do?
LISA (*turning to the girl and taking one menacing step in her direction*): Go away or I'll throw you down the stairs.

Rather than chase the girl, Lisa turns back to the door and enters Stefan's apartment.

50. *Cut to* MS *from within the apartment of Lisa as she walks into the kitchen.*

GIRL (*off-screen*): Are you crazy?

Background music begins on the soundtrack as the camera pans to follow Lisa. She walks through the kitchen and into a short connecting corridor that leads to the front entrance hall of Stefan's apartment. To her left off this corridor is a bedroom where she sees John laying the carpet. To the

*right of the entrance hall off another connecting corridor is the main
sitting room. She passes the door to the bedroom, enters the entrance
hall, then enters the other connecting corridor, and looks into the main
sitting room through a glass door.*

51. *Cut to a* MCU *of Lisa from inside the room through the glass doors. The
shot is framed by the door frame, Lisa's face is pressed against the glass,
and she grimaces as the door clicks and creaks when she turns the door
handle.*

52. *Cut to* MS *of Lisa from inside the room as she opens the door carefully to
make as little noise as possible and then slowly enters. The camera pans
with her as she walks into the room and looks around with great interest.
She turns her back to the camera to look at a piano in the background in
an adjoining room.*

53. *Cut to* MS *of a section of the adjoining room with a window in the
background through which the rooftops of buildings outside can be seen.
Just the top of a piano is visible in the lower left corner of the frame. Lisa
enters screen left, looks at the piano and at the sheet music in a holder on
top of it. She almost sits down on the piano stool, but instead turns to the
window, looks out and then around the room. The camera pans with her
as she goes behind the piano to examine the portraits of composers hanging
on the wall. As she studies them, she bumps into the lyre, and then her
attention is drawn to a large framed poster on the wall, which is an
announcement for one of Stefan's concerts. While examining a pile of
sheet music on a small shelf next to the poster, she tips it over and makes
a noise. Suddenly, the background music stops.*

54. *Cut to* MLS *of John startled by the noise as he lays the carpet in Stefan's
bedroom. He drops the carpet and walks quickly toward the camera.*

55. *Cut to* MLS *of Lisa, with her hand to her mouth looking very frightened.
The camera follows her as she kneels to pick up the sheet music.*

56. *Cut to* LS *from behind Lisa of John standing in the adjoining room
looking at her as she gathers together the music. When she sees him, she*

stands up and runs away.[26] *The camera pans with her to a doorway and watches from behind as she runs down the entrance hall to the front door. As she opens the front door in the background of the frame, John comes into the hall from a door in the middleground screen right and stands with his back to the camera watching her leave.*

57. *Cut to frontal* MS *of John as he stands with his arms folded and smiles after Lisa.*

58. *Cut to high angle* MS *through the bannister of the hall staircase of Lisa's mother being kissed by a man on the stairway. The sound of a door closing is heard off-screen, and they both look up at the camera. Frau Berndle is a large, rather stern woman and her beau is a fat, middle-aged, middle-class gentleman.*

59. *Cut to low angle* MS *of Lisa looking down at them from the landing at the top of the stairs.*

60. *Cut to previous high angle* MS *of Frau Berndle and the man looking up.*

> FRAU BERNDLE (*clutching her sweater together on her chest and looking very guilty*): Lisa! (*She turns to the man, gently pushes him to indicate that he should go, nods to him, and whispers something. He also nods, and she pushes him once more to hasten his departure. He then starts down the stairway as she, still clutching her sweater together at her chest, turns to Lisa and smiles.*) What are you doing up there?

61. *Cut to low angle* MS *of Lisa looking down at the floor.*

62. *Cut to high angle* MS *of her mother as she climbs the stairs. In the background, the man also can be seen going down the stairway and looking up at them. The camera pans with Frau Berndle to* MS *from behind Lisa, who stands on the landing at the top of the stairs as her mother continues to ascend the staircase.*

FRAU BERNDLE: Come, dear, I have something to tell you. (*She goes to Lisa and places her hand on her shoulder.*[27]) It's . . . it's really good news.

The camera pans to follow Lisa and her mother to a doorway screen left.

FRAU BERNDLE (*opening the door*): And I'm sure, if you think about it sensibly, you'll be very, very happy.

Both leave the frame through the doorway.

63. *Cut to* MLS *of Lisa and her mother entering the parlor of their apartment. The camera pans to follow them in profile as they walk across the room behind a large plant and a table in the foreground.*

FRAU BERNDLE (*to Lisa*): Sit down!

Lisa watches as her mother loosens her neckpiece and then opens the draperies screen right. As Lisa sits down she touches the table and dishes rattle. She sits on a chair next to the table, but with her back to it, her arms crossed, and her face and arms resting on the back of the chair. She looks at her mother who turns to her.

FRAU BERNDLE (*clutching a necklace at her throat and walking away from the window*): Well . . .

The camera pans to follow her as she walks screen left in the background behind and around the table and plant and then back screen right in the foreground.

FRAU BERNDLE: I can understand that you must have been startled when you saw Herr Kastner and me in the hall. (*Reaching the sofa against the wall screen right, she straightens a scarf on its back before she sits down.*) Perhaps it was my fault for not telling you something about it before. (*She moves a pillow from her left to her right side on the sofa, then sits with her legs crossed, one hand on the back of the sofa and the other nervously stroking her knee.*) You see, dear, your mother is

not really old. She can have admirers, too. She can even . . . well . . .
(*brushing her knee with her fingers*) . . . be in love with a man.

64. *Cut to* MS *of Lisa from over her mother's shoulder.*

FRAU BERNDLE: Someday, you'll understand better what that means.
Besides you know how hard it is for us to get along on my small
pension.

Lisa removes her hand from the back of the chair and looks down.

65. *Cut to reverse* MS *of Frau Berndle from over Lisa's shoulder.*

FRAU BERNDLE (*pulling on her collar as if it is too tight*): Herr Kastner
has a comfortable business in Linz, a military tailor. (*Sitting up very
straight and folding her hands on her lap.*) And he has . . . he has
done me the honor of asking me to marry him.

66. *Cut to reverse* MS *of Lisa from over her mother's shoulder.*

FRAU BERNDLE: Besides he's a kind man, and he likes you very much.
I'm sure with his help it'll be much easier for you to meet the kind
of . . .
LISA (*interrupting*): Mother?
FRAU BERNDLE: What is it?
LISA: Would we have to go to Linz? Would we have to live there?
FRAU BERNDLE: But why not? What is there to keep us here?
LISA (*rising from her chair and with a voice that cracks with emotion*): I
won't go! I won't go![28]

*Lisa runs out of the frame behind a wall, and the camera pans quickly
around the room to the doorway where she comes into the background
from behind the wall screen right. She runs to the door, opens it, and
goes out, slamming the door behind her.*

FRAU BERNDLE (*off-screen*): Lisa, what's the matter? (*As Lisa slams the
door in the background, her mother comes into the frame in the
foreground. She runs toward the door with her back to the camera*

holding up her skirts. Now in MS, *she stands by the locked door, trying the doorknob.*) What is it?
LISA (*faintly, off-screen*): I won't go! I won't go!
FRAU BERNDLE: Lisa! (*She shakes the doorknob.*) Now, Lisa, do be reasonable! Tell your mother!
LISA (*faintly, off-screen*): I won't! I won't! I won't!
FRAU BERNDLE: Lisa!

Frau Berndle shakes the doorknob and knocks on the door.

67. *Dissolve to* LS *of Herr Kastner in a white straw hat, with a cigar in his mouth, and with his coat draped over his arm. He has just purchased tickets at a ticket window in a train station. Laughing as he leaves the window, he puts the tickets in his wallet and mumbles to himself while counting his money. The camera pans with him as he walks to a counter screen right where Lisa and her mother await him in* MS. *Lisa is in the background piling her bags on the counter, and her mother is in the foreground as Herr Kastner comes to stand just between them and begins to speak to an official who is behind the counter handling their luggage.*

HERR KASTNER: That will go with us in our compartment. Let's see, we had eleven all together. (*Taking his cigar from his mouth, he begins to count their bags, turning around in order to point to the various pieces as he counts them.*)

FRAU KASTNER (*interrupting his counting*): The trunks, dear! The trunks, dear!
HERR KASTNER: Now don't worry, dear. I'll take care of everything. (*He walks away, and the camera pans with him, eliminating Lisa and her mother from the frame.*) The expressman promised the trunks at . . . (*He stops, looks up, and then looks back at his watch as a whistle blows.*) Oh, either I've lost half a minute, or the station clock's ahead.
FRAU KASTNER (*faintly, off-screen*): Oh, me!

Herr Kastner walks back toward the counter as a porter pushing a cart comes into the frame in the background. Herr Kastner, now in MLS, *reaches into his pocket.*

HERR KASTNER (*putting his cigar back in his mouth*): How much will that be, please?

PORTER: That's up to you, sir.

HERR KASTNER: Up to me, good heavens! One kroner should be enough. (*He walks back to the counter, and the camera pans with him. Now in* MS, *he speaks to his wife.*) I promise you the trunks will be here on time. About the boxes . . . one, two, three . . . (*He circles the boxes as he counts them and then runs back to the counter to talk to the official.*) Ah, how long will it take if we send them to Linz third class?

68. *Cut to* MCU *of Lisa as she clings to one of her bags which is resting on the counter.*

OFFICIAL (*off-screen*): Two weeks, maybe.

HERR KASTNER (*off-screen*): Two weeks. Very good. Mark each of these second class . . . (*laughs*) . . . third class.

OFFICIAL (*off-screen*): Each of these second class . . . third class.

69. *Cut back to previous* MS *of Herr Kastner, Frau Kastner, and Lisa at the counter with the official just in the frame behind the counter.*

HERR KASTNER: Third class, yes. (*He notices something behind him.*) Ha, what did I tell you? (*The camera pans with him as he walks off to meet in* MLS *the expressman who has just entered screen right pushing a cart full of trunks.*) When you're going to do a thing, do it on time. That's always been my system. (*To the expressman.*) You can unload those right here. Our train doesn't leave until twelve. (*He walks back to the counter with the camera panning to follow him.*)

FRAU KASTNER: Yes, twelve, of course, darling, but sharp, sharp.

HERR KASTNER (*taking out his watch again*): Twelve, yes, of course, I'd almost forgotten. Well, now let me see . . .

FRAU KASTNER: Ya.

The camera leaves them as they continue to discuss the luggage, and it pans with the official who leaves the counter and walks screen right in the foreground. In the background, Lisa is also seen walking away.[29] *The camera follows the official to a wall beyond which Lisa can be seen looking around the corner. Her mother and Herr Kastner are heard still talking about the luggage off-screen as background music begins on the soundtrack, and Lisa turns her back to the camera and runs through a doorway in the background.*

VOICE-OVER (*beginning as Lisa runs out of the train station*): Suddenly, I knew I couldn't live without you.

70. *Dissolve to* LS *at night of a streetcar pulling into the frame screen right. Lisa jumps from it onto the street, drops her purse, picks it up, and then begins to walk toward the camera.*

VOICE-OVER: I didn't know what I had in mind or what my parents would do when they found me missing.

Lisa walks down the sidewalk toward the camera as a cat crosses the street from right to left.

VOICE-OVER: All I wanted was to see you once more, to be near you again, to throw myself at your feet, and cling to you and never leave you. Nothing else, nothing else mattered.[30]

As Lisa crosses the street, the camera pans to watch her from behind. She walks to an iron gate where she rings a bell.

71. *Cut to* MS *of Lisa through the grating of the gate as she waits and again rings the bell.*

72. *Cut to reverse* LS *through the gate. The porter enters from the shadows screen right holding a candle and walks toward the camera. As he approaches the gate, the camera tracks back to reveal Lisa waiting there.*

PORTER: Alright, alright, I'm coming. Oh. it's you, Lisa. I thought by now you were already halfway to Linz. Didn't your train leave about . . .

As the porter opens the gate, Lisa quickly slips through and runs with her back to the camera toward the doorway to the building in the background screen left.

LISA (*softly as she runs*): I forgot something.

73. *Cut to high angle* LS *from the landing above the staircase of Lisa climbing the stairs in the darkened hallway. The camera pans with her as she ascends the staircase and then as she runs to the door of Stefan's apartment. When she reaches the door, she knocks and then nervously begins to straighten her clothes and hair. When no one answers, she knocks several times and listens at the door, then she turns, and the camera pans after her to the stairway. First, she looks down at the empty hall, then she starts down the stairs, the camera panning to frame the beginning of her descent.*

74. *Cut to* MLS *through the doorway of Lisa opening the glass door to the building. After walking through the doorway, she walks toward the garden gate with the camera panning to follow her.*

75. *Cut to* LS *of Lisa entering the garden. The camera pans behind her as she walks to the stairway and cranes up as she climbs the stairs. At the top, in low angle* LS, *she knocks on Stefan's back door, but again receives no answer.*

76. *Cut to* MCU *of Lisa from within Stefan's apartment through the window of the door and framed by the window's checked curtains.*

77. *Cut to low angle* MLS *of Lisa walking along the balcony at the top of the stairs to screen left. In the foreground obstructing the camera's view are tree branches and leaves.*

78. *As she walks into the shadows screen left, cut to* MLS *of Lisa now in her old apartment. The camera pans to follow her as she walks through its empty hallways.*
    VOICE-OVER: These rooms where I had lived had been filled with your music.

The Liszt étude begins on the soundtrack.

VOICE-OVER: Now they were empty.

The camera pans to watch Lisa enter a large empty room with a step ladder in the center, a large window in the background, and a wooden beam dividing the frame in the foreground.

VOICE-OVER: Would they ever come to life again? Would I? Only you could answer. (*Lisa goes to the ladder and sits down on it with her hands in her lap.*)[31] So I waited . . . (*whispered*) . . . waited.

The camera holds on Lisa in LS.

79. *Slow dissolve to MS of Lisa in the darkened hallway outside Stefan's apartment. She sits in profile on the stairs just above Stefan's door.*

VOICE-OVER: For what seemed like endless hours, I sat outside your door trying to keep myself awake, afraid I might fall asleep and miss you. Then . . .

The sound of a latch being opened is heard, and the background music stops. Lisa rises and looks down the stairway as she hears faint off-screen voices.

CONCIERGE: Who is it?
STEFAN: Brand.
CONCIERGE: Good morning, Mr. Brand.

Lisa slowly creeps up the stairs above Stefan's door, the camera panning and craning up with her.

80. *Cut to high angle LS from over Lisa's shoulder looking down the stairway to the door of the building. The stairway banister can be seen in the lower foreground and Lisa's back in the upper foreground as a woman in a white evening dress enters through the doorway followed by Stefan, who is also in evening clothes. They leave the frame bottom screen left, and*

the camera pans to the top of the stairs. The woman is heard laughing off-screen. Lisa is still seen from behind and in the shadows screen left as Stefan and the woman enter screen right. Stefan stops when almost at the top of the stairs, takes out his key, offers the woman his hand, and leads her up the last few steps and off screen left. Stefan whispers and the woman giggles; the sound of a key in a lock is heard. Lisa, left alone, slowly begins to walk down the stairs with her back to the camera as background music begins on the soundtrack.

VOICE-OVER: And so there was nothing left for me. I went to Linz.

81. *Blur and dissolve to blurred, gradually clearing* MCU *of Stefan, who is still seated at his desk reading the letter. The background music continues through the dissolve.*

VOICE-OVER: You who have always lived so freely, have you any idea what life is like in a little garrison town? (*Stefan turns the page of the letter and holds it up as he reads.*) I was eighteen now and was expected to take my place in society.[32]

The soundtrack music stops and is replaced by the sound of church bells ringing.

82. *Blur and dissolve to blurred, gradually clearing* LS *of Lisa, her mother, and Herr Kastner as they walk, dressed in their Sunday best, down a provincial street toward the camera. Lisa is wearing a white dress and carries a matching white parasol. Frau Kastner is also in white, but with a dark parasol, and Herr Kastner is dressed in a dark suit and alpine hat.*

FRAU KASTNER: Come now, Lisa, don't look down at your feet. Please be tactful and let him do the talking . . .

83. *Cut to* MCU *of Lisa who looks very uncomfortable.*

FRAU KASTNER (*off-screen*): . . . but not all the talking. Do you hear me, Lisa?

84. *Cut to* MLS *of Lisa and her parents. As Lisa looks down at her feet, her parents look up.*

FRAU KASTNER: Good morning, Colonel.
HERR KASTNER: Good morning, Colonel.

Quick pan right and crane up to a long shot of the colonel and the lieutenant both in dress uniforms as they stand on a balcony above the street.[33]

COLONEL (*saluting*): Good morning.

The colonel, followed by the lieutenant, descends the stairs screen right, and the camera pans and cranes down to follow them. The colonel salutes first Lisa's mother, Lisa, and then Herr Kastner each in turn.

COLONEL: Frau Kastner, Fraülein Kastner, Herr Kastner, may I have the honor to present my nephew, Lieutenant Leopold von Kaltnegger.
LIEUTENANT (*very stiffly walking up to Lisa's mother and saluting her*): I have the honor to kiss your hand. (*He kisses her hand, and she smiles.*) I'm very pleased to make your acquaintance. (*He steps back.*)
FRAU KASTNER: Thank you, lieutenant.
COLONEL (*turning and nodding to Herr Kastner as he introduces him to the lieutenant*): Herr Kastner.
LIEUTENANT (*to Herr Kastner*): I have the honor, sir. (*Herr Kastner removes his hat.*) I'm very pleased to make your acquaintance.

HERR KASTNER (*smiling and nodding*): Thank you, Lieutenant, thank you. (*Looking at Lisa.*) Allow me to present our daughter, Lisa. (*Introducing the lieutenant to Lisa.*) Lieutenant Leopold von Kaltnegger.

Lisa curtsies, and the Lieutenant salutes. As Herr Kastner makes the introduction, a peasant cart crosses the frame in the foreground, forcing the group to move back and temporarily obstructing the camera's view. After the cart passes, the lieutenant can be seen kissing Lisa's hand. The colonel then motions with his hand to lead her parents away across the

*street. Lisa follows with the lieutenant as her parents and the colonel
leave the frame screen right with Herr Kastner chattering on.*

HERR KASTNER: I've been meaning to tell you for quite some time
how impressed I was with your parading the morning of the emperor's
birthday . . .

The camera tracks with Lisa and the lieutenant in MS *as they cross the
street. When they reach the sidewalk, the lieutenant maneuvers himself
behind Lisa so that he can walk on the outer part of the sidewalk next to
the street.*

LIEUTENANT: Excuse me.

They walk on in silence with the camera tracking them.

LIEUTENANT (*as they walk, finally breaking the silence*): Do you like it here in Linz?

LISA: Quite well.

LIEUTENANT: It must seem very restful after living in Vienna.

LISA: I liked Vienna.

LIEUTENANT (*in mild disbelief*): Indeed! What did you like about it?

As they cross the street, they also cross before the camera, which then begins to track them from their left rather than from their right as previously.

LIEUTENANT (*having received no answer from Lisa*): Perhaps, you were fond of the music?

LISA: Yes.

LIEUTENANT: We also have good music here. Every . . . every other Saturday afternoon they have a concert on the Courso.

LISA: Oh, really!

LIEUTENANT: Perhaps someday, you'll allow me the honor of escorting you.

LISA: Very nice of you.

LIEUTENANT: When I was a cadet, I took part myself. I played second trumpet.

LISA: Oh, how nice!

LIEUTENANT: I must say I'm glad we both like music.

As the camera tracks with Lisa and the lieutenant, Lisa's parents come into the frame in MS. They stand in profile facing each other in the foreground as Lisa and the lieutenant walk into the background and out of the frame screen left.

FRAU KASTNER: You see there's nothing wrong with the child if she only meets the right people.

Herr Kastner nods. They turn their backs to the camera and walk away into a crowd of people who are walking in the background across the frame. The camera pans to follow them, a fountain intervenes in the

foreground, and the camera moves past it to hold as Herr Kastner and Frau Kastner approach a stairway.

85. *Dissolve to* MS *of the conductor of a military band. With his baton held high, he strikes up the band.*

CONDUCTOR: Hup, hup, hup!

The instruments which surround him in the frame are raised at this command, and the band begins to play a popular rendition of "Song to the Evening Star" from Wagner's Tannhäuser.

VOICE-OVER: The lieutenant was right. Linz was a musical town, so twice a month that summer we listened, the lieutenant and I.

Lisa and the lieutenant enter in the background behind the band and walk across the frame with the camera panning to follow them. They turn, walk around the band, then move toward the camera through a group of pigeons on the ground. The camera tracks back slowly as they approach. Lisa and the lieutenant turn slightly screen right to greet some soldiers and their female companions who are just in the frame. The lieutenant salutes, Lisa nods pleasantly, and then she and the lieutenant leave the frame in the foreground screen right. As they leave, revealed in the background are Herr Kastner, Frau Kastner, and the colonel, who sit in MLS *in an outdoor cafe.* [34]

FRAU KASTNER: Before the afternoon is over, I'm sure we will have an announcement. (*She takes a sip from her teacup.*)

HERR KASTNER: Nothing could please us more, Colonel. (*Meekly.*) Isn't that right, my dear?

All nod and look off-screen right in the direction taken by Lisa and the lieutenant.

86. *Cut to* LS *through the bushes of Lisa and the lieutenant as Lisa sits down on a park bench and the lieutenant on her left salutes her and then begins to sit down himself.*

87. *Cut to* MS *of Lisa and the lieutenant seated on the bench.*

LIEUTENANT: Miss Lisa.

LISA (*turning her head slightly to look at him, faintly*): Uh-huh.

LIEUTENANT: This is a subject which I wished to bring up for some time. I trust you'll forgive me if I presume to mention a hope I've allowed myself . . .[35]

Lisa begins to look nervously agitated, moving her head from side to side, looking at him and then down at the ground. He, on the other hand, seems to be trying very hard to look relaxed with his arm resting casually on the back of the bench.

88. *Cut to* MS *of the lieutenant with Lisa in profile in the foreground.*

LIEUTENANT: It may be unnecessary for me to mention that ever since you first came to my attention, I've been most favorably impressed . . .

LISA (*turning to look at him and nodding*): Thank you.

LIEUTENANT: And I have every reason to believe that your parents are not opposed to my keeping company—that is steady company—with you.

LISA (interrupting him): But, Lieutenant, I . . .

LIEUTENANT (*interrupting her by raising his hand and cutting the air with it*): Oh, please allow me to finish. As far as my prospects are concerned, you must be aware by now that it's generally believed by my uncle and others that I have the qualifications for an outstanding military career.

LISA: Well, there's no doubt of that.

LIEUTENANT: Naturally, it's too soon to discuss any definite steps.

89. *Cut to reverse* MS *of Lisa from over the lieutenant's shoulder.*

LIEUTENANT: We should know each other for a reasonable time . . .

LISA (*shaking her head*): But lieutenant, I'm sorry. It's impossible.

LIEUTENANT (*softly*): Impossible?

LISA (*now very nervous, nodding several times, fidgeting with her hands, looking back at him and then away*): Please don't ask me to explain, but . . .

LIEUTENANT: But I certainly must insist. Is there someone else?

90. *Cut to* MCU *of Lisa about to say no and then changing her mind just as she is about to speak.*

LISA: Yes, I'm engaged to be married. (*She swallows hard.*)

LIEUTENANT (*off-screen, in a shocked tone*): Engaged to be married?

LISA: I should have told you before, but I didn't realize how . . .

LIEUTENANT (*interrupting her*): The whole time you've been in Linz I haven't seen you in anyone's company.

LISA (*still fidgeting and talking very quickly from nervousness*): He doesn't live in Linz. He lives in Vienna.

LIEUTENANT: Vienna?

Lisa nods.

LISA (*still talking very quickly*): He . . . ah . . . writes music. He's a
musician. (*She smiles nervously.*)
LIEUTENANT: But how can that be? Your mother and father, they have
given my uncle every encouragement . . .
LISA (*interrupting him*): They don't know about it.
LIEUTENANT: You mean you're engaged to a man and your parents don't
even know him?

She nods.

91. *Cut to previous* MLS *of Lisa and the lieutenant sitting on the bench.*

LIEUTENANT: Oh!
LISA: I'm sorry. I . . .
LIEUTENANT (*As he stands up, his head rises above the frame, and he
very stiffly offers his arm to Lisa*): Oh, then please.

92. *Cut to previous* MLS *of Lisa's mother, Herr Kastner, and the colonel at
their table in the cafe.*

HERR KASTNER (*standing up anxiously*): It won't be long now!
FRAU KASTNER: The wine!
HERR KASTNER (*looking very excited*): The wine, waiter! The wine!
The wine!

93. *Cut to* LS *of Lisa and the lieutenant leaving the bench and walking screen
right. The camera pans to follow them from behind. As they approach a
garden gateway, the camera holds. Lisa and the lieutenant walk through
the gateway while in the background beyond it the band can be seen just
finishing. In the foreground, a cannon and people sitting next to it at
tables in a cafe are visible at the bottom screen right. As Lisa and the
lieutenant leave the frame, the band finishes playing and applause is
heard.*

94. *Cut to previous* MLS *of Lisa's parents and the colonel. A waiter hands a
bottle of wine to Herr Kastner, who then begins to pour it. Frau Kastner
looks over her shoulder expectantly as applause is still heard off-screen.*

95. *Cut to* LS *of the band.*

CONDUCTOR: Hup, hup, ahup!

*The band begins to play the Radetzky March and to march across the
frame. As the first members of the band begin to leave screen right,
Lisa and the lieutenant enter screen left in* MS *in profile with the camera
tracking to follow them. As they walk, Lisa and the lieutenant interrupt
the parade of marching musicians in order to approach the table where
Lisa's parents and the colonel are seated in the background. When they
reach the table, the lieutenant takes the colonel aside. The band continues
to march across the frame in the foreground. What is said between the
lieutenant and the colonel cannot be heard over the band music, but the
colonel nods, salutes Lisa and her parents, and both he and the lieutenant
leave screen left. The band music becomes faint and gradually fades
away as the parade of musicians and townspeople following them goes off
screen right.*[36]

HERR KASTNER: But I don't understand.
FRAU KASTNER: Lisa, what happened?

*Lisa sits down next to the table in the chair that was previously occupied
by the colonel.*

FRAU KASTNER (*standing over Lisa*): Answer me! What happened?
LISA: Nothing.

The camera slowly tracks in, the band music gradually fading away.

HERR KASTNER: But after all . . .
FRAU KASTNER: But you must have said something. What did you say
    to him?
LISA: Well . . . I . . . I only told him the truth.
FRAU KASTNER (*very angry, almost screaming*): The truth! What do
    you mean the truth? What did you say to him?
LISA: I told him I wasn't free.

During the above conversation, the camera has gradually tracked in to MS *of Lisa surrounded by her parents on both sides of the frame.*

FRAU KASTNER: What?

Blur and dissolve as the voice-over begins.

VOICE-OVER: My poor parents, for them this was the end. For me, it was a new beginning.

96. *Dissolve to blurred, gradually clearing* MS *of Stefan reading the letter. His elbows rest on the desk, and he rubs his chin with the back of his hand as he reads. Background music begins on the soundtrack during the dissolve.*

   The camera pans right to the door where John can be seen entering the room carrying a bottle of cognac and glasses on a tray. Then it pans with him back to the desk he places the tray on, lowering to reframe Stefan with the tray to his right.

   VOICE-OVER: Vienna, when I saw it again, seemed to have taken on a new splendor.

   The camera tracks in to MCU *of Stefan reading.*

   VOICE-OVER: All the time I'd been away I thought of it longingly as your city. Now it was our city.

97. *Blur and dissolve to a gradually clearing* MLS *of a woman laughing as she tries on a dress. The shot is framed by draperies which hang on both sides of the doorway through which the camera looks.*

   VOICE-OVER: Madame Spitzer's, where I found work, was the kind of establishment where one learns many things.

   The camera pans left to the next opening in the draperies where Lisa in

MLS *again framed by the draperies can be seen adjusting her dress and looking into a full length mirror.*

MADAME SPITZER (*off-screen*): Miss Lisa, please!
LISA (*turning toward the camera and looking out through the doorway while still adjusting her dress*): Coming!

Lisa picks up a full length cloak and exits through the doorway while she is still putting on the cloak. The camera pans to follow her as she meets a woman dressed as a maid who helps her button the garment. In the bottom foreground, another woman can be seen working at a sewing machine.

MAID: Now, hold your breath.

Lisa picks up a teacup and drinks from it.

MADAME SPITZER (*off-screen*): Miss Lisa, we are waiting!

98. *Cut to* MLS *of Lisa entering screen left through a curtained doorway and then walking across the frame with the camera panning to follow her. She ascends a small staircase to a slightly elevated platform which is the showroom of the fashion salon in which she is employed. Gracefully circling the room in long shot, she shows the dress to a woman sitting and a man standing in the background. The proprietress of the salon, Madame Spitzer, stands next to a metal railing in the foreground of the frame. As the camera looks through the railing, Lisa circles the room and Madame Spitzer walks slowly to screen left.*

WOMAN: Very pretty.
MAN: Yes . . . (*coughs*) . . . very.

99. *Dissolve to* MLS *of Lisa bending over a table in the salon. The camera rises with her as she straightens up upon hearing a knock at the window above her. Outside the window, two men in military uniforms stand smiling down at her. They nod and one man tips his hat, but Lisa abruptly pulls the draperies closed.*

100. *Dissolve to* MS *of Lisa now in a white evening gown. Again she is looking into a mirror and adjusting her dress.*

101. *Cut to* LS *through the banister of the salon platform. Lisa stands before the mirror. An elderly military man and a woman can be seen on the extreme right watching her. The man rises from his seat and walks across the frame in the foreground as the camera pans with him. When he reaches the banister, he leans against it to talk to Madame Spitzer, who is seated at a desk on the lower level of the room just below the banister.*

> MILITARY MAN (*leaning casually against the banister with a cigarette in his mouth*): Very charming, very charming indeed. (*He looks over his shoulder back in Lisa's direction.*) Do you think . . .
> MADAME SPITZER (*not even bothering to look up from her work*): She is not like that. I don't understand that girl, but every evening as soon as the shutters are closed, off she goes straight home.
> MILITARY MAN (*amazed*): Really! (*He turns and looks back in Lisa's direction.*)

102. *Dissolve to* LS *of women leaving the back door of Madame Spitzer's shop in the evening after work. The soundtrack music stops and is replaced by the sound of women talking and laughing. Two women come through the door in the center of the frame and walk out screen left. Another woman comes out to be met by a woman entering screen right.*

> VOICE-OVER: Madame Spitzer spoke the truth. I was not like the others. Nobody waited for me.

Lisa walks out of the door in a long black cloak and muffler. She turns and walks down a sidewalk with small piles of snow in the background. The camera pans to follow her in MLS.

> VOICE-OVER: Off I went, not home, but to the only place that had ever seemed home to me.

The camera now frames Lisa from behind as she walks down the street toward an archway in the background.

VOICE-OVER: Night after night . . .

103. *Dissolve to* LS *of Lisa standing on a street corner next to a wall with snow on the ground in small piles around her. The music of street musicians playing and singing begins to be heard as they enter the frame screen left.*

VOICE-OVER: . . . I returned to the same spot, but you never noticed me until one evening . . .

As the musicians walk across the frame in the background, one man leaves the group to pick up a coin in the snow near Lisa. The coin has apparently been tossed from the window of one of the adjacent buildings. As he reaches down, he raises his hat in a gesture of thanks and then rejoins the others. They move slowly on as Lisa stands in the foreground screen right next to the wall.

104–105. *Cut to* MLS *of Lisa and then to* LS *of Stefan entering from around a corner in the background. He walks down the sidewalk toward the camera with his hands in his overcoat pockets, casually looking into the windows of a restaurant as he passes. The camera begins to pan with him in* MS *as he continues down the sidewalk. He passes Lisa, who is standing in the background, and does not notice her. The camera continues to pan with him, excluding Lisa from the frame, as he walks on toward the street musicians, who now are seen in* LS. *Stefan reaches into his pocket to find some money to give them.*

106. *Cut to* MLS *of Stefan giving the money to a small boy among the musicians, patting the child on the shoulder, and then looking fixedly off-screen right.*[37]

107–108. *Cut to* LS *of Lisa still standing in the corner and then to* MCU *of Stefan looking in her direction with evident interest. He begins to move toward the camera.*

109. *Cut to* LS *of Lisa from over Stefan's shoulder as he approaches her. The camera tracks in with him to* MCU *of Lisa.*

> STEFAN (*removing his hat*): I've seen you before . . . (*She looks down.*)
> . . . a few nights ago . . .

110. *Cut to* MCU *of Stefan smiling.*

> STEFAN: . . . right here. Oh, you live near here?
111. LISA (MCU): No.
112. STEFAN (MCU): Do you like to listen to street singers?
113. LISA (MCU, *looking down*): Yes.
> STEFAN: Neither do I.

Both laugh.

114. *Cut to* MS *of Lisa and Stefan as Stefan puts on his hat and they walk down the street toward the camera, which tracks back as they approach.*

STEFAN (*stopping, removing his hat, and turning to Lisa*): Oh, I should introduce myself.
LISA: No, I know who you are.

They begin to walk on again in silence.

STEFAN: I suppose sooner or later we'll have to decide where we're walking to.

Lisa laughs.

STEFAN (*looking off-screen left*): I have something I should call off. Well, I almost never get to the place I start out for anyway.

• *They both laugh again, he takes her arm, and they walk away with their backs to the camera.*

115. *Cut to LS through the windows of a restaurant as Lisa and Stefan enter screen right. As they walk across the frame, the camera, still looking through the windows, pans to follow them. Background music is still heard on the soundtrack, but more faintly than previously and with the sounds of people talking and laughing and of dishes clinking in the restaurant heard above it.*

Stefan and Lisa enter the restaurant through the glass door in MLS. Stefan continues toward the camera and leaves Lisa standing next to the door. The camera remains on Lisa in the doorway as Stefan leaves the frame screen left.

116. *Cut to LS of Stefan from behind as he descends a small flight of stairs and enters the main dining area of the crowded restaurant. As he passes a waiter, he looks around the room and then calls a boy over to him. After Stefan whispers something to the boy, the boy runs off into the background screen right, and Stefan turns to look back at the camera in Lisa's direction.*

117. *Cut to* MLS *of Lisa at the door as a man with his back to the camera leaves the restaurant.*

118. *Cut back to* LS *of Stefan as a waiter approaches him and they begin to talk.*

119. *Cut to previous* MLS *of Lisa at the door as two men enter the restaurant.*

FIRST MAN (*to Lisa*): Pardon.
SECOND MAN (*also to Lisa*): Excuse me.

120. *Cut to* MS *of Stefan and the waiter.*[38]

WAITER (*looking toward the camera in Lisa's direction and then back at Stefan after having put on his pince-nez*): Very charming.
STEFAN (*looking down with mild embarrassment, but also with a self-satisfied smile, speaking in a low voice*): Thank you.
WAITER: Anything else I can do for you, Mr. Brand?
STEFAN (*taking a cigarette from his cigarette case and putting it in his mouth*): Will you please tell Balish I won't be at the rehearsal this evening?
WAITER (*lighting Stefan's cigarette*): Oh, congratulations!

121. *Cut to* LS *of a man sitting at a table reading a newspaper. The heads of other diners are visible in the lower foreground.*

MAN: Fritz, is the Journal free now?

122. *Cut to previous* MS *of Fritz and Stefan as they both look off-screen left in the direction of the man.*

FRITZ: Just a moment, sir. Don't you see I'm busy with Mr. Brand? (*Looking back at Stefan.*) Now, how about Lelia?
STEFAN: Yes, there's Lelia.
FRITZ: Yes, there's Lelia. Well, if she comes, what am I going to tell her?
STEFAN: Well, tell her . . .

FRITZ: Ya, I'll tell her . . . I'll tell her it was most important, and you had to work tonight.

STEFAN: Yes, that's it. That's fine.

FRITZ: I'm sure she will understand.

STEFAN (*handing him a coin*): I'm sure.

FRITZ (*as Stefan begins to walk away*): Thank you.

STEFAN: Bye.

The camera pans to follow Stefan as he walks away. When he begins to ascend the staircase with his back to the camera, he is stopped from behind by a man entering screen right.

MAN (*a cigarette in a cigarette holder dangling from his mouth*): Oh, Stefan!

STEFAN (*turning to face him*): Yes.

MAN: I missed you yesterday. I . . . I have to talk to you.

STEFAN: Well, later.

MAN: I saw the manuscript of a concerto. It's a young man I met. His father owns half of the train line to Schonbrunn. I thought perhaps it . . . it was something for one of your concerts. If you just glance at it . . .

STEFAN: Well, I'll talk to you tomorrow, huh?

MAN (*repeating in confirmation*): Tomorrow.

Stefan walks up the stairs and across the doorway. As the camera pans with him a large plant with long spiked leaves intervenes in the fore-ground. Stefan puts on his hat and walks out through the doorway with Lisa. The camera pans right to frame them in LS through the restaurant window as they enter a carriage.

123. *Dissolve to frontal LS of Lisa and Stefan as they sit behind a table in an opulent restaurant. They sit in an ornately decorated booth with partially drawn draperies hanging on either side of the frame. During the dissolve the background music changes to a waltz.*

The camera tracks in to just within the draperies.

STEFAN (*as he ties a napkin around Lisa's neck*): Now, don't be frightened. Even if it's not becoming, the lobster will pay no attention. (*Studying Lisa.*) I was wrong, it is becoming.[39]

Lisa laughs.

The camera continues to track in slowly.

STEFAN (*picking up a menu from the table*): Now let's see, when do they have lobster again? Friday. How about Friday? (*Not waiting for an answer.*) A whole week is a long time. How about Wednesday? That's venison, or there's pheasant on Monday. Could you possibly make it on Monday?

124. *Cut to* MCU *of Lisa from over Stefan's shoulder.*

   LISA: I've no engagements at all.

125. *Cut to reverse* MCU *of Stefan from over Lisa's shoulder.*

   STEFAN: Well, I don't either. We'll have dinner tomorrow night—wienerschnitzel.

126. *Cut to frontal* MTS *of Lisa and Stefan sitting behind the table. Stefan replaces the menu as a waiter enters screen right. He crosses the frame in the foreground, passing in front of the table, and stands screen left next to Stefan. The camera tracks out to* MLS *framed by the draperies.*

   WAITER: Excuse me, Herr Brand, but the lady in the next room—if I'm not mistaken, it's Countess Rudentsky—wonders if you'd do her the favor of signing her program of this afternoon's concert.

127. *Cut to* CU *of the program with Stefan's photograph on the cover as he signs.*

   STEFAN (*off-screen*): Certainly.

WAITER (*off*): She said Mozart himself could not have done better.
LISA (*off*): How nice of her!

128. *Cut to previous* MLS *framed by the draperies.*

STEFAN (*to the waiter*): There you are. Thank the countess for the
   compliment. (*He hands back the program.*)
WAITER: Thank you, Herr Brand.
STEFAN (*to Lisa as the waiter leaves and Stefan pours the wine*): Even
   though it's not in the least deserved.

*The waiter leaves through the draperies, which he pulls closer together as
he goes.*

LISA: Four years ago, when you played the D Minor . . .
STEFAN (*interrupting her*): You remember that?
LISA: . . . the Morning Review also compared you to a young Mozart.

The camera begins to track in again.

STEFAN: I was very young. There was that much resemblance. (*Lisa
   takes a sip of wine.*) You like it? (*Lisa nods. He also drinks.*) It's called
   Valpolicella. The first vineyard you see when you come down the other
   side of the Alps. (*He reaches to the center of the table, picks up a
   lobster, and pulls off a claw. With a nutcracker, he cracks it and then
   places it on Lisa's plate.*) The Italians say it's such a good wine because
   the grapes have their roots in the valley and their eyes on the mountains. (*He reaches for another lobster claw.*)
LISA: Please . . .
STEFAN: Please, what?
LISA (*as she places her wine glass on the table*): Please, talk about
   yourself.
STEFAN: I believe you really want to hear about me. Why?

129. *Cut to* MCU *of Lisa from over Stefan's shoulder. His face can be seen in
   the foreground in profile.*

STEFAN: Oh, never mind why. (*He looks thoughtfully into the distance.*) Well, the truth is I've had rather an easy time of it. People accepted my music very quickly, perhaps too quickly. Sometimes, it's easier to please others than oneself.

130. *Cut to reverse* MCU *of Stefan from over Lisa's shoulder.*

STEFAN: What were you going to say? You know you don't talk very much.
LISA: Well, I can't say it very well, but . . .
STEFAN: Yes.

131. *Cut to reverse* MCU *of Lisa from over Stefan's shoulder.*

LISA: . . . sometimes I felt when you were playing that . . .
STEFAN (*listening intently*): Go on.
LISA: . . . that you hadn't quite found—I don't know what it is—what you're looking for.

132. *Cut to previous* MCU *of Stefan. As he speaks, he leans back in his seat, and the camera pans to reframe him and then tracks back out to* MS.

STEFAN (*leaning back in his seat*): How long have you been hiding in my piano? Never mind explaining, I'll just assume you're a sorceress and that you can make yourself very tiny. (*Lisa laughs nervously and looks down and away from Stefan as he continues with mock seriousness.*) It might be a good thing to have a sorceress for a friend. Who knows, you may be able to help me someday.

133. *Dissolve to* MCU *of the face of a carriage driver. In this darkly lit night scene, the camera pans left and drops down to reveal Lisa and Stefan in* MS *in the back seat of a moving carriage. Stefan is looking off into the distance thoughtfully, and Lisa is looking at him.*

LISA: How could I help you?
STEFAN (*looking back at her*): So that's what you've been thinking about.

(*She smiles and sighs.*) You're a very strange girl, whoever you are and
wherever you came from. Don't you have any problems?

LISA: Not important ones. (*She reaches over and tenderly tucks Stefan's
scarf into the collar of his overcoat.*)

STEFAN: It's a long while since anyone did that for me.

Lisa looks down, and Stefan looks off into the distance again.

134. *Cut to* LS *as the carriage enters the frame screen right on a dark deserted
street.*

STEFAN (*to the driver*): Stop here, please!

DRIVER: Whoa!

*The carriage stops at a street corner. The frame is divided by a lamppost
in the foreground as Stefan gets out of the carriage and walks toward the
camera, which pans to follow him.*

FLOWER SELLER (*off-screen*): Good evening, Mr. Brand.

STEFAN: Good evening.

He walks to a flower stand attended by an old woman who is seen in MLS
from over Stefan's shoulder.

FLOWER SELLER: Roses?

STEFAN: Yes, please.

135. *Cut to reverse* MLS *of Stefan from behind the flower seller's shoulder.*

FLOWER SELLER: Red roses?

STEFAN: No, red is the wrong color. (*Pointing.*) A single, white rose,
that's perfect!

*The flower seller begins to extract a single white rose from a vase of
flowers.*

136. *Cut to* MS *of Lisa who is still sitting in the carriage looking after Stefan.*

STEFAN (*off-screen*): This is a special occasion. (*Lisa smiles.*)

137. *Cut to previous* MLS *of Stefan and the flower seller from over Stefan's shoulder.*

STEFAN (*holding the flower in one hand and paying the woman with the other*): There you are. Goodnight. (*He leaves the frame screen right as the flower seller warms her hands over a fire.*)
FLOWER SELLER: Goodnight, Mr. Brand. Enjoy yourself!

138. *Dissolve to* MCU *of Lisa and Stefan in the carriage again.*

STEFAN: Did I guess right? Is it your flower?
LISA (*fondling the rose*): From now on, it will be.

139. *Cut to* MS *of Lisa and Stefan in the carriage with the driver bending down into the frame in the upper left corner. He points with his whip to the carriage top which is folded down behind Lisa and Stefan.*

DRIVER: Would you like me to close it?
STEFAN: No.
DRIVER: And now to the fairgrounds.

Stefan takes Lisa's hand, and they stare into each others' eyes as the carriage pulls out of the frame screen left.

DRIVER (*to the horses*): Yup!

140. *Dissolve to* LS *of Lisa and Stefan walking in a snowy country landscape.*[40] *The scene is framed by trees on each side and a small spiked iron fence in the lower foreground. In the extreme background, a motionless ferris wheel can also be seen and carnival music is heard on the soundtrack. The camera tracks with Lisa and Stefan as they walk and look about them.*

141. *Cut to* MS *of Lisa and Stefan as they stop, turn around, and look at the landscape.*

LISA (*referring to the fairgrounds*): Do you think it will all be closed?
STEFAN: I hope not.

Stefan takes Lisa's arm, and they begin to walk again with the camera tracking them in MS.

STEFAN: I never come here in the season. It's more pleasant in the winter. I don't know why.
LISA: It's perhaps because you prefer to imagine how it will be in the Spring because if it is Spring, then there's nothing to imagine, nothing to wish for.
STEFAN (*putting his arm around Lisa as they walk and smiling affectionately*):[41] Is there anything about me you don't know?
LISA: A few things.

As a glass case containing life-sized wax figures comes into the frame in the background, Stefan leaves the frame screen right, and Lisa walks to the case.

LISA (*looking at the wax figures*): For instance, I don't know if one day they'll make a wax figure of you and put you in there because you'll be so famous.

142. *Cut to* MLS *of Stefan standing next to the glass case. He laughs, walks over to Lisa, takes her arm, and leads her away. The camera pans with him.*

STEFAN: Well, if they do, will you pay your penny to come in and see me?
LISA: If you'll come alive.

Both laugh.

After Lisa and Stefan have passed the glass case, the camera stops to watch them from behind as they walk into the background.

143. *Cut to* MS *of two carnival workers in an elevated booth. The man farthest from the camera is pulling taffy, while the one closest to it is preparing a*

carmel apple. He places the apple in a long-handled basket and hands it down to Lisa with the camera panning to follow the basket from the man's hands to Lisa's. As she takes the apple from the basket, she stands below the booth and looks up at the men working.[42]

STEFAN (*who can be seen in profile in the foreground of the frame*):
   Now, I see you as a little girl.
LISA (*smiling and holding her apple*): You do?

144. *Dissolve to* MLS *with the camera tracking out slightly as Lisa and Stefan are seen in profile facing each other in a mock railroad car. Behind them is a large curtained window through which painted scenery is passing. The music on the soundtrack changes to the hurdy-gurdy melody of "The Carnival of Venice."*

LISA (*fondling her rose*):[43] When my father was alive, we traveled a lot. We went nearly everywhere. We had wonderful times.

STEFAN: I didn't know you'd traveled so much.

LISA: Well, yes.

STEFAN (*moving to sit on the edge of his seat*): Perhaps we've been to some of the same places.

145. LISA (MS): No, I don't think so.

146. STEFAN (MS): Where did you go?

LISA (*off-screen*): Well, it was a long time, but . . .

147. *Cut to* MS *of Lisa.*

LISA: . . . for instance, there was Rio de Janeiro, beautiful exotic Rio with its botanical gardens, its Avenue of Palms, Sugar Loaf Mountain, and the harbor where you could look down and see the flying fish.

148. *Cut to previous* MLS *of Lisa and Stefan.*

LISA (*turning to look at the painted scenery which has stopped moving behind them*): We're in Venice.

STEFAN: Yes, we've arrived. Now, where would you like to go next? France? England? Russia?

LISA: Switzerland.

149. *As Stefan rises from his seat, cut to* LS *through the windows of the compartment door.*

STEFAN: Switzerland. Excuse me one moment while I talk with the engineer.

Stefan opens the compartment door, walks out, and goes to a booth in which an old woman is seated. As he walks with the camera panning to follow him from behind, he takes out a cigarette and puts it in his mouth.

OLD WOMAN: You and the lady, are you enjoying the trip?

STEFAN (*with the cigarette dangling from his mouth*): Very much. We've decided on Switzerland. (*He reaches into his pocket, takes out some money, and hands it to the old woman.*) There you go, thank you.

OLD WOMAN (*as Stefan turns and walks away*): Oh, thank you.

The camera pans with Stefan now seen in frontal shot as he begins to walk back to the compartment.

150. *Cut to* MS *of the old woman looking out from the booth.*

OLD WOMAN (*shouting*): Switzerland!

151. *Cut to* LS *of a tired-looking old man working the machine that moves the scenery. He leans against the machine and holds a teacup in his hand.*

OLD MAN (*answering the woman with an obvious lack of enthusiasm*): Switzerland. (*Now calling as if he were a conductor on a train*) Switzerland!

He moves a lever to change the scenery on the machine, blows a whistle, begins to pedal a bicycle that makes the scenery move, and then turns a wheel to start the music. When he turns the wheel, the background music temporarily swells.

152. *Cut to previous* MS *of Lisa and Stefan in the compartment.*

STEFAN: So you were looking down at the flying fish, then what? (*Getting no answer from Lisa.*) Aren't you going to finish the trip?
LISA: Well, there weren't any trips. Do you mind? You see, my father had a friend in a travel bureau. My father worked across the street. He was an assistant superintendant of municipal waterworks, and he used to bring folders home with him with pictures in them. We had stacks of them.

153. LISA (MS): And in the evening, he would put on his traveling coat. That's what he called it. Of course, I was very young.

154. *Cut to* MS *of Stefan as he smokes his cigarette and listens.*

LISA (*off-screen*): And he would say, "Where should we go this evening?" And I would say Vera Cruz because it's a beautiful name, and then he would say . . .

155. LISA (MS): . . . "Um, it's Summer there. You don't want to roast like a coffee bean, do you?"

156. STEFAN (MS): So, you never did get there?

    LISA (*off-screen*): No, it was just like our trip to the "Land of the Midnight Sun."

    STEFAN: What stopped you this time?

    LISA (*off-screen*): The weather.

157. LISA (MS): I thought of India, but then father remembered it was the rainy season.

158. STEFAN (MS): Your father was an expert on climates.

159. LISA (MS): My mother used to say that he knew what the weather was everywhere except home.

Lisa laughs and looks at the painted scenery as it passes behind the window.

160. *Cut to previous* MLS *of Lisa and Stefan in the compartment.*

    LISA: What mountain is that?

    STEFAN: That's the Matterhorn.

    LISA: Have you climbed it?

    STEFAN (*nodding*): Um-hum.

    LISA: Tell me, when you climb up a mountain, what then?

    STEFAN: Well, you come down again.

Stefan puts out his cigarette in an ashtray on the windowsill and then moves across the compartment to sit next to Lisa. The camera pans to reframe them in MS *as a whistle blows.*

    STEFAN (*holding Lisa's hand*): Tell me more about your father.

    LISA: Well, then he finally did go away.

161. *Cut to* MCU *of Lisa and Stefan.*

    LISA (*looking down*): He had the nicest eyes.

    STEFAN: Yes, I can see them.

    LISA: Why do you like to climb mountains?

    STEFAN: Oh, I suppose because no matter how high you climb there's always a higher one.

LISA: And you like to imagine that the other one's even more wonderful, like the spring in the fall.

STEFAN (*pulling her to him*): Now, you know far too much about me already, and I know almost nothing about you . . . uh . . . except that you've traveled a great deal.

As the whistle blows again, Lisa and Stefan stare into each other's eyes, he blows on her hair, and they both laugh.

162. *Cut to* LS *of the old man operating the machinery.*

OLD MAN: End of the line!

163. *Cut to* MLS *of the closed door of the mock train compartment.*

OLD MAN (*off-screen*): All change! All change!

Finally, Stefan emerges through the doorway, and the camera again pans with him as he walks back to the old woman in the booth.[44]

OLD WOMAN: What now?
STEFAN: Where haven't we been?
OLD WOMAN: We have no more countries left.
STEFAN: Then we'll begin all over again.
OLD WOMAN: Oh!
STEFAN (*taking a coin from his pocket and handing it to her*): There you are. Thank you.
OLD WOMAN: Oh, thank you.

The camera pans to follow Stefan back to the compartment.

STEFAN: We'll revisit the scenes of our youth.

164. *As Stefan opens the door and goes into the compartment, cut to* LS *of the old man starting up his apparatus again.*

165. *Dissolve to* MLS *of a uniformed all-female orchestra. The music on the*

soundtrack changes to a waltz, and the frame is divided by a wooden post in the foreground.

166. *Cut to high angle* LS *from behind the orchestra of Lisa and Stefan as they dance together alone on the dance floor.*

167–168. *Cut to previous* MLS *of the orchestra and then quickly to* MCU *of four of its members.*

> FIRST CELLIST (*reaching down to pick up a glass and taking a quick drink from it*): I don't know about them, but I'm going home right after this number.
> SECOND CELLIST: Me, too, if he's not paying me fifty kroner.

169. *Cut to* MCU *of two other musicians.*

VIOLINIST (*to the pianist*): I like to play for married people. They've got homes.

The pianist nods.

170–172. *Cut to* MS *of the first celloist picking up a sandwich and stuffing it quickly into her mouth so that no one will notice, back to previous* LS *of Stefan and Lisa dancing, and then to previous* MLS *of the orchestra. When they finish playing, they immediately begin to pack up their instruments.*

173. *Cut back to* MLS *of Stefan and Lisa having just stopped dancing.*

STEFAN (*clapping*): You are a sorceress. Now, I'm sure. How else could we dance this way unless we've danced together before? (*Lisa looks down, and Stefan places his finger under her chin to lift her face up to him.*) And yet if we had, I should have remembered.

Stefan is about to begin clapping for the orchestra, and he turns to look in the direction of the bandstand.

174–175. *Cut to* MLS *of the empty bandstand, and then quickly back to previous* MLS *of Stefan and Lisa on the dance floor.*

LISA (*motioning for Stefan to move screen right*): Please?

The camera pans with Stefan as he walks to an old piano and sits down to play the same waltz the orchestra had been playing. As he plays the out-of-tune piano, Lisa enters the frame in the background screen left and gradually makes her way closer to him, going first to a table and chair and leaving her jacket, her purse, and her white rose there, and then pausing next to a post in the middle distance as a man enters in the back-ground to extinguish the lamp on another post. Lisa slowly moves in to stand next to the piano and finally to kneel with her face next to the keyboard.[45] As she looks up adoringly at Stefan, the camera pans and tracks in to reframe them in high angle MS *and then tracks in slowly as they talk.*

STEFAN (*as he plays*): Promise me something.
LISA: Anything.
STEFAN: And I don't even know where you live. Promise me you won't
  vanish.
LISA: I won't be the one who vanishes.

176. *Cut to high angle* CU *of Lisa, her face just next to the keyboard, Stefan's
     fingers gliding over the keys in the foreground. She gazes with love up at
     Stefan and then at his hands on the keyboard.*

177. *Cut to previous high angle* MS *of Lisa and Stefan. As he plays, Stefan
     looks lovingly down at Lisa.*

178. *Cut to* LS *through an iron gate at night. A carriage pulls into the frame
     screen right. The waltz music continues on the soundtrack as the carriage
     stops at the gate and its door opens.*

DRIVER: We're here!
STEFAN: Thank you.

179. *Cut to* MLS *again through the iron gate as Lisa and Stefan emerge from the carriage. Stefan walks into the background to pay the driver, and Lisa walks up to the gate where she turns to look at Stefan.*

180. *Cut to previous* LS *through the gate as Stefan joins Lisa.*

    DRIVER: Thank you.

    Stefan unlocks the gate and he and Lisa walk into the courtyard. The camera pans with them in LS *as they walk to the glass door. As they approach the door, the voice of the concierge is heard.*

    CONCIERGE (*off-screen*): Who is it?
    STEFAN (*turning to look behind him*): Brand.
    CONCIERGE (*off-screen*): Good morning, Mr. Brand.

    Stefan and Lisa walk through the doorway into the hall.

181. *Cut to a darkly lit high angle* LS *from the landing above the hall stairway with the banister visible in the foreground. Lisa and Stefan enter through a doorway in the center of the frame and exit at the bottom. The camera pans to the top of the stairway as Lisa and Stefan reenter at the bottom screen right. Stefan leads Lisa up the stairs and then to the doorway of his apartment screen left.*

182. *Cut to* MS *from within Stefan's apartment of Lisa and Stefan as they enter. Stefan reaches to help Lisa with her coat, but instead he takes her in his arms, they kiss passionately, and the screen fades to black as the background music swells.*

183. *Fade in to* MS *of a closed drapery as the background music stops on the soundtrack.*[46]

    MADAME SPITZER (*off-screen*): Please be seated. It will be just a moment.

Suddenly, the drapery parts, and Madame Spitzer enters the frame.

MADAME SPITZER: Lisa!

The camera pans with her in MS *as she walks screen left.*

MADAME SPITZER (*to Lisa*): Leave it on! (*She helps Lisa as she puts a white fur jacket back on.*) Someone wants to see it, a new customer. Looks like a good one.

The camera pans to follow Madame Spitzer as she walks back to the drapery screen right. When she exits through it, the camera holds on the closed drapery.

MADAME SPITZER (*off-screen*): It won't take a moment.

184. *Cut to* MLS *of Madame Spitzer in the showroom of the salon. She holds a chair for a man who enters screen left and sits down with his back to the camera. Madame Spitzer then walks screen left with the camera panning to follow her.*

MADAME SPITZER: You'll like this one, I'm sure.

As Madame Spitzer exits through the drapery, Lisa enters. While climbing the small flight of stairs to the showroom, she sees Stefan and stops. Regaining her composure, she walks toward him, modeling the dress. The camera pans with her until it frames her with Stefan.

STEFAN: I like it very much . . . (*Lisa walks around his chair, still modeling the dress, as he turns to her and whispers*) . . . very much.
LISA (*still pretending to show the dress, but also whispering*): How did you find me?
STEFAN: I'm a good detective, what do you think?
LISA: You are.

Stefan stands up and walks over to sit on the edge of a table.[47]

STEFAN (*still whispering*): I'm afraid we'll have to . . .

185. *Cut to* MS *of Stefan from over Lisa's shoulder. Lisa's face is reflected in a small oval mirror next to Stefan on the table.*

STEFAN: . . . put off our plans for tonight. I couldn't go away without seeing you.
LISA: Where are you going?
STEFAN: Milan.

186. *Cut to reverse* MS *of Lisa from over Stefan's shoulder.*

STEFAN (*looking down*): The whole orchestra is going. We're to play at La Scala.
LISA (*looking away, almost in tears, but trying to hide her disappointment*): That's wonderful!

187. STEFAN (MS): I'd forgotten all about it. It won't be long, just two weeks.

188. *Cut to previous reverse* MS *of Lisa.*

   STEFAN: The train leaves at 5:30. Do you suppose you could see me off?
   LISA: I'll try.

189. *Cut to previous* MLS *of Lisa and Stefan as Stefan rises to go.*

   STEFAN: I'll look for you there. (*He turns and walks toward the camera, now speaking loudly.*) Goodbye, thank you. (*Lisa curtsies as he leaves the frame screen left.*)

190. *Cut to* MS *of Stefan from behind as he walks to the door. At the door, he turns to look back at Lisa once more.*

   STEFAN: Goodbye. You'll be there?

191. *Cut to* MS *of Lisa as she watches him leave.*

   MADAME SPITZER (*off-screen*): How did it go?

   Lisa turns, and the camera pans with her as she walks over to the banister that surrounds the upper level of the showroom. Madame Spitzer comes into the frame on the lower level below the banister.

   LISA: He wasn't interested in the suit, but, Madame Spitzer, could I leave a little earlier today?
   MADAME SPITZER: How early?
   LISA: About five.
   MADAME SPITZER: Yes, sure.

   Lisa walks down the steps and to the doorway behind Madame Spitzer. When she reaches the drapery that covers the doorway, she stops and looks back.

LISA: Thank you.

MADAME SPITZER (*as Lisa exits through the drapery*): Congratulations, my dear!

192. *Dissolve to* MLS *through a glass door into the street. Lisa enters screen left, walks to the door, opens it, and goes through. She runs through the train station with the camera tracking her in profile. A train whistle and a bell can be heard periodically throughout the sequence as Lisa runs to catch Stefan's train before it leaves. As she runs, a spiked iron fence comes into the frame in the background.*[48] *Lisa runs along the fence and stops at its open gate to look for Stefan.*

193. *Cut to* LS *of a crowd of people boarding a train. Stefan emerges from the crowd as a woman's voice can be heard calling him back.*

WOMAN (*off-screen*): Stefan, the train is leaving!

The camera pans with Stefan as he throws away his cigarette and walks away from the crowd.

STEFAN (*calling back*): Just a minute! (*He takes off his hat and approaches Lisa*): How long have you been standing here? (*He takes her hand, and she looks down.*) I don't want to go. Do you believe that?

The camera tracks in slowly to MCU *as Lisa and Stefan talk.*

LISA (*nodding and then looking down*): I'll be here when you get back.

MAN (*calling, off-screen*): Brand!

STEFAN: Yes.

WOMAN (*off-screen*): Stefan, hurry, please!

STEFAN: I still know so little about you.

LISA (*looking down*): You like mystery.

STEFAN (*putting his arm on the fence and leaning closer to Lisa*): That a woman like you exists, and I've found you, that's mystery enough. (*He places his fingers under her chin and raises her face to his.*) Say "Stefan" the way you said it last night.

LISA: Stefan.

STEFAN (*shaking his head*): It's as though you said it all your life.

CONDUCTOR (*walking behind them in the background*): Better hurry,
   sir!

STEFAN (*to the conductor*): Yes. (*To Lisa, kissing her hand.*) Goodbye.

WOMAN (*calling, off-screen*): Stefan!

STEFAN (*to the woman*): Yes. (*Starting away, to Lisa.*) Goodbye.

Stefan runs toward the train, and the camera pans with him.

194. *Cut to* MCU *of Lisa with the spikes of the fence close to her face as she
   watches Stefan go and as off-screen voices welcome him back to the crowd
   waiting to board the train.*

STEFAN (*off-screen, calling back to Lisa*): It won't be long! I'll be back
   in two weeks!

Lisa smiles and waves.

195. *Cut to* LS *of the train pulling out of the station with Stefan jumping on just in time.*

   STEFAN (*hanging from the train*): Goodbye! Two weeks!

196. *Cut to previous* MCU *of Lisa with the camera tracking in slowly. She watches as the train leaves, then looks down, and begins to cry. She turns and walks slowly with her back to the camera along the spiked fence as background music begins on the soundtrack.*[49]

   VOICE-OVER: Two weeks. Stefan, how little you knew yourself. That train was taking you out of my life.[50]

   The image blurs and fades to black.

197. *Fade into* LS *of a nun in habit walking toward the camera down a shadowy, darkly lit corridor as she holds a candle before her. During the fade, the music on the soundtrack stops and is replaced by the sounds of nuns chanting off-screen. The nun in the corridor goes to a chalkboard on the wall and writes on it. She then enters a doorway in the right foreground, the camera panning with her as she goes into a ward of curtained bed-chambers.*[51] *She goes to the first curtain, looks at a paper hanging there, and tears it off. She walks in among the curtained enclosures with the camera panning to follow her as she walks behind some curtains, closes others, and pulls down another piece of paper. The sound of the nuns chanting stops as a voice is heard off-screen.*

   SECOND NUN (*off-screen*): He was a married man? Does he live here in Vienna?

   The first nun leaves the frame bottom screen right as the camera tracks in and up to CU *of a chalkboard on which is written:*
   Name: Stefan
   Born: 12 November
   Mother: Lisa Berndle
   Father:

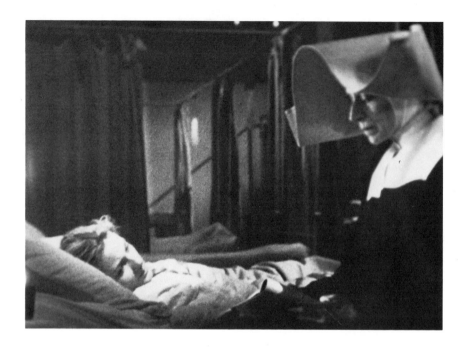

SECOND NUN (*off-screen*): If we knew who he was, he might be willing
to accept his responsibility.

198. *Cut to* MLS *of Lisa lying in a bed in one of the curtained chambers with a
nun sitting at her bedside. The bedchamber is darkly lit and in deep
shadow, but Lisa's face and the nun's are brightly lit. The first nun walks
across the frame in the foreground, temporarily obstructing the camera's
view of Lisa and the second nun.*

SECOND NUN: You won't tell us his name? (*Lisa shakes her head weakly.
The nun touches her pen to her lips and then writes in a notebook on
her lap.*) But you haven't the means to take care of the child.

199. *Cut to* MCU *of Lisa from over the nun's shoulder.*

LISA: We'll get along.

SECOND NUN: It's your duty to tell us. When a man does this sort of thing . . .

LISA (*interrupting*): Please, I'm feeling tired. Would you go?

The nun leaves, crossing in the foreground from left to right. The camera remains in MCU *of Lisa as background music begins on the soundtrack.*

VOICE-OVER: You may wonder why I never came to you for help. I wanted to be one woman you had known who asked you for nothing.

200. *Dissolve to* MS *of Stefan reading the letter at his desk.*

VOICE-OVER: My deep regret is that you never saw your son.

201. *Cut to* CU *of a picture of a small boy seen through Stefan's magnifying glass.*

VOICE-OVER: There were times during those years I prefer not to remember.

202. *Cut to previous* MS *of Stefan as he looks at the picture through the magnifying glass.*

VOICE-OVER: But I can assure you . . .

203. *Cut to another* CU *of a picture seen through the magnifying glass: Lisa and the boy (who looks slightly older) in a mock hot air balloon.*

VOICE-OVER: . . . whatever the cost, he repaid me a thousand times.

204. *Cut to previous* MS *of Stefan.*

VOICE-OVER: You would have been proud of him, too.[52] When he was about nine . . .

205. *Cut to* CU *of a picture again seen through Stefan's magnifying glass of a still older boy posing very formally.*

VOICE-OVER: . . . as much for his sake as mine, I married.

206. *Cut back to previous* MS *of Stefan who is smiling tenderly down at the picture.*

VOICE-OVER: You know who my husband is.

207. *Dissolve to* LS *at night of the ornate iron gate to an opulent mansion. The lighted windows and a vague outline of the house can be seen in the background.*

VOICE-OVER: Johann Stauffer married me, knowing the truth about us and about our child.

208. *Dissolve to* MCU *of Lisa who looks considerably more mature and sophisticated.*[53]

LISA (*referring to a string of pearls that she holds in her hand*): Oh, how lovely! (*She looks over her shoulder and gives Johann the pearls.*) Thank you, Johann. (*As he puts the pearls on her neck.*) What a nice birthday! This, and Stefan home.

The camera tracks back to MS *of Lisa sitting before a bedroom mirror and dressing table with Johann behind her standing very erect in his military dress uniform.*

JOHANN: You know I'm not good at saying such things, but . . .

Lisa rises and walks across a large, luxurious bedroom with the camera panning to follow her in MLS. *She can now be seen to be wearing a flowing white evening gown.*

JOHANN (*off-screen*): Lisa, I want you to be as happy as you've made me.

Lisa goes through a curtained doorway screen left.

LISA: If I were really a deserving wife, I'd be ready on time.

She emerges from the doorway carrying a white fur coat, and the camera pans with her as she walks back across the room to Johann. As she approaches him, she gives him her coat, which he drapes over her shoulders.

JOHANN: You are happy? (*Lisa walks to the bed where she picks up her gloves and purse. Johann goes to the door and waits for her there. When she reaches the doorway with her back to the camera, he blocks her way.*) You are?

209. *Cut to reverse* MS *through the doorway from the hall behind Johann.*

LISA (*smiling*): Why shouldn't I be?

Harmonica music can be heard as Lisa and Johann enter the hall. The camera pans with them as they walk through the hallway and past the staircase.

LISA: Let's say goodnight.

Johann nods and when they reach a door screen right, he opens it for Lisa.

210. *Cut to* MLS *from inside Stefan junior's room of Lisa and Johann entering through the doorway.*[54]

LISA (*as they walk in*): Hello. (*She walks out of the frame screen right.*)
JOHANN (*to Stefan*): Still another talent?

The camera pans with Johann as he walks to the bed where Lisa and Stefan come into the frame. Stefan sits on the bed in his pajamas, playing the harmonica while his mother stands over him next to the bed.

LISA: He has a lot of talents, but not for finishing his milk. (*She picks*

up a glass of milk from the nightstand next to the bed and hands it to Stefan, who stops playing.)
JOHANN (*holding out his hand*): May I see it?
STEFAN (*handing the harmonica to Johann and speaking as he drinks his milk*): Um-hum.
LISA (*as Stefan finishes his milk*): Or for brushing his teeth.

Stefan gets up from the bed and crosses the room with Lisa and Johann following him. The camera pans with them.

JOHANN: Made in Switzerland, hum!
STEFAN: Switzerland must be a very nice place, don't you think?

Stefan stands in MLS at a small table next to the door and begins to brush his teeth. Lisa and Johann stand on both sides of him.

LISA (*patting Stefan affectionately on the head*): Who gave it to you, darling?
STEFAN: Herr Frank.
JOHANN: Who is Herr Frank?
LISA (*to Johann*): His music teacher.

211. *Cut to MS from over Johann's shoulder of Lisa standing behind Stefan.*

STEFAN: He says he thinks I have a natural talent.
JOHANN: For the harmonica?
STEFAN (*laughing*): No, for music.

212. *Cut to reverse MS of Johann from behind Lisa and Stefan.*

JOHANN (*looking at Lisa with mild displeasure evident on his face*): Oh!
(*He puts down the harmonica and then shakes Stefan's hand.*)
Goodnight, Stefan.

213. *Cut to MLS of Lisa, Stefan, and Johann as Johann turns, pats Stefan on the head, and walks to the door.*

STEFAN: Goodnight, sir.

LISA (*bending to kiss Stefan as Johann leaves the frame through the doorway screen left*): Goodnight, darling.

STEFAN: Goodnight, mother.

Lisa leaves the room as Stefan remains at the washing stand.

214. *Cut to* MLS *of Lisa walking to the staircase, the camera panning to follow her. She goes down the first few steps with Johann awaiting her just below.*

STEFAN (*calling, off-screen*): Mother!

Lisa looks back over her shoulder.

LISA (*to Johann*): I'll be right down.

Johann nods, and the camera pans with Lisa as she walks back to the door of Stefan's room.

215. *As she begins to open the door, cut to* LS *of Stefan sitting on the bed and Lisa looking in through the doorway.*

LISA (*laughing*): Yes.

STEFAN (*putting his head to the side pleadingly*): You remember the last time, the first night I was home from school.

LISA: Um-hum, what about it?

STEFAN: When you went out, you let me sleep in your room.

LISA: Well, all right, as a special concession because it's your first night home. But hurry, I'm late. (*She walks toward the bed.*)

216. *Cut to* MLS *through the doorway of Stefan's room. The boy runs with the camera panning to follow him through the doorway, across the hall, and through another open doorway into Lisa's room. He then jumps into her bed with the camera watching him from the hall through the doorway. In the foreground of the frame, Lisa enters from screen left in the hall, goes to the railing of the stairway, and looks down.*

LISA (*calling down the staircase to Johann*): In just a minute!

217. *Cut to* LS *of Johann, who is standing below the staircase in the entrance hall, holding his coat, and looking up.*

> JOHANN: There's no hurry. (*He walks slowly toward the camera.*)
> STEFAN (*off-screen*): Goodnight, sir.
> JOHANN (*stopping and looking up the staircase*): Goodnight.

218. *Cut to* MLS *of Lisa as she stands at the top of the stairs. In the background through the open doorway, Stefan can be seen lying on her bed. As she goes to the doorway, a maid walks out of the room, crosses behind Lisa, and exits screen left. Lisa enters the room and sits on the bed next to Stefan.*

219. *Cut to* MS *from within the bedroom of Lisa and Stefan talking.*

LISA: You know, Stefan, it might be nice if you could say "goodnight, father" instead of "goodnight, sir."

STEFAN (*putting his head to one side again*): But I've always said it that way.

LISA (*holding Stefan's hand and playing with his fingers*): I think he'd like it if you could manage a change. Supposing you said to me "goodnight, madam." It would sound pretty silly, wouldn't it? (*She gets up and walks around the bed with the camera panning to follow her in* MLS.) Now, promise me that you'll go to sleep and not wait up for me. (*She goes to the wall screen right and turns off a light there.*)

STEFAN: I promise. Will you bring me a program at the opera?

LISA: I promise.

The camera pans with her as she puts out the light next to the bed and then walks back around it.

STEFAN: Goodnight, madam.

LISA: Goodnight, sir. (*Standing at the door.*) After all, when a person treats you so much like a son, he is in a sense your father.

STEFAN: All right, mother, if you say so. Goodnight.

LISA (*softly*): Goodnight.

Lisa closes the door, and the camera pans back to the bed in the darkened room as harmonica music is heard on the soundtrack.[55]

220. *Dissolve to* CU *of a large poster in the foyer of the opera house.*[56] *It announces* Die Zauberflöte *as the opera being performed. In the background, a man in evening dress stands looking at his program with a pince-nez as the sounds of an orchestra tuning up can be heard on the soundtrack. A woman enters from behind the poster, and she and the man walk away together screen left. The camera pans with them in* MLS. *They pass a man standing in the foreground with his back to the camera, and then they leave the frame screen left. As they leave, the camera picks up two women and a military officer who enter as the others leave. As they walk across the frame, the camera now pans with them.*

VOICE-OVER: The course of our lives can be changed by such little things.

The officer and ladies exit screen right as the camera begins to pan with two young officers who have just entered the frame. The officers walk screen left passing behind several people standing in the foreground.

VOICE-OVER: So many passing by, each intent on his own problems. So many faces that one might easily have been lost.

The camera tracks in to MS *as it pans to follow the officers who are ascending a winding staircase. They leave the frame screen left as two women enter. The camera pans with the women as they descend the stairway, turn, and then ascend another stairway.*

VOICE-OVER: I know now that nothing happens by chance. Every moment is measured; every step is counted.

As the two women ascend the crowded staircase, Lisa and Johann enter the frame as part of a group of people in the background who are approaching the staircase. The camera cranes up to follow Lisa and Johann from behind as they ascend the staircase.

OFF-SCREEN VOICES (*shouting, repeating several times*): Curtain, curtain going up! Second act!

As the camera cranes up, a chandelier and then the banister of the stairway obstruct the camera's view of Lisa and Johann, and at the top of the staircase they disappear entirely, first behind a pillar and then a group of people standing next to the banister.

WOMAN (*one of the group of people standing next to the banister who are off-screen as she begins to speak, but come into the frame as she continues*): Look, isn't that Stefan Brand?
FIRST MAN (*standing to her right*): He returned last week.
SECOND MAN (*to her left, smoking a cigar*): A concert tour?
WOMAN: Pleasure trip most likely.

SECOND MAN: The way he's burning himself up it's a wonder he's still alive.

The camera pans right and Lisa comes into the frame at the railing just next to the group of people who have been discussing Stefan.

221. *Cut to high angle* LS *of Stefan in conversation with a woman on the staircase.*

222. *As he kisses her hand, cut to* CU *of Lisa looking down from the balcony.*

SECOND MAN (*off-screen*): Ten years ago, he showed great promise.

223. *Cut to high angle* LS *of Stefan as he leaves his female companion and begins to ascend the staircase.*.

SECOND MAN (*off-screen*): Too bad. With that talent, he could have been a great pianist.

224. *Cut to* MS *of Lisa standing at the railing. The group of people who have been discussing Stefan move off into the background behind her.*

FIRST MAN: Perhaps talent is not enough.

They laugh.

WOMAN: Perhaps he has too many talents.

After the group passes across the middle of the frame, Johann is seen behind them in the background waiting for Lisa. She turns and goes to him.

VOICES (*off-screen, shouting*): Second act! Curtain going up!

225. *Cut to* MS *of Lisa and Johann entering their opera box. As they move to their seats, the camera tracks out to* MLS *and an officer in the box stands to greet them.*

OFFICER: We missed you at the buffet.
WOMAN (*sitting next to Lisa*): You know the colonel and his cognac.
OFFICER (*standing behind the woman*): General Hazendorf was asking for you. You've made a conquest.
WOMAN: My dear, you should have joined us.

Off-screen, act two of Die Zauberflöte *begins—incorrectly—with "Ein Mädchen oder Weibchen" performed in Italian.*[57]

226. *Cut to* MS *of Stefan from behind in profile as he sits in the shadows of his box.*[58] *Only his face is brightly lit as he moves up in his seat, stares screen left, and then settles back into his chair.*

227. *Cut to* MLS *of Lisa with Johann sitting just behind her as the camera tracks in to* MCU.

VOICE-OVER: Suddenly in that one moment everything was in danger, everything I thought was safe. Somewhere out there were your eyes . . .

228. *Cut to* ECU *of Stefan's face.*

VOICE-OVER: . . . and I knew I couldn't escape them.

229. *Cut to previous* MCU *of Lisa.*

VOICE-OVER: It was like the first time I saw you. The years between were melting away.

Lisa gets up and turns toward the back of the box.

230. *Cut to* MLS *of Lisa through the curtained doorway at the back of the box. She stands in profile talking to Johann.*

LISA: I have a headache.
JOHANN: I'll take you home.
LISA: No, please, don't. I'll be all right . . .
JOHANN (*interrupting her*): Lisa!
LISA: . . . if I lie down for a few moments. Please stay with them.

The camera pans with Lisa as she walks out of the box, goes through the vestibule behind it, and leaves through another curtained doorway.

231. *Cut to previous* MCU *of Stefan in profile from behind in the shadows of his box with his face brightly lit. He looks off-screen left.*

232–234. *Cut to* LS *of Lisa's box with her empty chair, back to previous* MCU *of Stefan, and then to* MLS *of Lisa as she walks toward the camera in the foyer of the opera house.*

LISA (*speaking to someone who stands before her just off-screen*): Would you be kind enough to give my husband a message. He's in seventeen. (*A black porter enters in the foreground screen left with his back to the*

*camera. Lisa searches in her purse and then hands him some money.
He takes the tip and bows slightly.*) Not now, but after this act. Tell him
I've decided to go home and not to worry.

Lisa turns to leave as the porter bows to her.

PORTER: Thank you.

235. *Cut to* LS *of Lisa walking to the staircase. The camera pans with her
and the banister of the staircase intervenes in the foreground of the shot.
When she begins to descend the stairs the camera cranes down to follow
her. At the bottom of the staircase, she walks toward the camera and begins to speak to another porter who enters the frame in the foreground,
having gotten up from a chair just off-screen.*

LISA: Would you call my carriage, please?
PORTER (*exiting screen right*): Yes, Madame Stauffer.
LISA (*walking into the background with her back to the camera*): The
  side entrance.
PORTER: Yes, madame.

236. *Cut to previous* LS *of Lisa's box with her empty chair. Johann rises from
his seat and exits through the curtained doorway in the background.*

237. *Cut to* LS *at night of Lisa leaving the opera house and pacing back and
forth on the veranda with the camera panning to follow her. The music
from the opera can still be heard faintly in the background. As she paces,
she passes behind pillars that temporarily obscure the camera's view. She
turns, and suddenly Stefan's voice is heard off-screen.*

STEFAN: Excuse me.

*Lisa goes to him, and they stand facing each other framed between two
pillars, Stefan with his back to the camera.*

STEFAN: You realize where there is a pursued, there must also be a
  pursuer.

238. *Cut to* MCU *of Stefan from over Lisa's shoulder.*

   STEFAN: I've seen you somewhere, I know.

239. *Cut to reverse* MCU *of Lisa.*

   STEFAN: I followed you upstairs and watched you in your box.

240. *Cut to previous* MCU *of Stefan.*

   STEFAN: But I couldn't place you, and I had to speak with you. Oh, I know how this sounds. I assure you in this case it's true. You believe that, don't you?

241. LISA (MCU): Yes.
   STEFAN: Thank you. (*Lisa begins to walk toward the camera, but he stops her by gently putting his hand on her arm.*) Now please, just a moment.

242. STEFAN (MCU): Is there anyplace we could have met, that I might have seen you? Like one of my concerts. It must have been some time ago. I haven't given any concerts in Vienna lately—or anywhere else for that matter.

243. LISA (MCU): You don't play anymore?

244. STEFAN (MCU): Oh, it's not quite as final as that. I always tell myself I'll begin again next week, and then when next week comes, it's this week, so I wait for next week again.

245. LISA (MCU, *shaking her head*): What are you waiting for?

246. STEFAN (MCU): That's a very disturbing question.
   LISA (*interrupting him*): My carriage.
   STEFAN: You can't ask such a question and just walk away.

247. STEFAN (CU): I have a feeling—please, don't think I'm mad. I know it sounds strange, and I can't explain it, but I feel that you understand what I can't even say, that you can help me.

248. *Cut to reverse* CU *of Lisa from over Stefan's shoulder.*

   STEFAN: Have you . . . have you ever shuffled faces, like cards, hoping to find the one that lies somewhere just over the edge of your memory, the one you've been waiting for.

249. STEFAN (CU): Well, tonight when I first saw you and later when I watched you in the darkness, it was as though I had found that one face among all others. Who are you?

250. *Cut to previous reverse* CU *of Lisa turning to leave and then to* MS *as she walks away from Stefan.*

    STEFAN: Promise I'll see you again. I must see you.
    LISA (*turning her head slightly to look back at Stefan, but walking away quickly*): I don't know.

    The camera pans with her as she leaves. Suddenly, her carriage comes into view in MS *with Johann sitting in it waiting for her. Lisa gasps when she sees him, he holds out his hand to her through the now open door, and she enters the carriage. A porter closes the door, and the camera looks in through the window at Lisa and Johann in profile. The carriage pulls out of the frame screen left as the sound of hooves beating on the pavement is heard. The camera pans to watch the carriage from behind in* LS *as it pulls away into the background streets. The porter enters screen right and stands in the foreground directing traffic.*

251. *Fade to a darkly lit frontal* MTS *of Lisa and Johann in the carriage. The dots of light in the previous street scene fade into the shining buttons on Johann's uniform as he sits very stiffly in the carriage. During the fade, the soundtrack music stops.*

    LISA: Johann, you don't think I wanted this to happen?
    JOHANN (*looking ahead, not at Lisa, and smoking a cigarette*): No. (*Pause.*) What are you going to do?
    LISA: I don't know.

252. *Cut to* MS *of Lisa and Johann in profile. She looks down and then at him as he begins to speak. He looks only straight ahead, never at her.*

    JOHANN: Lisa, we have a marriage. Perhaps it's not all you once hoped for, but you have a home, and your son, and people who care for you. (*As he finishes speaking he puts his cigarette to his mouth with his gloved hand.*)

LISA: I know that, Johann. I'd do anything to avoid hurting you, but I can't help it.

JOHANN: And your son, you think you can avoid hurting him?

LISA: He won't be harmed. I'll see to that.

253. *Cut to frontal* MTS *of Lisa and Johann.*

JOHANN: There are such things as honor and decency.

LISA: I told myself that a hundred times this one evening.

JOHANN: You talk as though it were out of your hands.

254. *Cut to* MTS *of Lisa and Johann in profile.*

JOHANN: It's not, Lisa. You have a will, you can do what's right, what's best for you, or you can throw away your life. (*He smokes his cigarette.*)

255. LISA (MCU): I've had no will but his, ever.

JOHANN (*off-screen*): That's romantic nonsense.

LISA (*turning her head to look at him*): Is it, Johann? I can't help it. I can't. You must believe that.

256. *Frontal* MTS, *Johann and Lisa.*

JOHANN: What about him? Can't he help himself either?

257. LISA (MCU): I know now that he needs me as much as I've always needed him.

258. *Frontal* MTS, *Johann and Lisa.*

JOHANN (*smoking his cigarette*): Isn't it a little late for him to find that out?

DRIVER (*off-screen*): We're home, sir.

259. *Cut to* MCU *through the window of the door with the lamp on the near side of the carriage prominent in the extreme foreground. Johann rises, opens the door on the far side, and they exit.*

260. *Cut to a long shot with the carriage in the foreground and Lisa and*

Johann in the background walking away from the camera toward the door of their home. Music begins on the soundtrack.

JOHANN (*to the driver*): Goodnight.
DRIVER: Goodnight, sir.

261. *Cut to* LS *inside the house through a doorway from the study into a foyer. In the foyer, a servant opens the front door and Lisa and Johann enter. They walk toward the camera into the study. The camera tracks in to* MLS *of Lisa and Johann, still in their coats as they stand at Johann's desk. Lisa stands in front of the desk in the foreground with her back to the camera. Johann faces her in profile from the side of the desk. On the wall behind them, dueling pistols and swords are hung.*[59]

JOHANN: Lisa, if you do this, you can never turn back. You know that, don't you?
LISA: Yes.

Johann walks behind the desk.

262. *Cut to* MS *of Lisa.*

JOHANN (*off-screen*): I warn you . . .

263. *Cut to* MS *of Johann in profile as he stands behind the desk with crossed swords hanging behind him on the wall.*

JOHANN: . . . I shall do everything in my power to prevent it.

264. *Cut to previous* MS *of Lisa and then back to previous* MS *of Johann as they exchange silent stares with the background music prominent on the soundtrack.*

265. *Cut to* MLS *of Johann from behind Lisa who stands in the foreground with her back to the camera. She slowly walks screen right toward the staircase, and the camera pans to follow her from behind.*

266. *Dissolve to frontal* LS *of Lisa entering her bedroom. Stefan is asleep on*

the bed in the lower foreground. Lisa walks to the bed where she in MLS *removes her wrap, bends down, kisses her child on the forehead, and wakes him up.*

LISA: Hello, darling, wake up. It's time to go to your own room.

She takes off his blanket, helps him up, and leads him out of the room.

267. *Cut to* LS *in the hallway with the banister of the staircase in the lower foreground. Lisa holds Stefan's hand as they leave the bedroom and enter the hallway.*

STEFAN (*rubbing his eyes*): Did you have a nice time?
LISA: Yes, darling.

The camera pans with them as they cross the hallway.

STEFAN (*calling down the stairway*): Goodnight, father.
JOHANN (*off-screen*): Goodnight.
STEFAN: Did you hear? I just said it.
LISA: Yes, darling.
STEFAN (*as they enter the doorway to Stefan's room with their backs to the camera*): Tell me about the opera.

268. *Cut to* MLS *of Lisa and Stefan from inside Stefan's room as Lisa guides him to his bed.*

STEFAN: Was it exciting?

The camera slowly tracks in to MS *as Lisa tucks Stefan into bed. A lamp on the nightstand next to the bed is prominent in the foreground.*

LISA: There, how's that?
STEFAN: You're wonderful.
LISA (*bending over him*): You're wonderful. (*She walks around the bed.*) You've always been a wonderful boy. (*She stands behind the head of the bed holding on to the headboard and looking down at Stefan.*) You don't know how much that's meant to me to be so proud of you always. (*She starts to say more, but her voice breaks, and she is unable to go on.*)[60]

As she looks down, she notices that Stefan has fallen asleep. She then shuts off the light next to the bed, and the room darkens. She goes to the window behind her, opens it slightly, stands there holding on to the curtains, glances back at Stefan, and then looks out of the window. Suddenly, she breaks into tears as she clings to the window frame and buries her face in the curtains. Fade to black.

269. *Fade in to* MLS *from within the train compartment with the camera looking out through the window.*[61] *The music on the soundtrack is replaced by the sounds of a busy railroad station with a train whistle blowing periodically. A conductor opens the door of the train compartment from the outside and guides Stefan junior and Lisa into it. Stefan enters first, sits on the seat screen right, and places his small bag on the handle of his seat. Lisa sits down next to him on his right.*

STEFAN: Don't worry, mother. You'll see, two weeks will go like an express train. (*The conductor enters with a large suitcase which he places on a rack above them.*) You're sure you're coming?

270. *Cut to* MS *of Lisa and Stefan from outside the compartment through the open doorway from which the conductor now emerges.*

LISA: Of course, I promise. (*Unbuttoning Stefan's jacket.*) You can even get my room in the village for me.
STEFAN: I'll get you the same one you had last time. . . . (*Lisa strokes his hair affectionately; the conductor has closed the door of the compartment, and the frame of the window now frames the shot.*) The one with the balcony.

271. *Cut to* MS *of the conductor who had escorted Lisa and Stefan to their compartment. He stands with his back to the camera just outside of the train as a second conductor enters screen left.*

SECOND CONDUCTOR: Didn't I tell you that compartment was quarantined? (*He walks off screen right as the first conductor watches him go and people walk across the frame in the foreground.*)

272. *Cut to previous* MS *of Lisa and Stefan from within the compartment. The second conductor with a cigar in his mouth is seen through the window as he enters screen left.*

SECOND CONDUCTOR (*tipping his hat*): I'm sorry, ma'am, but this compartment has to be closed up. (*He opens the door.*) I'll take you to the next car forward.
STEFAN (*as he and Lisa prepare to leave*): That's good! I'll be nearer the locomotive.

The conductor chuckles, and Lisa points him to Stefan's bags on the overhead rack.

SECOND CONDUCTOR (*getting the bags down*): I'll take them for you.

Lisa and Stefan leave the compartment through the doorway and then exit screen left with the conductor following behind them.

273. *Cut to* MLS *of Lisa, Stefan, and the conductor walking toward the camera along the side of the train.*

STEFAN (*to the conductor*): Do we have two locomotives on our train?
SECOND CONDUCTOR: We usually get along with one, but I'll talk to the engineer. (*Pointing to the train.*) How about that one over there? You can have two seats in there. (*They stop, and the conductor opens the door of the new compartment.*)
LISA (*as Stefan enters the compartment, to the conductor*): He's traveling alone.
SECOND CONDUCTOR: Don't worry, madam, I'll take good care of him.

274. *Cut to* MS *from within the compartment of Stefan and Lisa entering as the conductor holds the door for them.*

SECOND CONDUCTOR: We leave in about a minute. Better hurry and get your seat.

Lisa and Stefan sit on opposite sides of the compartment as the conductor stands between them and places Stefan's luggage on an overhead rack.

LISA (*to Stefan*): You can see better if you sit over here, and if you get too cold, put up the window. (*She motions to the window.*)
STEFAN: Yes, mother.

The conductor leaves through the doorway, and Stefan crosses the compartment to sit next to Lisa. As he does, Lisa takes his hands, and background music begins on the soundtrack.

LISA: Stefan . . .
275. LISA (MCU): . . . you know how I . . . I've longed so for your being home, and now I can't even explain. Maybe someday very soon, I'll be able to give you a reason . . .

276. *Cut to* MS *of Lisa as she gently pulls Stefan down to sit beside her.*

    LISA: . . . but now you'll just have to believe that it's for your own good.

277. *Cut to* MCU *of Stefan from over Lisa's shoulder.*

    STEFAN: I don't mind going back so much, especially when you're coming so soon.

278. *Cut to reverse* MCU *of Lisa from over Stefan's shoulder as she removes his scarf from his neck.*

    STEFAN: It'll be like two vacations.
    LISA: You're right, darling.

    A whistle blows.

    STEFAN: Then I'll show you the new walk we found since you were there last time.
    LISA: Oh, yes.

279. *Cut to* MS *of Lisa and Stefan from within the compartment. The second conductor passes outside the door.*

    SECOND CONDUCTOR: Better get out, lady.

    Lisa and Stefan both rise and embrace as the background music swells. Lisa goes out through the doorway and closes the door behind her. Stefan stands at the door talking to her through the window. A whistle blows again.

    LISA: You'll write me often, won't you?

280. *Cut to* MS *from outside of the compartment behind Lisa. Lisa and Stefan stand at the compartment door holding hands and talking through the window.*

STEFAN: Yes, mother, but I can't write very often . . . (*the train begins to pull away*) . . . not in two weeks.

Lisa is left standing in MS *with the train pulling away in the background.*

STEFAN (*off-screen*): Bye, mother! Two weeks!

Lisa waves.

281. *Cut to* MLS *of the train pulling away with Stefan waving through a window. A lamppost is prominent, dividing the frame in the foreground.*

282. *Cut to previous* MS *of Lisa looking anxiously after the departing train. She waves and continues to look after the train as smoke curls behind her. Then she turns away.*

283. *Cut to* LS *of Lisa as she walks slowly toward the camera. Absorbed in her thoughts, she walks beside a spiked iron fence, the camera panning with her now in* MS. *She passes two men, one in civilian and the other in military dress, who stand at the fence. As she leaves in the foreground screen left, the camera tracks in on the two men.*

CIVILIAN: What is it? What's happened?

Both men turn to look behind the fence in the background where a stretcher is being carried across the frame.

WOMAN (*off-screen*): Someone's hurt?

The camera pans with the stretcher.

CONDUCTOR (*walking next to the stretcher*): No reason to be alarmed.

The camera frames in MS *another group of people, two women and a man who are also standing at the fence.*

MAN: They say it's a case of typhus.

WOMAN (*whispering*): Typhus?
MAN: Yes, typhus on the train.

In the background, the stretcher is carried through a doorway screen left.[62]

284. *Dissolve to* LS *through a window of Lisa entering the restaurant she and Stefan visited briefly at the beginning of their one evening together.*[63] *The background music is also the same as that played by the street musicians that night. When she enters the restaurant, she passes behind a large plant with thin pointed leaves dominating the foreground. The camera pans with her as she walks to a stairway. When she begins to walk down the stairs, she is met by a waiter.*

WAITER: Yes, madam.
LISA: Is Mr. Brand here—Stefan Brand?
WAITER: Brand? One moment please. (*He turns and calls behind him.*) Fritz!

285. *Cut to* MLS *of Fritz, the waiter who talked with Stefan about canceling his engagements for his evening with Lisa. Fritz is seated with his back to the camera at a table where he is dining with another waiter. Another plant similar to the one at the door is behind them. Fritz turns in his chair.*

286. *Cut to previous* MLS *of Lisa standing on the steps with the first waiter before her. He nods, and she walks down the stairs, passing him as he walks up a few stairs and then stops to look back at her.*

287. *Cut to* MS *of Lisa approaching Fritz's table.*

LISA: Could you tell me . . . (*Fritz rises and bows*) . . . has Mr. Brand been here this evening?
FRITZ: Oh, Mr. Brand is no longer a customer of ours, not for some time. Mr. Brand these days is more likely to be found at the Ritz.
LISA: Thank you. (*She turns to leave.*)

288. *Cut to* MLS *as Lisa walks to the stairway, up the stairs, and to the door with the camera panning to follow her. She leaves the restaurant in* LS *with the spike-leafed plant again prominent in the lower foreground.*

289. *Cut to* MS *of the outside wall of the restaurant at night. Lisa comes into the frame in the background, walks toward the camera down the sidewalk next to the wall, and stares fixedly before her. The music on the soundtrack swells.*

290–291. *Cut to low angle* LS *of a lighted upper-story window in one of the townhouses that line the street and then to previous* MS *of Lisa as she walks toward the camera and stops.*

FLOWER SELLER (*off-screen*): Good evening, ma'am, I still have nice flowers left.

292. *Cut to* MS *of the flower seller sitting on the steps of a building. A lamppost in the foreground divides the frame.*

FLOWER SELLER (*arranging his flowers*): I'm closing up, and I'll sell you a nice bouquet very cheap.

The camera pans left, rises up, and tracks back to reframe Lisa as she walks toward it.

LISA: I'll take those, the white ones. (*The flower seller reaches down and comes up with a bouquet of white roses in his hand.*) Don't bother to wrap them up. It doesn't matter.

Lisa pays the flower seller, he hands her the flowers, she nods, and he tips his hat. She then turns back to look in the direction of the window. The background music swells on the soundtrack as Lisa crosses the street with the camera panning to follow her. She hesitates a moment, looks up in the direction of the window, and then walks toward the iron gate.

293. *As she leaves the frame screen right, cut to* MS *of Lisa through the grating of the gate where she stands ringing the bell. The sound of a door*

opening can be heard, and Lisa's face is suddenly illuminated from off-screen right.

294. *Cut to* LS *of Lisa from behind as she goes through the now open gateway. A quick pan to* MS *of a carriage just down the street reveals Johann's face in the carriage window.*

JOHANN (*to the driver*): Now, you can drive on.

The carriage pulls off-screen right.

295. *Cut to* MS *of Lisa climbing the stairway to Stefan's apartment. At the top of the stairs in* MLS, *she walks to Stefan's door and rings the bell.*

296. *Cut to* MS *from within Stefan's apartment of John looking out through a small curtained window in the door. When he opens the door, Lisa enters the frame and stands in the doorway.*

LISA (*to John*): Stefan Brand, is he . . .

John nods before she can finish, Lisa enters the apartment, and he closes the door behind her. The glass door to Stefan's study can be seen in the background of the frame as John walks to it and reaches for the doorhandle.

297. *Cut to* MCU *of Lisa walking through the doorway as John holds the door open for her; she smiles as she hears it squeak just as it did years before.*

LISA (*to John as she enters the room*): Thank you.

The camera pans to follow her into Stefan's study. She stands in the middle of the room in MLS *as the squeak of the closing door can be heard off-screen. When John enters screen right, Lisa smiles again. He passes before her in the foreground, motions to her to remain in the room, and leaves through the open door screen left. After John has gone, Lisa begins to examine the room just as she did when she was a girl.*

298. *Cut to* MCU *of Lisa. The camera pans with her and then tracks her from behind as she enters the adjoining room, places the flowers that she has brought on a table, then walks to the piano, and finally goes to a window in the background. When the sound of a door opening off-screen is heard, she turns to the camera, unbuttoning her jacket and looking up expectantly.*

299. *Cut to* MS *of Stefan, wearing a smoking jacket and ascot and casually entering the room with his hands in his pockets. When he sees Lisa, he smiles slightly and walks purposefully to her. The camera pans with him as background music begins on the soundtrack.*

STEFAN: Well, this is a surprise, but I assure you a very happy one. (*Stefan goes to Lisa, who has now removed her jacket. He takes her arm and leads her to a chair in the background.*) And John didn't prepare me for such a pleasant occasion.

The camera tracks in to MLS *of Stefan as he escorts Lisa to a chair and then stands beside her.*

STEFAN: I thought last night the darkness . . . (*reaching behind him, Stefan turns on a light, and the room brightens*) . . . might have played tricks on my eyes. (*Lisa smiles up at him.*) You're even more beautiful than I imagined.
LISA: Very kind of you.

Stefan walks across the foreground, passing before Lisa. The camera pans with him and eliminates Lisa from the frame.

STEFAN (*as he walks away from Lisa*): This is just the hour for a little late supper . . . (*turning back to her*) . . . or is it too late? Well, it makes no difference. You're here, and as far as I'm concerned, all the clocks in the world have stopped. Excuse me a moment.

The camera pans to follow Stefan to an open door and then holds as he walks down a hallway into the background.

STEFAN (*calling*): John! (*John enters the hall in the background from another doorway screen left.*) John, I'm sorry to send you out so late . . .

300. *Cut to* MS *of Lisa as she awaits Stefan's return.*

STEFAN (*off-screen*): . . . but would you go down to the corner and get a few things? We're going to have some supper, the usual things.

Lisa abruptly rises and walks to the window behind her.

301. *Cut to* MCU *of Stefan as he reenters the room. The background music stops on the soundtrack.*

STEFAN (*walking to Lisa*): John makes life possible for a hopelessly single man.

The camera pans with him as he walks, and then it rests in MLS *on Lisa, who is seen from over Stefan's shoulder standing in the middleground with a table behind her. On the table, a lamp and a terra cotta bust of an ancient goddess can be seen. Stefan, in the foreground with his back to the camera, leans his elbow on the piano, upon which rests a large vase that is prominent in the foreground of the shot, dividing the frame evenly between Stefan and Lisa.*

STEFAN (*looking at the statue*): She fascinates you, too. You remember the Greeks built a statue to a god they didn't know, but hoped someday would come to them.

302. *Cut to* MS *of Lisa listening to Stefan.*

STEFAN (*off-screen*): Well, mine happens to be a goddess.[64]
LISA (*smiling*): And you never found her.

303. STEFAN (MS, *looking down pensively, still leaning on the piano*): For years, I never woke in the morning, but I said to myself, "Perhaps today she will come . . ."

304. *Cut to previous* MS *of Lisa listening.*

> STEFAN (*off-screen*): ". . . and my life will really begin." Sometimes it seemed very near.

305. *Cut to* MS *of Stefan.*

> STEFAN: Well, now I'm older and I know better.

306. *Cut to previous* MLS *of Lisa from over Stefan's shoulder. She walks toward the camera, which pans to frame her with Stefan behind the piano in* MLS. *The vase on the piano is again prominent in the foreground, dividing the frame between Stefan and Lisa.*

> LISA: Even for yourself, you don't play anymore?
> STEFAN: Oh, I remember last night you were kind enough to be interested.

(*He tries to open the cover over the piano keys.*) I forgot John locked it when I went away. Nowadays, I'm away quite a lot of the time. Oh, I'll ask him for the key when he comes back. (*Suddenly, changing to a softer tone and leaning toward Lisa.*) You're very lovely. Beautiful dress.

LISA (*looking down*): Thank you. How could you do that, give it up altogether?

STEFAN: Well, if you're so curious, I'll tell you.

307. *Cut to* MS *of Stefan leaning against the piano with the vase again prominent in the foreground. He walks around the piano and then into the background behind Lisa. The camera pans with him.*

STEFAN: One night I came back to this room. I'd given a concert like all the others, not better, not worse. (*He begins to pace back and forth, the camera panning with him, with Lisa's back visible in the foreground.*) Afterwards, they'd said all the usual things, the things you say when you're not really convinced. So I happened to look in the mirror, this one here. (*He looks at a mirror in the background and then looks down.*) The young prodigy was no longer young, certainly wasn't prodigious. (*He walks to Lisa and puts his arms around her in* MCU.) Since then I found other things to do, more amusing things.

308. *Cut to* CU *from over Stefan's shoulder of Lisa. Stefan lifts the veil that covers her face, and background music begins on the soundtrack.*

STEFAN: I knew last night, didn't you? (*They kiss passionately, and after the kiss, he gently removes her hat.*)[65] I haven't even offered to fix you a drink. (*He walks toward the door with his back to the camera, which pans to follow him.*)

LISA (off-screen): Stefan.

He turns, framed by the doorway, and looks back at her in MLS.

STEFAN: Yes.

309. LISA (CU): I came here . . . I have something to tell you.

310. STEFAN (MLS): If it has to do with you, I'm very interested.

311. LISA (CU): It has to do with us.
312. STEFAN (MLS): Now we can't possibly be serious this early in the morning . . . (*he walks through the doorway into the hall in the background where he bends to open a chest against the wall*) . . . at least not without a glass of champagne. It won't take a minute.

313. *Cut to previous* CU *of Lisa.*

STEFAN (*off-screen*): Champagne tastes much better after midnight, don't you think?
LISA (*trying to smile*): Much better.
STEFAN (*off-screen, laughing*): I just came back from America. It's a fascinating country. The men are fond of money, and their wives are fond of Europeans.[66]
LISA (*almost in tears, her voice breaking*): It must have been a wonderful trip.
STEFAN (*off-screen*): So you travel a great deal?[67] (*Lisa cannot answer him.*) Well, I suppose you won't believe me, but I couldn't get you out of my mind all day.
LISA (*faintly, beginning to cry*): No, I don't believe you.[68]

314. *Cut to* LS *taken from the front entrance of the apartment of Stefan in the hallway preparing two glasses of champagne. Lisa can be seen in the extreme background watching him from the far side of the piano.*

STEFAN: If only I had known you were coming, but to tell you the truth, I never dared hope you could arrange it so soon. (*He walks with a champagne bottle in his hand toward the camera and into the adjoining corridor.*) But you're so clever. You managed so beautifully. (*He goes to a mirror screen left with the camera panning to follow him, looks at himself in the mirror, and runs his fingers through his hair.*) You know, you're a very strange woman.
315. LISA (CU): Am I?
STEFAN (*off-screen*): Something you said last night keeps running through my mind.
LISA: What was that?

316. *Cut to* MLS *of Stefan from behind as he walks across the corridor to the doorway to the kitchen screen right. The camera pans with him.*

     STEFAN: I'll tell you in just a moment as soon as I get the ice.

317. *Cut to previous* CU *of Lisa.*

     STEFAN (*off-screen*): Are you getting lonely out there?
     LISA (*her voice breaking again*): Very lonely.

318. *Cut to* MS *of Lisa as she turns away from the camera and walks to a chair in the background where she picks up her purse and coat. She then leaves the room through the glass doors with the camera panning to follow her.*

     VOICE-OVER: I'd come to tell you about us, to offer you my whole life, but you didn't even remember me.

319. *The camera tracks in to* CU *of the roses Lisa had brought. They lay in a pile on a chess table next to a vase.*[69]

320. *Cut to* MLS *of Lisa as she leaves Stefan's apartment. She descends the staircase in the darkened outer hallway as background music plays on the soundtrack. When she is halfway down the stairs, she meets John coming up with a tray of food covered with a white cloth. He steps aside to let her pass and then watches as she continues down the stairway and leaves the frame screen left.*

321. *Cut to* LS *of Lisa as she leaves Stefan's building and walks across the street. As she enters the frame in the background coming out of the courtyard of Stefan's building into the darkened street, a staggering man in uniform also enters with his back to the camera in the foreground. They walk toward each other and meet in middleground. He turns as she walks by and salutes her. She walks on without even noticing him, so absorbed is she in her thoughts, but he begins to follow her.*

M A N: Take you somewhere, young lady, anywhere at all. (*She stops now in* MS *and turns to him.*) Makes no difference.

322. *Cut to* MCU *of Lisa. She first looks at the man and then up in the direction of Stefan's window. Suddenly, she bursts into tears and runs off into the background with the man turning to watch her go.*

323. *Cut to* MLS *of Lisa running through the darkened streets.*[70] *The camera pans to follow her from behind as she runs to a stairway in the background of the frame.*

324. *Cut to high angle* LS *of Lisa walking near a large fountain.*

VOICE-OVER: I don't remember where I went. Time moved past me not in days or in hours, but in the distance it put between us. When I could think again, I went to my son, but it was too late.

325. *Dissolve to* MLS *of a crucifix hanging on an empty wall with a burning candle beneath it.*

   VOICE-OVER: He died last night of typhus without even knowing I was there.

326. *Dissolve to* LS *of an empty bed with four burning candles at its corners. The crucifix hangs on the wall behind the bed and an empty wooden chair stands against another wall.*

   VOICE-OVER: Now I'm alone. My head throbs and my temples are burning. Perhaps God has been kind, and I too have caught the fever.[71]

   The camera pans right and then drops down to frame Lisa, who is sitting at a desk writing the letter. A desk lamp in the foreground partially obscures the camera's view of her.

   VOICE-OVER: If this letter reaches you, believe this—that I love you now as I've always loved you. My life can be measured by the moments I've had with you and our child. If only you could have shared those moments, if only you could have recognized what was always yours, could have found what was never lost. If only . . . (*Lisa stops writing and raises her hand to her forehead, too exhausted to go on.*)

   The image blurs and dissolves.

327. *Dissolve to* CU *of the final page of the letter as the background music builds on the soundtrack. The letter ends abruptly in a blot of ink and is unsigned, but the camera drops down to a note clipped to the bottom of the last page. It contains the cross circled by the name St. Catherine's Hospital that was seen on the first page of the letter. The note reads in typed letters:*
   This letter was written by a patient here. We believe it was meant for you as she spoke your name just before she died.
   Added in handwriting is:
   May God be merciful to you both.
   Mary Theresa
   Sister in Charge

328. *Camera tracks in to* MCU *of Stefan with tears glistening in his eyes.*[72]

329–336. *Dissolve to a series of flashbacks accompanied by background music which combines the Liszt étude with the waltz played as Lisa and Stefan danced on their one evening together. Dissolve first to* CU *of Lisa from over Stefan's shoulder as he lifts the veil from her face during her final visit to his apartment; then to* MLS *of Lisa, again seen from over Stefan's shoulder, with the camera tracking in to* MS *as Stefan walks toward her on the street corner; to* LS *of Lisa and Stefan dancing; to* MCU *of Lisa and Stefan together in a carriage; to* MS *of the carnival workers making the caramel apple and handing it down to Lisa; to previous* LS *of Lisa and Stefan dancing; to* CU *of Lisa kneeling next to the piano as Stefan plays; and finally to* MCU *of Stefan sitting at his desk with the letter before him. Overcome, he covers his face with his hands.*

337. *As church bells are heard chiming in the distance, cut to* MS *of John in profile as he enters the room. The camera pans with him as he walks to Stefan's desk. He taps Stefan on the shoulder to get his attention as the bells chime again. Stefan raises his head and looks at John.*

338. *Cut to a high angle* MS *of Stefan from over John's shoulder.*

STEFAN (*looking up questioningly at John*): You remembered her?

John nods and Stefan looks away. Picking up a pad of paper and a pencil from the desk, John begins to write.

339. *Cut to* ECU *of the pad of paper as John writes "Lisa Berndle."*

340. *Before he finishes completely, cut to previous* MS *of Stefan from over John's shoulder.*

STEFAN (*slowly*): Lisa. (*Turning from John and looking down at the desk.*) Lisa.

The sound of horses' hooves is heard in the distance.

341. *Cut to* MS *of Stefan and John as they both look off-screen right. Stefan*

rises to his feet, walks around the desk, and goes to the window.[73] *The camera pans with him, excluding John from the frame.*

342. *As the sound of the horses is heard again, cut to* CU *of the horses' hooves beating against the cobblestone streets. The legs of the horses and the wheels of the carriage pass across the frame, and the carriage stops with the camera framing its rear wheel. The camera is then raised to look over the top of the wheel as three men enter the frame. Johann's second, dressed in military attire, enters in the foreground screen left, crosses in front of the wheel, and then stands next to it. Stefan's two friends, dressed in long black coats, then enter in the background screen right, stop and look at each other. Johann's second retraces his steps back to the carriage door and Stefan's friends enter the gateway to his building. The camera pans with Johann's second back to the carriage door where Johann very solemnly sits. They nod to each other.*

343. *Cut to previous* MLS *of Stefan still looking out of the window. He looks down, turns to John, and begins to unbutton his vest.*

STEFAN (*to John*): Bring my things.

344. *Cut to* MLS *of Stefan's friends on the stairway to his apartment. The camera, looking through the banister, cranes up to the landing where they walk with their backs to the camera to Stefan's door and ring the bell.*

345. *Cut to* MS *of Stefan and John as John affectionately squeezes Stefan's arm. John then walks into the background and leaves the frame through a doorway. As he closes the door behind him, the doorbell rings.*

346. *Cut to* MS *of Stefan's friends with their backs to the camera as they wait outside the door. John opens the door and nods to them. They take off their hats and solemnly enter the apartment. The camera pans with them through the wall as they enter. John stands in the background facing the camera and holding open the door.*

347. *Cut to* MLS *through a doorway of Stefan in a black overcoat as he walks toward the camera.*

STEFAN: Ready, gentlemen.[74]

The camera pans with him as he walks to a table where the bouquet of white roses that Lisa brought is now arranged in a vase. He takes out one rose and holds it as background music plays on the soundtrack.[75]

VOICE-OVER: Oh, if only you could have recognized what was always yours, could have found what was never lost.

348. *Cut to previous* MLS *of John holding the door open for Stefan's friends, who walk into the hall.*

349. *Cut to previous* MLS *of Stefan holding the rose. He places it in his lapel button hole, turns, and walks with his back to the camera through a doorway. The camera pans with him to the doorway and then holds. Stefan is seen as he walks down a hall into the background.*

350. *Cut to* MLS *of Stefan as he opens the glass door of his study and enters the entrance hall where John awaits him. He stops to shake John's hand, puts on his hat, and walks out of the door. The camera pans with him until he leaves the frame through the doorway. It then holds on John as he closes the door after Stefan.*

351. *Cut to* LS *through the half-opened outer glass door to the building as Stefan walks down the last few steps of the hall staircase and then goes out through the doorway. The camera pans with him in* MS *as he walks across the courtyard to the iron gate where he stops in* MLS. *He looks back toward the camera in the direction of the door. Behind him in the street, a carriage is waiting.*

352. *Cut to* MLS *of Lisa's image as Stefan first saw her, standing shyly behind the door. Gradually, the image fades.*

353. *Cut to* MCU *of Stefan as he smiles sadly, closes his eyes and looks down.*

354. *Cut to previous* MLS *of Stefan at the gate. He turns his back to the camera, walks through the gateway and around the back of the waiting carriage.*

355. *Cut to* LS *of Stefan in the darkened street as he walks toward the camera to his carriage door. In the background, Johann's carriage can be seen with his second standing at the door. Stefan enters his carriage and is followed by one of his friends. As he enters, Stefan's friend snaps his fingers to the driver as a signal for him to drive off. Johann's second then gets into the other carriage and both vehicles pull into the distance as the background music swells on the soundtrack.*

Notes on the Shooting Script

1. Shooting script (hereafter SS) reads: "Then you've made up your mind. You're going to leave the choice to him."

2. SS continues the conversation:

   FIRST MAN: This isn't a joking matter.
   STEFAN: I suppose it isn't.

3. This scene between the two men in the carriage is not in SS. When Stefan leaves, they merely look at each other and shake their heads.

4. In SS, Stefan only tells John "I'm all right" as he walks into the apartment. He does not philosophize about his situation as in continuity script (hereafter CS).

5. In SS, the letter begins with the note which in CS is attached to the end of the letter and is not read until shot 327. The note reads:
   This letter was written by a patient here. We believe it was meant for you as she spoke your name just before she died.
   SS also does not begin the letter proper with the very dramatic "By the time you read this letter I may be dead" since it is already clear from the note that the author of the letter is dead. It begins rather with "I have so much to tell you . . ."

6. This instance of voice-over narration is not in SS.

7. The SS version of this scene varies considerably and combines elements from this scene in CS and the encounter between Lisa and John at the top of the stairs (CS, shots 12–14). The SS version is here quoted in full:

> INTERIOR MOVING VAN
>
> At first we see only the dark cavernous walls of the van. Then as though conscious memory were commencing, objects begin to take shape. We become aware that we are inside a moving van and that its contents are household furnishings.
>
> A moving man materializes in the dim light. He picks up an armful of leather-bound books. The camera pans with him as he carries them to the mouth of the van. We perceive now that it is bright sunlight outside and we begin to hear street noises—children's voices, etc.
>
> Framed in the lighted area, supervising the moving, is John, fourteen years younger than when we first saw him. A second moving man appears beside John, taking the stack of books from his fellow worker's arms.
>
> 2ND MOVING MAN: Where do these go?
>
> John, who has a pencil and pad in his hand, writes briefly on his memo, then holds it out for the other to see.
>
> 2ND MOVING MAN: (reading aloud) The study. (turns and starts away)
>
> At this juncture, from behind the camera, the first moving man reappears in the lighted area. We see that he is carrying a gracefully-wrought antique lyre. As he gets it to the light, he regards the instrument quizzically, then holds it to his breast and looks upwards angelically.
>
> 1ST MOVING MAN: Do I look like one?
>
> John smiles and nods agreeably as much as to say, "That's right, you do." The moving man stands the instrument gingerly on the lip of the van, ready to be carried on the next trip.
>
> The camera moves forward and pans down until we see, standing close to the mouth of the van, a slim, intense girl of fifteen, Lisa

Berndle. From the young girl's enthralled expression and from her neat but patched dress, we can guess her own circumscribed and pinched existence. Apparently the precious objects emerging from the van hold a fascination for her. More than house furnishings, they are the romantic props of a fairy-tale world.

Involuntarily her hand moves out toward the wire strings of the lyre as though magnetized. Only by dint of willpower does she resist touching the beautiful instrument.

The camera draws back to an angle that includes John, who is dusting off some books. Apparently in his own unobtrusive way he has been watching the intense absorption of the girl. After she draws her hand back, she glances toward him and is rewarded by the ghost of a smile, which though seeming to compliment her for the slight act of self-denial, does not encourage her to take any liberties with his master's possessions. However, she gives him a slight smile in return, and from that moment a friendly bond between them is established.

The moment is interrupted by a woman's voice from off scene.

FRAU BERNDLE'S VOICE: (over scene) Lisa!

The girl looks up.

8. This instance of voice-over narration is not in SS.

9. In SS the concierge leaves the hallway and enters a courtyard. There the following scene, which is not included in CS, is enacted:

The concierge turns and starts toward the courtyard in the background, still grumbling to himself. We now become aware of other activity in the courtyard.

The concierge's daughter, Marie, a girl around Lisa's age, is in a boy-girl argument with a callow youth a year or so older. Lisa appears in foreground of shot, crossing toward the door opening to the stairway which leads to her apartment. In the background, Marie begins to scuffle with the boy who grabs her around the waist. Giggling, she pulls away, starts to run, with the boy after her. Out of the corner of her eye Marie spots Lisa, calls out in simulated alarm.

MARIE: Lisa! Lisa, help me!

Lisa glances at the fleeing, giggling girl, decides she neither needs nor wishes her help. She continues to the stairway entrance.

Marie is the girl who will later be involved in the garden scene (CS, shots 20–37) and the rug beating scene (CS, shots 48–49).

10. SS does not include the scene with John at the top of the stairs. Some aspects of this scene are incorporated into an earlier scene in SS (see note 7). Instead SS includes at this point an extended scene in the Berndle apartment which is not in CS and is quoted here in full:

VESTIBULE OF BERNDLE APARTMENT
whose floor plan is a truncated duplicate of Stefan's apartment across the hall. However, the contrast between his furnishings and the frugal

middle-class pieces of the Berndle's is as great as the contrast in their lives. Lisa enters the vestibule, walking toward the door of her mother's bedroom and overhearing a woman's voice chattering off scene.

FRAU MOMBERT'S VOICE: (over scene) They say on the first day he played in the Opera House, the Director General came back to congratulate him. Frau Mendel was there and saw it with her own eyes . . . I think I'll drop the skirt another half inch to be on the safe side . . . And I also heard that the Aide-de-camp of the Arch-Duke paid him a personal call. . . .

FRAU BERNDLE'S BEDROOM
furnished in keeping with the period and with their circumstances. A seamstress, Frau Mombert chats with Frau Berndle as she finishes measuring her skirt. Frau Mombert, an ample figure, is no more a busybody than any other seamstress of the time and place; she is expected to convey gossip from house to house, collecting it as she goes—that is her function in Viennese society. And the heroes of the period, being artists and cultural leaders, receive the lion's share of attention. Today's subject is naturally the advent of a celebrity into this very house.

FRAU MOMBERT: (continuing) The Concierge told that to Herr Boehn and he told his wife . . . the fat one who always wears poppies on her hat. But I'm not surprised. Brand has a pianissimo as I've never heard for thirty-five years . . .

The seamstress notices Lisa who now stands in the doorway, listening.

FRAU MOMBERT: Come, Lisa, we're just ready for you.

Lisa glances inquiringly at her mother who nods.

FRAU BERNDLE: You're going to have a new dress.

Lisa's expression lights up, then changes to a puzzled frown. Frau Berndle and the seamstress exchange a look as though sharing a secret.

FRAU MOMBERT: Come, child, take off your things.

Lisa slips off her dress obediently, but is about as fully clothed as before, wrapped as she is in layers of undergarments that were thought proper in the early years of the century. The seamstress winds her tape around the girl's hips.

FRAU MOMBERT: (disapprovingly) Mmm, still only thirty-two. You need to fill out . . . However, Frau Strobell says the new Paris styles favor slim hips. She was in Paris all winter. How she affords it I have no idea, although I've heard some things I wouldn't want to repeat.

FRAU MOMBERT: (continues measuring and making notations) Sleeve, eight inches . . . In France it seems they don't mind showing a girl's figure. Leave it to the French to save cloth at the expense of decency.

By now Lisa has forgotten her qualms and has a mounting feminine pleasure in the thought of new clothes.

LISA: What kind of dress will it be, Frau Mombert?

FRAU MOMBERT: One suitable for a wedding, at the same time can be altered for school.

LISA: (puzzled) Wedding?

A warning glance from Frau Berndle causes the seamstress to cover her careless slip.

FRAU MOMBERT: Well, you never can tell when one of your friends will get married.

This carries little conviction with Lisa, but she lets the matter drop. She glances toward the window as though remembering the incoming tenant.

LISA: (dreamily) What kind of clothes do the dancing-girls wear at the Opera?

FRAU MOMBERT: (surprised and a little shocked) Your dress will *not* look like theirs!

From the hall outside we hear voices.

VOICES FROM OUTSIDE: (shouting) Be careful of that . . . Look out where you're going . . .

Apparently the piano has now been hoisted the rest of the way to Stefan's apartment. Lisa and the seamstress turn toward the sound the piano makes—a sharp, discordant noise, as someone has evidently rubbed against the keys.

11. SS reads:

> VOICE-OVER: Next day you moved in. Though I was on watch, I
> couldn't get a glimpse of your face. Not this or for many days after. But
> I could listen to your playing . . . It sounded strange, as though you
> were searching for something that eluded you . . .
>
> After a dissolve to a shot of Lisa in the garden, the voice-over continues.
>
> VOICE-OVER: By this time I was so curious to see you I could hardly
> bear waiting.

12. In SS, Lisa and Marie, her girlfriend, are both seated on the same large
swing, and the shot is not described as framed by the fork of a tree trunk.

13. This series of shots (17–21) and all subsequent shots showing Stefan
playing and juxtaposing his playing with Lisa's swinging are not in SS.

14. In SS, Lisa does not push the girl, but instead answers: "I'm not—you . . .
you idiot." She then turns and runs up the stairs.

15. In SS, this instance of voice-over narration reads:

> Try to believe, if you can, that from that moment on, you have never left
> my thoughts. Perhaps it was because I was a starved and impressionable
> child. Perhaps it was the way you looked at me that first time. Even to
> this day when I remember your glance, it is as though I were bathed in
> fire. Or perhaps, as I now believe, it was something deeper than any of
> these things. Quite consciously, I began to prepare myself for you. I kept
> my clothes neater so you wouldn't be ashamed of me.
>
> It is accompanied by a sequence of shots not in CS in which John brings
> coffee to Stefan.

16. In SS, Lisa is not separated from the other dancers.

17. In SS, Lisa does not go to a library to learn about music, but rather to a
museum exhibition illustrating the life of Schubert.

18. In SS, Lisa and the man are inside the car, not standing on its rear platform.

19. In SS, Lisa does not replace the program in the man's pocket.

20. In SS, Stefan and his friends appear to be gathering for an informal evening and so are not formally attired.

21. SS reads instead: "I even had my likes and dislikes among them."

22. In SS, Frau Berndle is washing dishes at the kitchen sink as Lisa passes.

23. In SS, Lisa looks into Stefan's apartment through a small judas on one side of the door. She does not see him playing, but only sees the flickering candlelight in the room.

24. In SS, this scene begins with a sign hung on a side wall announcing "Rug Cleaning Day." Its opening is described as follows:

> Off scene we hear the repeated, explosive sounds of many rugs being beaten.
>
> LISA'S VOICE: (over scene) Then came a great day for me.
>
> The camera pulls back and pans to the iron apparatus where a line of rugs hang, with a tenant behind each one, pounding it with a rug-beater. The camera moves down the row and we discover Lisa among them, beating her small, frayed rug energetically. The camera continues to the end of the line where Marie is munching a piece of cake as she deals her rug some ineffectual, half-hearted blows.

25. This conversation between Lisa and the girl regarding John does not appear in SS; instead the girl annoys Lisa by rudely imitating John's muteness.

26. In SS, Lisa does not knock over the sheet music. John simply enters the room, sees her looking about, smiles, and leaves. She touches Stefan's piano, his reading chair, the terra cotta statue that will play a part in her final visit to Stefan's apartment, and Stefan's coat sleeve. Then she leaves the apartment.

27. In SS, Frau Berndle tries to kiss her daughter, but Lisa turns away.

28. Before she rises from her chair in SS, Lisa opens her hand in which she holds the remnants of a cigarette which she apparently took from Stefan's apartment and crushed during this disturbing conversation.

29. This elaborate pan with Lisa to the door of the train station is not in SS. Instead, Lisa's mother simply turns to look for her, and she is gone.

30. In SS, this voice-over begins: "If I weren't sure you were able to understand my feelings, I'd be afraid you'd laugh at this infatuation of a girl of fifteen."

31. In SS, Lisa does not sit on the ladder. She leaves the apartment after having walked through its rooms.

32. SS reads instead: "There is nothing more terrible than to feel yourself alone among human beings. I came to realize it during those three interminable years in the garrison town where my stepfather lived. When I became eighteen, my parents insisted that I take some part in the social life of the town."

33. In the "One Line" Continuity Breakdown (hereafter OL), Lisa and the lieutenant are introduced at a parade ground with the lieutenant on horseback participating in a jumping competition.

34. In SS, this scene begins with a close shot of a perspiring trumpeter, and Lisa and the lieutenant are part of a crowd of officers and their female companions. At this time in SS, the band marches across the frame and past the café in which the Kastners and the colonel sit. In OL, the Kastners and other prominent members of Linz society watch an archery contest.

35. In SS, the lieutenant continues: "I can imagine you must have been impressed with the fact that in the short time we've known each other, I have been extremely attentive. You must realize, please permit me to be quite frank, that in the past, I have not been entirely unsuccessful in my relations with the gentler sex."

36. In SS, the encounter described is as follows:

> LONG SHOT—THE COMMANDANT'S TABLE IN FRONT OF HOTEL
> As Lisa and Leopold approach, the others look up expectantly. The
> Commandant makes a welcoming gesture. In another moment their an-
> ticipation turns to consternation. The lieutenant escorts Lisa to her chair,
> bows formally to the table and then moves off, his manner leaving no
> doubt as to what occurred.
>
> In consideration of his nephew's feelings, the Commandant now rises,
> pays the waiter's bill, bows stiffly and without a word follows Leopold
> off. Lisa's parents look at her in bewildered anguish. The other couple at
> their table at first are uncertain what they should do. They glance around
> at the adjoining tables where there is already a buzz of conversation that
> suggests a scandal. The man evidently decides it is best to let the others
> know where he stands. Therefore he rises, bows stiffly to the Kastners
> and with his wife follows the Commandant out of scene.
>
> By now the poor Kastners are miserably aware that their new position in
> Linz society is at an end. They look as though they wished the ground
> would open up and swallow them. However, Lisa sits by herself in dig-
> nified and defiant silence.

37. In SS, Stefan's dealings with the small street urchin portray him in a less
sympathetic light:

> The street singer spots him [Stefan], advances toward him with out-
> stretched hat. Hardly slowing his step, Stefan reaches in his pocket for a
> coin and tosses it carelessly in the hat. The musician starts to thank him,
> but Stefan hurries on as though wishing to avoid any acknowledgement.

38. In SS, this restaurant is described as a "coffee house" and has a decidedly
more casual character than in CS. Patrons are seen playing chess and
writing letters, and the waiter, called Fritzel in SS, sits at a large desk.
When Stefan approaches him, Fritzel hands him his mail, which apparently
is delivered to the coffee house.

39. In SS, the scene begins with Stefan's unsuccessful attempt to teach Lisa
how to crack a lobster shell.

40. In SS, they stroll down the main avenue of the amusement park.

41. In SS, Stefan adds an unidentified quotation: "Expectation and desire and something ever more about to be."

42. In SS, Lisa merely watches the workers prepare the taffy apples. The pan down with the long-handled basket is not in SS.

43. In SS, Lisa is eating a taffy apple.

44. In SS, Stefan does not emerge from the compartment; instead the old woman goes to the door. When she knocks, Stefan and Lisa stick their heads out through the window and laughingly respond to her inquiries.

45. In SS, Lisa goes over to the piano with Stefan; she does not gradually follow him there; and she does not kneel next to him as he plays.

46. This scene begins in SS not with a shot of a closed drapery, but with Madame Spitzer "puffing" up the stairs. "Madame" Spitzer is "Frau" Spitzer in SS and is presented as a fat shop owner, not as the elegant salon proprietress of CS.

47. In SS, Stefan does not walk over to sit on the edge of the table, and Lisa continues to model the dress and to circle his chair throughout the scene.

48. In SS, Lisa stops to watch a young couple's affectionate goodbye, and she does not run beside a spiked fence.

49. In SS, Lisa walks along the side of the train as she waves to Stefan. The camera then leaves Lisa and holds on the train as it pulls into the distance. The fade out is not from Lisa walking slowly away, but from the fading tail light of the train.

50. The voice-over in SS continues: "But not quite all of you . . . the child, our son, was born in a charity hospital."

51. There is no mention of this ward of curtained bedchambers in SS.

52. The voice-over narration in SS reads: "Every year we celebrated a certain day. He never knew why." The camera then pans across the room until it rests on a vase of faded flowers.

53. In SS, it is Johann who is seen first as he walks up the winding staircase and enters the bedroom.

54. In SS, Lisa and Johann applaud as they enter the room, and the little signs of Lisa's motherly concern in CS (making Stefan drink all of his milk and brush his teeth) are absent.

55. In SS, Stefan disobediently gets up and runs to the window to watch Lisa and Johann leave. He is a somewhat more mischievous child in SS than he is in CS. In SS, for example, he does not eagerly rush to call Johann "father" in order to please Lisa as he does later in CS, and when she asks him to call Johann "father" he insists to her, "But he isn't."

56. In SS, this scene does not begin with a close-up of the poster, but with the camera immediately panning to follow groups of operagoers. Lisa's voice-over narration is also absent, and the mundane conversation of the operagoers is recorded instead. As Lisa and Johann approach the camera, they are discussing a possible family outing to Pressburg to see a new steamboat.

57. In SS, Act II, Scene 2 of *Die Zauberflöte*, entitled "Distant Thunder" and involving a comic scene with Papageno, is heard in English off-screen during this sequence.

58. This shot of Stefan in his box and those that follow are not in SS.

59. In SS, Lisa and Johann do not go into his study, but have their conversation at the foot of the staircase. When they are finished, Lisa walks up the stairs. As she passes through the upstairs hall, she notices swords and trophies on the wall, and "her expression shadows."

60. In SS, Lisa does say more: "Darling, you must have asked yourself sometimes about—many—about us and—who your father is . . ."

61. This scene (CS, shots 269–273) is very different in SS. Lisa and Stefan are first seen at a candy machine where Lisa buys Stefan caramels. They walk to the train and see a stretcher being carried off. The first part of their conversation takes place as they walk beside the train, not in the contaminated compartment as in CS. In SS, Lisa and Stefan never enter the quarantined compartment, but are warned off by a conductor just as they are about to go in. They are informed plainly that there was a typhus case on the train and are led to another compartment in which they then continue their conversation.

62. This scene (CS, shot 283) is not in SS. Instead the following scene is included:

BUFFET IN STATION WAITING ROOM—LATER THAT NIGHT
This is a dreary, uncomfortable room. Lisa sits at the counter, a cup of coffee in front of her. She looks as though she might have been there for hours, as a person often remains in a neutral place while putting off a vital decision. There are some dozen people in the room. Behind her at the counter, is a peasant couple with empty market baskets on the floor beside them. The woman holds a sleeping child. On a station bench opposite we catch a glimpse of a drunk stretched out. A trainman with a lamp strapped on his chest appears at the track entrance in the background. He rings a bell which jangles harshly in the quiet room.

TRAINMAN: (announcing) Local leaving on track 5 for Modling, Baden, Weiner Neudstadt and Graatz.

This brings a small flutter of excitement. The peasant couple rise hastily. The husband picks up the empty baskets. They start toward the train gate. At the same time a railway policeman, making his rounds, comes on the drunk, shakes him.

POLICEMAN: Come . . .

The drunk has quite a time getting to his feet. Partly supported by the policeman he makes his way out of the shot.

In the meantime Lisa has apparently remained oblivious to what is going on around her. The trainman regards Lisa curiously for a moment, then walks over to her.

TICKET AGENT: Have you your ticket, madam? (Lisa looks up as though at first not understanding him) This is the last train.

LISA: Oh . . . Thank you.

She turns to the waiter behind the counter.

LISA: My bill, please.

The trainman glances at her for another moment, then moves out of the shot.

WAITER: (figuring aloud) A cognac . . . four coffees. That'll be one krone, twenty.

Lisa puts a coin on the counter, rises, starts in the opposite direction from the train gate.

63. In SS, Lisa goes first to Stefan's apartment and then to the restaurant, but does not go into either.

64. In SS, this discussion of the statue ends at this point with the following exchange which is not in CS:

STEFAN: You know, you don't look so much unlike her.
LISA (trying to hide her deep hurt): Really? I wish that were . . . I wish I did.

65. In SS, Stefan neither removes Lisa's hat, nor lifts her veil. After they kiss, he tries to kiss her again, but Lisa turns away.

66. There are two versions of Stefan's line in SS: "I just came back from America. They're strange people. They drink either whiskey or water. I don't know which is worse for you . . ." This line is crossed out and replaced by: "It's quite a country. The men are very rich and the women are very—generous—especially with Europeans."

67. This line, which recalls their conversation in the mock train compartment and indicates clearly to Lisa that Stefan does not remember her, is not in SS.

68. In SS, Stefan laughs and answers: "Sooner or later one has to mean it."

69. The voice-over narration in shot 318 and the track in on the roses here are not in SS.

70. In SS, Lisa walks alone in a park. In voice-over narration, she confesses: "I hated you that morning as I never thought one could hate another human being." The SS suggests that she perhaps contemplates suicide as she stands on a bridge in the park, looks into the water, and says in voice-over: "I had so much to tell you that night—about us—about our little boy. But you treated me as a stranger—not even as a stranger." In OL, Lisa meets the soldier before going into Stefan's apartment.

71. SS continues: "Though things around me are becoming vague, the sight within me seems to grow clearer. I realize now that you're no more to blame than I . . . what happened must have its own reason beyond our poor understanding."

72. This close-up of Stefan and the series of flashbacks that follow are not in SS.

73. In SS, Stefan does not go to the window. Instead he looks down once again at the letter and says, "If I could have recognized what was always mine . . . found what was never lost . . ."

74. In SS:

    SECOND: You won't reconsider? You still have the right to choose your . . .

    STEFAN: No, the right is on the other side.

    SECOND: As you wish.

75. The SS ends here as follows:

    They [Stefan's friends] turn and start toward the door. Stefan is about to join them when something occurs to him. He crosses toward the piano.

The room is empty as the seconds go out through the vestibule and down the stairs.

MED. SHOT — AT THE PIANO

Standing in a vase are Lisa's white roses, a little wilted. Stefan comes into the shot, looks the roses over carefully, selects a bud that is still unfaded. He takes it out tenderly, fastens it to the lapel over his heart. The camera pans as he walks to the vestibule where John is waiting with his hat and coat. For one last moment their eyes meet in mutual under-standing, then Stefan turns and disappears into the dark hall. Music comes up—fragments of the piece Lisa heard Stefan play years ago. The camera moves in close to the white roses. From this angle, with the morning light full on them, they seem to recapture their freshness and beauty. Only underneath them on the piano top a few fragile, white petals have fallen.

Contexts

The Source

In retrospect it seems almost inevitable that Max Ophuls should have been selected to direct the film version of Stefan Zweig's 1922 novella (translated here by Jill Sutcliffe for a 1981 volume entitled *The Royal Game and Other Stories*). Zweig had been raised in turn-of-the-century Vienna, the setting of most of Ophuls's major films, and was a friend and follower of Arthur Schnitzler, whose work Ophuls had previously adapted for the screen. In addition, Zweig was an avid francophile, whose work and lifestyle reflected an Ophulsian commitment to internationalism. Born in 1881 of a wealthy Jewish family, Zweig, like Ophuls, escaped from the increasingly oppressive atmosphere of Germany to find refuge in the New World during the Second World War. Unlike Ophuls, however, Zweig found himself increasingly depressed by the events of the war and eventually committed suicide in 1942.

"Letter from an Unknown Woman" ("Brief einer Unbekannten") first appeared in a volume of stories entitled *Amok: Tales of Violent Feeling* (*Amok: Novellum einer Liedenschaft*). The book became Zweig's first great international success, followed by many others. A consistently productive writer, Zweig steadily turned out criticism, literary biographies, poems, and stories. During the early part of the century, this output won him a distinguished international reputation and considerable fame, though he is not nearly so widely known today.

Ophuls and scriptwriter Howard Koch modified the story in significant ways to bring it into line with their own preoccupations and the demands of cinematic form. The two main characters are no longer anonymous, Stefan borrowing Zweig's given name. Though Zweig's hero is a writer like himself, Ophuls and Koch turn him into a musician. Lisa undergoes a change of profession from courtesan to model. The film's more "proper" Lisa also acquires a husband and does not sleep with Stefan during their final rendezvous. The settings, too, have been altered. Most strikingly, the movie adds the much lauded set pieces in Linz, the Prater and the opera, thereby opening up the story scenically and creating opportunities for humor to vary the tone of Zweig's relentlessly somber narrative. Perhaps most significantly, a framing story has also been added, concluding with a duel, a device Ophuls has favored in other films as well.

Letter from an Unknown Woman

Stefan Zweig

When the celebrated novelist R. returned to Vienna early in the morning after a refreshing three-day trip in the mountains, he bought a newspaper. He was reminded, as soon as he glanced at the date, that it was his birthday. It was his forty-first, he reflected rapidly, and was neither glad nor sorry at this observation. Cursorily he turned the crackling pages of the paper, and then took a taxi to his flat. His manservant told him there had been two visitors and some telephone calls while he was away, and brought him the accumulated post on a tray. Looking idly at what had been put before him, he opened one or two envelopes that interested him on account of who had sent them. He put aside for the time being one letter which looked too bulky, addressed in unfamiliar handwriting. Meanwhile tea had been brought. He leaned back comfortably in his armchair, glanced through the newspaper again, and some circulars; then he lit a cigar and picked up the letter he had put aside.

There were about two dozen hastily written pages in an unfamiliar, shaky, feminine hand, a manuscript rather than a letter. He examined the envelope again automatically, to see if a covering letter had been left inside. But it was empty, and as with the pages themselves, it carried no sender's address or signature. Strange, he thought, and took up the manuscript again. At the top, as an opening, it said: 'To you who never really knew me.' Surprised, he paused. Did that refer to him, or to an imaginary person? His curiosity was suddenly aroused. He began to read.

'My child died yesterday. For three days and nights I struggled with death over this small, fragile life. I sat by his bed for forty hours while influenza shook his poor body with its fever. I put cold compresses on his burning forehead and held his restless little hands day and night. On the third evening I was in a state of collapse. I couldn't keep my eyes open and involuntarily I fell asleep. I must have slept on the hard chair for three or four hours and during that time death took him. There he lies, the poor, sweet boy, in his narrow bed, just as he died; only

From *The Royal Game and Other Stories* (New York: Harmony Books, 1981), pp. 216–250.

someone has closed his eyes, those intelligent, dark eyes, and folded his hands over his white nightshirt.

'Four candles—one at each corner of the bed—burn brightly. I dare not look; I am afraid to move. When the candles flicker, shadows flit over his face and his closed lips, and it seems then as if his features move; and I can almost imagine he isn't dead, that he'll wake up again and say something childishly tender to me in his clear voice. But I know he is dead. I won't look again, so as not to revive my hopes, and be disappointed once more. I know, I know, my son died yesterday— now I have only you left in all the world, only you, who know nothing about me. You, who meanwhile amuse yourself all unawares or trifle with people and things; only you, who never knew me, and whom I always loved.

'I have taken the fifth candle and put it here on the table on which I am writing to you. I can't be alone with my dead child without pouring my heart out to someone. And to whom should I speak at this terrible time if not to you? To you who were everything to me, and still are? Perhaps I can't make myself completely clear to you, perhaps you won't understand me. My head is so heavy; my temples twitch and throb; my limbs ache. I think I am feverish. Perhaps I have influenza, too. It is spreading from door to door now; and that would be good, for then I would go with my child and not have to kill myself. Sometimes everything goes dark before my eyes. Perhaps I shall not be able to finish this letter—but I want to summon up all my strength, this once, just this once, to speak to you, my darling, who never knew me.

'I want to speak to you alone, to tell you everything for the first time. You ought to know all about my life. It has always belonged to you and you knew nothing about it. But you shall know my secret only when I am dead, when you won't have to answer me, if what is making my limbs go hot and cold really is the end. If I must go on living I shall tear up this letter and keep silent, as I have always done. But if you hold it in your hands you will know that a dead woman is telling you the story of her life; the life that was yours all her waking hours. Don't be afraid of my words. A dead woman no longer wants anything—not love, or pity, or comforting words. There is only one thing I ask of you and that is to believe everything I tell you, everything the pain that flies from me to you reveals. Believe my every word, I ask nothing more of you: one doesn't tell lies at the deathbed of an only child.

'I will reveal my whole life to you, a life which truly began only on the day I first knew you. Before that everything was simply obscure and confused, in that my memory never surfaced from some kind of cellar filled with dusty, dull things and people, covered in spiders' webs, that my heart no longer recognises. When you came into my life I was thirteen years old and lived in the same house you live in now, the same house in which you are holding this letter—my last living breath—in your hand. I lived on the same floor, immediately opposite the door of your flat. You will certainly not remember us at all, the poor widow of an accountant (she always wore mourning) and the thin, half-grown child—we were very quiet, of course, immersed in our petty-bourgeois poverty. Perhaps you never heard our name: we had no nameplate on our door and no one came to visit us, no one inquired after us. It is also so long ago, fifteen or sixteen years. No, you certainly won't remember it now, my darling, but I, oh I remember passionately every little detail. I remember as though it were today, the day, no, the hour, I first heard of you, first saw you. Why shouldn't I, for it was then the world began for me. Have patience, my darling, I want to tell you everything, everything from the beginning. Don't tire of listening to me for a little while, I beg you. I haven't grown tired of loving you all my life.

'Before you moved in to our house, odious, nasty, quarrelsome people lived in your flat. Poor as they were, they hated most of all having poverty-stricken neighbours like us, because we didn't want to have anything to do with their depraved lower-class coarseness. The man was a drunkard and beat his wife. We were often wakened in the night by the noise of chairs being knocked over and the clatter of breaking plates. Once, after she had been beaten until she was bleeding, she ran out onto the stairs, her hair dishevelled, and with the drunken man bawling after her, until people opened their doors and threatened to call the police. My mother had avoided having anything to do with them from the start and forbade me to speak to the children, who as a result never missed an opportunity to take it out on me. When they met me in the street they shouted obscenities after me and once they threw such hard snowballs at me they made my forehead bleed. Everyone in the house instinctively disliked that family and breathed a sigh of relief when something happened to make them leave suddenly with their bits and pieces—I believe the husband was imprisoned for theft. For a few days a 'To Let' notice appeared on the front door, then it was taken down and the caretaker promptly let it be known that an author, a quiet bachelor, had taken the flat. That was how I heard your name for the first time.

'After a few days painters and decorators, cleaners and carpet layers came to renovate after the mess left by the former tenants. There was much hammering, banging, plastering and scraping but Mother was only too pleased, she said, that the unsavory goings-on over the way had come to an end. I didn't actually see you—not even while you were moving in. All the work was supervised by your manservant. That small, grave, greyhaired gentleman's gentleman directed everything in a quiet business-like, superior way. He impressed us all very much, firstly because in our suburban dwelling a gentleman's gentleman was something of a novelty, and then because he was so very polite to everybody, without in any way putting himself on a level with the servants, or descending to familiar gossip. From the very first he treated my mother as a lady, with respect, and he was always friendly and serious, even to a little shrimp like me. If he mentioned your name it was always with a certain reverence, with particular esteem. It was evident that he was attached to you far more than was usual with servants. And how I have loved good old John for that, though I envied him because he could always be near you, and do things for you.

'I am telling you all this, my darling, all these little, almost silly things, so that you will understand how right from the start you were able to gain such power over the shy, timid child I was. Even before you actually came into my life, there was a prestige about you, an aura of opulence, of being special and mysterious. Everyone in the small suburban house waited impatiently for you to move in (people who live narrow lives are always curious about new neighbours), and I first felt this curiosity about you when I came home from school one afternoon and the furniture van was standing outside. The removal men had already taken up most of the heavy furniture and were carrying in a number of small things. I stood at the door to marvel at everything, for all your things were so very different from anything I had ever seen. There were Indian idols; pieces of Italian sculpture; large pictures in dazzling colours; and then, finally came the books, so many and so beautiful, I wouldn't have believed it possible. They were all piled up at the door, where the manservant took charge of them and carefully removed the dust from every single one with a feather duster. I loitered near the ever-growing pile with curiosity; the manservant didn't send me away, but neither did he encourage me. I didn't dare touch anything, although I would have loved to handle the soft leather of some of them. I just looked shyly at the titles on the spines; there were French and English books among them, and many in languages I didn't understand. I believe I would have looked at them all for hours but Mother called me in.

'I thought about nothing else but you all the evening; even before I knew you. I myself possessed only a dozen cheap tattered books with cardboard covers which I loved more than anything else and had read over and over again. And then I wondered what the man must be like who owned and had read all those wonderful books, who knew all those languages, and was so wealthy and knowledgeable at the same time. A sort of supernatural awe combined with the idea of all those books. I tried to picture you in my mind. You were an old man with glasses and a long, white beard, like our geography teacher, only much kinder, more handsome and gentler—I don't know why I was already sure then that you must be good-looking, when I still thought of you as an old man. That night, still without meeting you, I dreamt about you for the first time.

'The next day you moved in, but in spite of being on the look-out all the time, I wasn't able to catch a glimpse of you—which only increased my curiosity. At last, on the third day, I saw you; and what a tremendous surprise it was, to discover how different you were, so completely unrelated to my childish picture of a godfather. I had imagined a bespectacled, kindly, old man, and then you appeared—you, exactly as you still are today, unchangeable, on whom the years sit lightly! You were wearing fashionable, light-brown country clothes and ran up the stairs two at a time in your inimitable, easy, boyish way. You carried your hat in your hand so I was able to see, with amazement I could scarcely hide, your open, lively face and your youthful hair: really, I was taken aback to see how young, how handsome, how willow-slim and elegant you were. And isn't it strange: at that first moment I saw clearly what I and everyone else came to see in you so uniquely time and time again, but with some astonishment—that somehow you are two people in one, a passionate, happy-go-lucky young man given over to pleasure and adventure, and at the same time as far as your writing is concerned a relentless, serious, responsible, extremely well-read and educated man. Unconsciously I felt what everyone sensed about you, that you led a double life, a life which presented to the world a light-hearted, open face and an obscure life known only to yourself. I, the thirteen-year-old, magically attracted, felt this profound duality, this secret of your existence, at my first sight of you.

'Do you understand now, my darling, what a marvel, what an alluring enigma you must have been for me, as a child? Suddenly to discover that a man everyone held in respect because he wrote books, because he was famous in that great world outside, was a young, stylish, boyishly high-spirited, twenty-five-year-old! Do I have to tell you that from that day on nothing else in our house, in my entire wretched childish world, interested me except you, that the entire obduracy, the whole intense tenacity of a thirteen-year-old revolved more and more around your life, your existence? I watched you, I observed your routine, noticed the people who visited you; and all that only increased my curiosity about you, instead of diminishing it, for the two sides of your character were revealed by the diversity of those visitors. There were young people, friends of yours, with whom you laughed and were in high spirits; shabbily dressed students; and then again there were ladies who drove up in cars; once the Director of the Opera, the great conductor whom I had only looked at respectfully from afar on his rostrum. Then there were also young girls still attending commercial school, who scurried in the door looking embarrassed. Altogether there were many, very many, women. I didn't think anything about this particularly, not even when, as I was on my way to school one morning, I saw a heavily-veiled lady leave your flat. I was only thirteen and too innocent to know that the intense curiosity with which I watched and spied on you was already love.

'But I know exactly, my darling, the day and the hour when my heart was lost to you for ever. I had been for a walk with a schoolfriend and we were standing at the gate chatting. A car drew up, stopped, and you jumped from the running board in that impatient, buoyant way that thrills me about you even today, and made for the door. Instinctively I was impelled to open it for you and so I stepped in your path and we nearly collided. You looked at me with that warm, soft, covert expression, which was like a caress, smiled at me tenderly—yes, I can't put it any other way—and said in a very soft and almost intimate voice, "Thanks very much, young lady."

'That was all, darling; but from that moment when I met your gentle, caressing eyes, I was yours. Later, of course, it was not long before I discovered you look this way at every woman who passes by. You give them a glance intended to attract and trap them. It takes in everything they are wearing and at the same time strips them naked. It's the look of the born seducer. You give it to every shopgirl who serves you, every maid who opens the door for you. It signifies little more to you than desire and curiosity, but it shows simply that your fondness for women quite unconsciously makes your expression caring and warm, when it is turned on them. But I, the thirteen-year-old child, did not suspect this: it was as though I had been plunged into fire. I thought the tenderness was for me alone, and at that moment the woman in me, the adolescent, awoke and that woman was yours for ever.

"Who was that?" my friend asked.

'I couldn't answer straightaway. It was impossible to speak your name. At that one, unique moment your name was already sacred, had become my secret. "Oh, some man who lives in the house," I stammered awkwardly.

"Well why did you go so red then when he looked at you?"

'My friend teased me with all the mischievousness of an inquisitive child. And the thought that she was making fun of my secret made me blush even more. Feeling embarrassed, I was rude. "Stupid fool," I said angrily: I would have liked to have strangled her. But she only laughed louder and more scornfully, until I felt the tears well up in my eyes with impotent rage. I left her standing there and ran upstairs.

'I have loved you ever since that moment. I know women have often told you they love you, you pampered man! But believe me, no one has loved you as slavishly, with such dog-like devotion, as the creature I was, and have always been. Nothing on earth equals the unseen, hidden love of a child, because it is so without hope, so servile, so submissive, so observant and intense, as the covetous and unconsciously demanding love of a grown woman never is. Only lonely children can maintain their passion completely. The others rid themselves of emotion by chattering with their companions; they smooth it away in confidences. They have heard and read so much about love and know it is the fate of all. They play with it, as though it were a toy, they boast of it like boys with their first cigarette. But I had no one in whom to confide. No one advised or warned me; I was inexperienced and unsuspecting; I fell headlong into my destiny as into an abyss. Everything that grew and blossomed within me centered trustfully on you, and the dream of you. My father had long been dead; my mother was a stranger to me with her everlasting, wretched depression, and worries about her pension. The half-corrupted schoolgirls repelled me, as they played so unscrupulously with what was to me the ultimate passion. And so I turned everything that would normally have scattered and divided, towards you—my whole concentrated and ever-impatiently growing personality. You were to me—how shall I put it? No comparison is good enough—you were indeed everything, my whole life. Nothing existed unless it related to you. My whole existence made sense only if it was connected with you. You transformed my whole life. Until then apathetic and only average in school, I suddenly came first. I read a thousand books far into the night, because I knew you loved books. Much to my mother's astonishment I began to practise the piano with almost mulish tenacity, because I thought you were fond of music. I mended and pressed my clothes, just so that I would look neat and pleasing to you; I thought it terrible that my school overall (it was made out of one of my mother's dresses) had a square patch inserted on the left-hand side. I was afraid you might notice it and despise me. So I always covered it with my satchel when I ran up the stairs, trembling with fear in case you saw it. But how silly that was: you hardly ever looked at me again.

'But I, on the other hand, really did nothing all day but wait and watch for you.

There was a small brass peep-hole in our door and through this round hole it was possible to see your door. That peep-hole—no, don't laugh, darling, even today I am not ashamed of the hours I spent!—was my eye on the world outside. During those months and years I sat whole afternoons there in the icy hall on the alert, a book in my hand, afraid my mother would be suspicious. I was like a taut string, vibrating if your presence touched it. It was always tense and agitated whenever I was near you, but you could no more have felt it than you did the tension of the spring in the watch you carried in your pocket. It patiently counts the hours for you in the darkness and ticks them off, accompanying you on your way with inaudible heartbeats, and you give it only a quick glance once in a million ticking seconds. I knew all about you, knew all your habits, all your suits and ties. I knew and soon made distinctions between your various friends and divided them into those I liked and those I disliked. From the time I was thirteen until I was sixteen my every hour was yours. Oh, what follies I committed! I kissed the door-handle your hand had touched, I picked up a cigarette end you had thrown away in the entrance, and it was sacred to me because your lips had touched it. In the evenings I ran down into the street a hundred times, on any pretext, to see in which of your rooms the light was burning, and so be party to your invisible presence. And during the weeks you were away—my heart always stopped with anguish when I saw John faithfully carrying your yellow traveling bag outside— in those weeks my life was desolate and without meaning. I went about sullen, bored and bad-tempered and had to take care all the time that Mother did not notice how my eyes were red with crying and from that see my despair.

'I know I am telling you about childish follies, extravagant over-enthusiasm. I ought to be ashamed of them but I am not ashamed, for my love for you was never purer and more passionate than at the time of those childish excesses. I could tell you for hours, for days, how I lived with you then. You scarcely knew me by sight, for if I met you on the stairs and could not avoid you, I ran past with my head lowered, afraid of meeting your ardent look, like someone jumping into water to avoid being scorched by fire. I could tell you about those long-since vanished years of yours for hours, for days on end, and unroll the entire calendar of your life; but I won't bore you, won't distress you. I'll confide to you only the most wonderful experience of my childhood; and please don't deride me because it is such a small thing. To me, as a child, it was of infinite importance. It must have been on a Sunday. You were away and your manservant was pulling the heavy carpets, which he had been beating, through the open door of the flat. The good fellow found it hard work and in a fit of rashness I went over and asked if I could help. He was astonished but let me do it, and so—if only I could find words to tell you with what awe-struck, indeed devout, reverence—I saw the inside of your flat. I saw your world, the writing-table at which you were accustomed to sit, with a blue crystal vase on it containing a few flowers, your bookcases, your pictures, your books. It was only a fleeting, surreptitious glance into your life, as the faithful John would certainly have prevented me from making a closer inspection. But with this one glance I absorbed the whole atmosphere and had nourishment for my endless dreams about you, waking or sleeping.

'These fleeting moments were the happiest of my childhood. I wanted to tell you about them so that you, who didn't know me, will at last begin to understand how a life ebbed and flowed with you. I wanted to tell you about them and about that other, most dreadful hour, which unhappily was so near. Because of you—I have already told you—I had forgotten everything else. I had paid no attention to my mother and concerned myself with no one. I didn't notice that an elderly gentleman, a businessman from Innsbruck, distantly related to my mother by marriage, was calling more often and staying longer. Indeed I was only too pleased that he sometimes took Mother to the theatre and I could then be alone, thinking of you and watching out for you—my greatest, my only happiness. Well, one day my mother called me to her room with a certain formality; she had something serious to say to me. I went pale and heard my heart start to pound: had she noticed something, guessed something? My first thought was of you, the secret that linked me with the world. But mother was herself embarrassed, she kissed me tenderly once or twice (which she hardly ever did), she sat me close beside her on the sofa and began hesitantly and shamefacedly to tell me that her relative, who was a widower, had made her an offer of marriage, and she had decided, mainly on my account, to accept. My heart beat very fast: only one thought came into my head, the thought of you. "But we'll stay here, won't we?" I just managed to say.

"No, we'll move to Innsbruck. Ferdinand has a beautiful house there."

'I didn't hear anything else. Everything went black before my eyes. Later I knew I had fainted. I heard mother quietly telling my future stepfather, who had been waiting behind the door, that I had suddenly thrown up my hands, stepped backwards and then fallen down like a lump of lead.

'I cannot describe to you what happened in the next few days, how I, an impotent child, resisted their all-powerful intentions. My hand still trembles as I write, thinking about it. I could not betray my real secret, so my resistance merely appeared obstinate, wicked and insolent. No one spoke to me any more about it; everything was done behind my back. They used the time I was at school to expedite the removal. When I came home, yet another piece of furniture had been removed or sold. I saw how the flat, and with it my life, was disintegrating. And then one day when I came home to lunch, the removal men had been and taken everything away. Packed suitcases and two camp beds for Mother and me stood in the empty rooms. We were to sleep there for one more night—the last—and travel to Innsbruck in the morning.

'I decided all of a sudden on this last day that I could not go on living without being near you. You were my only refuge. How I was thinking and whether I was capable of thinking clearly at that desperate time, I can never say. But I stood up, wearing my school clothes—Mother had gone out—and just as I was, on the spur of the moment, I went across to you. No, I didn't go: I was impelled towards your door as though mesmerised; my legs were stiff and I was trembling. I have already told you I didn't know clearly what I wanted: to fall at your feet and ask you to keep me as a maid, as a slave. I am afraid you will laugh at this innocent fanaticism of a fifteen-year-old, but—my darling, you wouldn't go on laughing if you knew how I stood there outside in the icy hall, rigid with fear and yet pushed forward by a power I could not comprehend, and how my trembling arm seemed to tear itself loose from my body, lifted itself up and—it was a struggle that lasted through an eternity of terrible seconds, pressed the doorbell. It still rings in my ear today, that shrill sound of the bell, and then the silence that followed, while my heart stood still and my blood froze, and I just listened to see if you would come to the door.

'But you didn't. Nobody came. You were obviously out that afternoon and John away on an errand; so I stumbled back into the desert of our empty flat, with the dead note of the bell reverberating in my ear, and threw myself exhausted on a travelling rug, worn out with the four steps I had taken, as though I had been walking for hours in deep snow. But beneath this exhaustion there still burned undiminished the determination to see you, to speak to you, before they tore me away. I swear there was nothing sexual in it. I was still ignorant, just because I thought of nothing but you. I wanted only to see you, to see you once more, to cling to you. The whole night, the whole long, frightful night, I waited for you, my darling. Scarcely had Mother gone to bed and fallen asleep than I crept into the hall to listen for your return. I waited the whole night, and it was a bitterly cold January night. I was tired, my limbs ached and there was no longer a chair to sit on. So I lay down on the cold floor, stretched out in the draught that came under the door. I lay there in my thin clothes, on the painfully cold floor, without putting on any covering. I didn't want to be warm for fear of falling asleep and not hearing your footsteps. Oh how painful it was, I had cramp in my feet, my arms shivered; I had to keep standing up, it was so cold in the frightful darkness. But I waited, waited, waited for you, as for my destiny.

'At last—it must have been two or three o'clock in the morning—I heard the lock turn in the front door and then steps coming up the stairs. The cold vanished, warmth spread over me, I opened the door softly meaning to throw myself upon you, to fall at your feet . . . Oh I don't know what I should have done in my childish foolishness. The footsteps came nearer, candle-light flickered. Trembling, I held on to the door-handle. Was it you climbing the stairs?

'Yes, it was you, darling—but you were not alone. I heard a soft, sensual laugh, a rustling of silk, and your voice speaking quietly—you had come home with a woman. I don't know how I lived through that night. The next day, at about eight o'clock, they took me off to Innsbruck: I had no more energy to resist.

'My child died last night—now I shall be alone again, if I really must go on living. In the morning strangers will come, bulky men in black, bringing a coffin in which they will place my poor child, my only child. Perhaps friends will come, too, bringing wreaths, but of what use are flowers on a coffin? They will comfort me, and say a few words. Words, words! But how can they help me? I know I must be alone again. And there is nothing more terrible than to be alone with people all around. I experienced it before, in those endless two years from sixteen to eighteen in Innsbruck, where I lived with my family like a prisoner, an outcast. My stepfather, a very easy-going, taciturn man, was kind to me. My mother, as if to atone for an unwitting injustice, seemed ready to grant my every wish. Young people tried to be helpful but, fiercely stubborn, I rebuffed them. I didn't want to be happy, to be content away from you; I buried myself in a dark world of self-torment and loneliness. I did not wear the pretty clothes they bought me. I refused to go to concerts or the theatre, or to join in companionable excursions. I rarely left the house. Would you believe it, my darling, I didn't know ten streets in that small town, where I lived for two years? I grieved, and I wanted to; I wallowed in every deprivation I inflicted on myself while I thought about you. And then, I didn't want to allow anyone to turn me from my passion to live only for you. I sat alone at home, hour after hour, day after day, and did nothing but think of you; again and again I revived my hundred small recollections of you, every encounter, all the times I waited, and played over those little events as though I were in a theatre. It is because of the innumerable times I re-enacted every second of those days that my whole childhood has remained such a glowing memory. I feel every minute of those past years are as alive and active as if I had experienced them yesterday.

'I lived only through you in those days. I bought all your books; if your name appeared in the newspaper it was a red-letter day. Will you believe it when I tell you that I know every line of your books by heart, I have read them so often? If someone were to wake me in the night and quote one of your lines at random I could continue it, trance-like, even now, today, after thirteen years. Your every word was holy writ to me. The whole world existed only with reference to you. I read in the Viennese newspapers about concerts and first nights, thinking only which would have interested you, and when evening came, I accompanied you from afar: now he is entering the concert hall, now he is taking his seat. I dreamt that a thousand times, because I had seen you once at a concert.

'But why should I recount all this, this raving, self-destructive, so tragic, hopeless fanaticism of a forsaken child? What is the good of telling someone who never suspected it, never knew? Was I really still a child then? I was seventeen, eighteen—young men in the street began to turn and look at me, which only annoyed me. For love, or even flirting with the idea of it, with anyone other than you was so unimaginable, so unthinkable, so foreign to me, that even the temptation seemed to me like a crime. My passion for you remained constant; only it changed as I matured physically, as my senses awoke and became more ardent, more physical, more womanly. And what the innocent, unaroused child who had rung your doorbell could have had no inkling of, was now my only thought: to give myself to you, to surrender to you.

'People around me considered me shy, and said I was timid (I had kept my secret to myself). But I developed a firm resolve. All my thoughts and endeavours were stretched in one direction: back to Vienna, back to you. And I achieved my purpose, however foolish and incomprehensible it must have seemed to the others. My stepfather was well off. He looked on me as his own child. But I was bitterly obstinate and insisted I wanted to earn my own living, and eventually I succeeded in coming to Vienna as an employee in a large, ready-to-wear dress business belonging to a relative.

'Need I tell you where I went first when—at last! At last!—I arrived in Vienna on a foggy autumn day? I left my cases at the station, rushed on to a tram—how long that journey seemed. I resented every stop!—and ran to the house. There was a light in your window. My whole heart sang. The city had been so alien, so mindlessly tumultuous to me, but now it came alive, as I did again, when I felt your presence, you, my everlasting dream. I didn't realise that in fact I was just as far away from your consciousness, beyond valleys, mountains and rivers, as I was when only the thin, glass window-pane, showing a light, was between you and my radiant gaze. All I did was to go on staring up; there was a light, the house, you, there was my world. For two years I had dreamed of this hour, now my dream had come true. All that long, soft, misty evening I stood in front of your window until the light went out. Only then did I look for my own lodging.

'Every evening I stood in front of your house like that. I had to work until six o'clock. It was hard, tiring work, but I liked it, as the turmoil there prevented me from feeling my own so painfully. And straightaway, as soon as the iron shutters rolled down behind me, off I ran to my beloved destination. Only to see you again, only to meet you once more; that was all I wanted, just to be able to look on your face from a distance. After about a week I did meet you at last. In fact it was just at a moment when I least expected it: while I was looking up at your windows, you actually crossed the street. And in an instant I became a child, that thirteen-year-old, again. I felt the blood rush to my cheeks. Involuntarily, against my innermost longing to feel your eyes on me, I bowed my head and ran past you like lightning, as though someone was chasing me. Afterwards I felt ashamed at running away like a shy schoolgirl, as now I knew exactly what I wanted: I really wanted to meet you. I looked for you, I wanted you to recognise me after all the accursed, yearning years, to notice me, to love me.

'But for a long time you didn't notice me, although I stood in your street every evening, even in flurries of snow and in the sharp, cutting Viennese wind. I often waited for hours in vain. You would come out at last with friends. I saw you twice with women, and then I felt my adulthood, experienced that new, different feeling towards you in the way my heart would suddenly quicken, tearing me apart, when I saw a woman I didn't know walking so confidently arm in arm with you. I wasn't surprised, I knew already from my childhood days about those endless lady callers, but now, somehow, it hurt me physically. Something was aroused in me, hostility and desire at the same time, in the presence of this public physical familiarity with someone else. One day, childishly proud as I was and perhaps still am, I stayed away from your house. But how awful that empty evening of defiance and revolt was. The next evening I stood once more humbly outside your house waiting, waiting, as it has long been my whole destiny to stand, outside your life which has been closed to me.

'At last, one evening, you noticed me. I had seen you coming from a distance and pulled myself together to prevent myself avoiding you. By chance the street was made narrower by a lorry that was unloading and you had to pass quite close to me. Your absent-minded glance skimmed over me so quickly and casually that hardly had you noticed how intently I was looking at you than it became that look you give all women—how the recollection terrified me!—tender, veiled yet unveiling, all-embracing and captivating—the look that awoke my passion for you as a child, and now did so for the first time as a woman. For one, perhaps two, seconds, your glance held mine in this way—I could not tear mine away, and did not want to—and then you had walked past me. My heart beat so fast that in spite of myself I had to slow my pace. When I turned round, overcome by irresistible curiosity, I saw you had stopped and were gazing in my direction. And by the way you were looking at me, with interest and speculation, I knew at once you did not recognise me.

'You did not recognise me then or ever—you have never recognised me. How can I describe the disappointment of those moments, my darling? That was the very first time I endured the fate of not being recognised by you, the first of many occasions I have lived through since, and a fate I shall die with—never, ever recognised by you. How can I describe that disappointment? Just consider, in those two years in Innsbruck, where I thought of you all the time and did nothing but imagine what our first reunion in Vienna would be like, my fancy ranged from the wildest to the most blissful possibilities, according to my mood. If I may put it this way, every fantasy passed through my mind. In my darkest moments I had imagined you would reject me, despise me for being too inferior, too ugly, too importunate. I suffered dreadful visions of all forms of your disfavour, coldness or indifference. But not in the darkest stirrings of my feelings, or in the uttermost awareness of my inferiority, had I ventured to consider this one most appalling possibility: that you had never actually noticed my existence.

'I understand now, of course—indeed you taught me to understand!—that a girl's or a woman's face must be extraordinarily changeable for a man, because it is mostly a mirror, now of a passion, now of childishness, now of exhaustion. It is gone as quickly as a reflection in a glass. You taught me that a man can easily forget a woman's face because her age changes with the light and shade, and her clothes provide a different setting from one occasion to the next. Those who are resigned to it are the truly wise. But I was a young girl then and couldn't understand how you could have forgotten. For somehow my excessive, endless preoccupation with you gave me the illusion that you must often be thinking of me and were waiting for me. How could I have gone on living, knowing for certain that I was nothing to you, that you never gave me the slightest thought? This realisation came to me from your glance, which showed that you had forgotten my existence and there was no thread of memory connecting your life to mine. That was my first plunge into reality, my first premonition of my destiny.

'You didn't recognise me on that occasion. And two days later when we met again and you looked at me as though you knew me, it was not that you recognised me as the one who loved you and whom you aroused, but simply as the pretty eighteen-year-old who passed you at the same place two days earlier. You looked at me with friendly surprise, a light smile playing round your mouth. You passed me again and slowed up immediately as before. I trembled, I was jubilant, I prayed you would speak to me. I felt you saw me as flesh and blood for the first time. I, too, walked slowly and did not avoid you. Suddenly, without turning round, I was conscious that you were behind me. I knew I would hear your dear voice speak directly to me for the first time. Anticipation paralysed me. My heart beat so fast I was afraid I would have to stop—there you were at my side. You spoke to me in your easy, cheerful way as though we were old friends—oh, you knew nothing about me, you never had any idea of what my life was like. You spoke to me in such a charming, free and easy manner that I was even able to answer you. We walked the whole length of the street together. Then you asked me if we might dine together. I agreed. How could I have refused you?

'We ate together in a small restaurant—do you still know where it was? No, of course not. You certainly won't distinguish it from other similar evenings, for who was I to you? One of hundreds, one flirtation in a never-ending chain. Why should you remember me? I said very little. I was so infinitely happy to have you near me, to hear you speak to me. I didn't want to waste a moment of it by asking questions or by foolish chatter. I shall never cease to be grateful to you for that hour. How fully you earned my warmest respect. How tender, how gentle, how tactful you were, entirely self-controlled, without trying to force caresses on me. And from the first moment you displayed such a confident, friendly intimacy that you would have won me, even if I had not already been yours with all my heart and soul. Oh, you don't know what a monster you exorcised, when you didn't disillusion me after five years of childish anticipation.

'It was late; we had finished eating. At the restaurant door you asked me if I was in a hurry or not. How could I conceal from you that I was ready to give myself to you! I said I had plenty of time. Then you asked me, after a moment's hesitation, if I would come home with you and talk. It was a foregone conclusion, feeling as I did, that I said, "With pleasure." I noticed at once that my prompt acceptance affected you somehow; you were either embarrassed or pleased. Anyway, you were visibly surprised. Of course, today I understand your astonishment. I know now it is usual for a woman, although she has a burning desire to give herself to a man, to hide her willingness, to feign alarm or indignation, which will only be calmed by urgent entreaties, lies, protestations and promises. I know that perhaps only professional prostitutes or naïve adolescents agree so readily to such an invitation. How could you know that for me it was only the outward expression, the outburst, of longing accumulated over a thousand lonely days. In any case, however, you were attracted and I began to interest you. As we walked along, talking, I felt you were somehow appraising me speculatively. Your instinct, your magically certain instinct about human nature, told you at once there was something unusual, some mystery, about this pretty, trusting girl. Your curiosity was awakened and I was aware from your indirect, searching questions, how you wanted to discover the secret of this mystery. But I was evasive. I preferred to appear stupid rather than reveal it.

'We went up to your flat. Forgive me, darling, when I say that you can't understand what that path, those stairs meant to me—how it disturbed me, such rapture, such frantic, agonising happiness—I nearly died. I can scarcely think of it now without crying; and I have no more tears. I only felt that every object there was steeped in my love. Everything was an emblem of my childhood and my longing: the gate, where I waited for you thousands of times; the stairs, which taught me to recognise your step and where I first saw you; the peephole, through which I spent my very soul looking for you; the mat in front of your door where I once knelt; the click of the key at which I always sprang up from my vigil. My whole childhood, all my passion, was centred on those few square yards. My whole life was there. And now it broke over me like a storm: I had achieved everything—everything—and I was going with you—you and I together—into your home, our home. Just think of it—it sounds banal, but I don't know how else to say it—outside your door lay reality, that dreary daily round that had been my whole existence; and at your door the magic kingdom of childhood began—Aladdin's Cave. Just think—that door, that threshold I now crossed with a feeling of intoxication, I had gazed at it a thousand times, with eyes aglow—and you will have an inkling, but only an inkling—you will never completely understand, my darling—what that tumultuous moment cost me.

'I spent the whole night with you. You had no idea that until then no man had touched me, caressed my body or seen it. But how could you possibly have suspected that, darling, since I offered you no resistance? I supressed all modesty, all hesitation, only to prevent you from guessing the secret of my love for you, as you would certainly have been alarmed. You care only for the superficial, the frivolous, the inconsequential. You are afraid of becoming involved in anyone's destiny. You want to squander yourself on everyone, on the whole world; and to accept no sacrifice. If I tell you now, darling, that I was a virgin when I gave myself to you, I implore you, don't misunderstand me! I'm not complaining. You didn't entice me, deceive me, seduce me—I forced myself on you, threw myself into your arms, went out to meet my fate. Never, never will I accuse you. No, I shall always be grateful to you, for how rich that night was for me, how it sparkled with pleasure, how blissful it was when I opened my eyes in the darkness and knew you were by my side. I felt so much as if I were in heaven that I was surprised not to find the stars all around me. No, I have never regretted it, my darling, never wished those hours undone. I only know that as you slept, as I heard you breathing and felt your body and mine so close, I wept for joy in the darkness.

'In the morning I hurried away early. I had to go to work and, besides, I wanted to be away before your man came. I didn't want him to see me. When I stood there, dressed to go out, you took me in your arms and looked at me intently; was it a faint and distant memory that stirred in your mind, or was it that, because I was so happy, you thought I looked beautiful? Then you kissed me. I freed myself gently from your embrace and was ready to leave. You then asked, "Would you like to take some flowers with you?" I said I would. You took four white roses from the blue crystal vase on the writing-table (how I knew that vase from the one glance I stole in childhood!) and gave them to me. I kissed them for days on end.

'We had first arranged another evening together. I came to your flat, and again it was wonderful. You gave me a third night. Then you said you had to go away— oh how I had hated those journeys, from my childhood on!—and you promised to tell me as soon as you returned. I gave you a *poste restante* address—I didn't want to give you my real name. I kept my secret. On parting, you gave me roses again—on parting!

'Every day for two weeks I asked—but no, what's the point of describing to you the agony of waiting, of despair? I'm not complaining. I love you as you are, passionate and forgetful, generous and unfaithful. I love you exactly as you have always been and as you still are. You had been back a long time. I saw it from your lighted windows. You didn't write to me. I have no letters from you to read in my final hours, not a line from you, to whom I gave my life. I waited, waited in desperation, but you didn't send for me. Not a line did you write . . . not a line . . .

'My child died yesterday—he was your child, too. He was your child, too, darling, conceived on one of those three nights: I swear it, and one doesn't tell lies in the shadow of death. It was our child, I give you my solemn word, for no man touched me from the time I gave myself to you until the child was wrested from my womb. Your touch sanctified me. How could I possibly have shared you, who were all the world to me, with others who only lightly brushed against my life in passing? He was our child, darling, the child of my conscious love and your carefree, abundant, almost instinctive embraces; our child, our son, our only child.

'You will ask now—perhaps you are shocked, perhaps merely surprised—you ask, my darling, why I concealed this child from you all these years. Why do I tell you about him only today, as he lies here sleeping in the darkness, asleep for ever, about to leave me for ever, never to return? But how could I have told you? You would never have believed me, the eager stranger who was all too willing to spend three nights with you and offered no resistance in giving herself. Yes, obviously willing. You would never have believed that the nameless woman of a fleeting encounter was faithful to you—to you, who were unfaithful. You would never have accepted the child as your own without misgivings. Even if what I said might have seemed plausible you would never have been able to put aside the secret suspicion that I was trying to foist another man's child on you, because you were wealthy. You would always have been suspicious of me. There would have been a shadow, a dreadful, hovering shadow of mistrust between us. I wouldn't have wanted that. Besides, I know you. I know you so well, perhaps better than you know yourself. I know it would have been embarrassing for you, who prefer love to be carefree, superficial and frivolous, suddenly to find you were a father, immediately responsible for another life. The real you can breathe only while you are free, and you would have felt somehow restricted with me. You would have hated me for this obligation—yes, I know you would—against your own conscious will. I would have been an encumbrance and you would have hated me, perhaps only for an hour or two, or perhaps only for fleeting moments, but in my pride I wanted you to think of me all your life without being worried. I preferred to take everything on myself rather than be a burden to you; to be the only one among all your women you always think of with affection and gratitude. But, to be sure, you have never thought of me. You have forgotten me.

'I'm not complaining, my darling. No, I'm not complaining. Forgive me if a drop of bitterness occasionally falls from my pen. My child—ours—lies here dead beneath the flickering candles. I have shaken my clenched fists at God and called Him murderer, my feelings are so confused and perplexed. Excuse the lamentations; forgive me! I am well aware you are a good man and helpful at heart. You help anyone who asks you, even the remotest stranger. But your generosity is so peculiar. It lies open to anyone who can take it, as much as a man can carry. Your generosity is large, infinitely large, but it is—excuse me—it is lazy. It has to be asked for, has to be taken. You help if someone calls for help, requests it. You help from a sense of guilt, from weakness, and not gladly. Let's be honest about it—you don't like the needy and the afflicted any more than you do your companions in good fortune. And people like you, even the most charitable, are difficult to ask for help.

'Once, when I was still a child, looking through the peephole, I saw how you gave something to a beggar who had rung your doorbell. You gave promptly, and indeed generously, even before he had asked, but you handed it to him with a certain anxiety and haste; so that he would go away again quickly. It was as though you were afraid to look at him. I have never forgotten your uneasy, reticent way of helping, retreating from being thanked. That's why I've never turned to you. Of course, I knew you would have stood by me at the time even without being certain it was your child. You would have comforted me, given me money, plenty of money. But it would always have been only with concealed impatience to shake off an embarrassment. I think you would even have tried to persuade me to have an abortion. That was what I dreaded most—for what would I not have done if you wanted it! How could I have refused you anything? But this child was everything to me. It was yours; it was you all over again: not the happy, carefree you whom I had no power to keep, but you given to me for ever—so I thought— implanted in my womb, bound up with my life. Now, at last, I had captured you. I could feel your life growing in my blood; I would be able to nourish you, suckle you, cuddle you, kiss you, whenever my heart yearned to do so. You see, darling, that's why I was so happy when I had your child, and why I didn't tell you about it: because now you could never run away from me. I admit, darling, they were not months only of happiness, as I had anticipated in my mind. They were also months of greyness and torment, full of loathing for the baseness of mankind. It wasn't easy for me. I couldn't go to work in the later months in case my relatives became aware of my condition and sent the news home. I wouldn't ask my mother for money—so I kept body and soul together until my time came by selling the few bits of jewellery I possessed. A week before the confinement a washer-woman stole my last few crowns from a cupboard, so I had to go to the maternity hospital. The child, your child, was born there—in the midst of the squalor of penury—where only the very poor, the outcast and the forgotten drag themselves in their need. It was a deadly place: everything was alien, completely alien. We were strangers to one another, lying there in our loneliness, and hating each other thoroughly. We were thrown together only by misfortune, by the same anguish, in that stifling, overcrowded room full of screaming and moaning, chloroform and blood. I experienced there what degradation, what spiritual and physical shame has to be endured by the poverty-stricken. I experienced it in the company of prostitutes and the sick, who created a baseness out of a common fate; in the cynicism of the young doctors who stripped the bedclothes off the defenceless women with an ironic smile and pretended to examine them scientifically; in the avarice of the nurses. Oh, there a person's shame was crucified with looks and scourged with words. The chart with one's name on it is the only indication that one still exists. For what lies in the bed is only a quivering piece of flesh to be handled by the inquisitive, an object to be exhibited and studied. Oh, women with husbands waiting lovingly for them to bestow children on the home, they don't know what it means to give birth to a child alone, defenceless, as though you were being experimented on! And even today if I read the word 'Hell' in a book, I can't help thinking immediately of that slaughterhouse full of shame, that overcrowded, steaming room, filled with groans, hysterical laughter and blood-curdling screams, where I suffered.

'Forgive me, forgive me for speaking of these things. I mention them only this once, but I shall never do so again. I have kept silent for eleven years and soon I shall be mute for all eternity. I had to proclaim it once, just once, how dearly I bought this child, who was all my joy and who now lies dead. I had already forgotten those hours. They were long forgotten in laughter, in the child's voice, in my delight. But now that he is dead, the torment has come alive again, and I had to cry out to you from the depths of my soul just this once. But I'm not blaming you—only God, only God, who made that torment futile. I swear I don't blame you, and I have never risen up in anger against you. Even at the time my womb was contorted in labour, when my body burned with shame under the devouring gaze of the students, even at the moment when the pain rent my soul, I never accused you before God. I have never regretted those nights, never gainsaid my love for you. I have always loved you, always blessed the hour you came into my life. And if I had to go through the hell of those hours again, and knew in advance what awaited me, I would do it, my darling, not once but a thousand times!

'Our child died yesterday—you never knew him. Your most casual glance never lighted on this small, blossoming human being, your creation, even in a fleeting chance meeting. I kept myself hidden from you for a long time as soon as I had the child. My longing for you became less painful. Indeed I think I loved you less ardently. At least I didn't suffer so much from my love, once I had the gift of the child. I didn't want to divide myself between you and him, so I didn't give myself to you who were happy and out of my life, but to this child, who needed me. He had to be fed, and I could kiss him and take him in my arms. I appeared to have been rescued from the disturbance you caused me, from my fate, saved by this replica of you. Moreover, he was truly mine. Only seldom now, very seldom, were my emotions directed humbly towards your home. I did just one thing, though. I always sent you a bouquet of white roses on your birthday, exactly like those you gave me after our first night of love. Have you ever asked yourself, in the last ten, eleven, years, who sent them? Have you remembered at all the girl to whom you once gave roses like those? I don't know and never shall. It was enough for me to send them to you out of the blue; that once a year the memory of that hour should be allowed to flower.
    'You never knew our poor child. I blame myself now for keeping him from you, for you would have loved him. You never knew him, the poor boy, never saw him smile, when he gently opened his eyes, his dark, intelligent eyes—your eyes!—and then cast a bright, happy light over me, over all the world. Oh, he was so cheerful, so lovable: all your easy grace was repeated in him in a child-like way. Your quick, lively imagination was renewed in him. He could play with things for hours, totally absorbed, as you play with life, and then sit earnestly again, his brow furrowed, with his books. He grew more and more like you. He soon also began noticeably to develop that double blend of seriousness and frivolity so characteristic of you. And the more he resembled you, the more I loved him. He was a good pupil. He chattered away in French like a little magpie, and his exercise books were the neatest in the class. How good-looking he was, how smart in his black velvet suit or his little white sailor-jacket. He was always the best dressed wherever he went. When I walked with him along the beach at Grado, women stopped and stroked his long, fair hair. At Semmering, when he went tobogganing, people looked round after him admiringly. He was so hand-

some, so gentle, so helpful. When he became a boarder at the Theresianum last year he wore his uniform and the little sword like an eighteenth-century page-boy—now he has nothing on but his little nightshirt, the poor child, lying there with pale lips and folded hands.

'But you will ask me perhaps how I could bring him up in such luxury, how I managed to allow him this lively, happy, well-to-do life. Dearest, I speak to you out of the darkness. I'm not ashamed. I will tell you. But don't be shocked, darling—I sold myself. I was not exactly what one calls a whore, a prostitute, but I sold myself. I had rich friends, rich lovers: at first I sought them out, then they sought me. I was—did you ever notice it?—very beautiful. Everyone to whom I gave myself grew fond of me, they all thanked me, they were all devoted, they all loved me—all but you, all but you, my darling!

'Do you despise me now because I have disclosed that I sold myself? No, I know you won't despise me. I know you understand everything and will also understand I did it only for you, for your other self, for your child. In that room in the maternity hospital I had once experienced the horror of poverty. I knew that in this world the poor are always the downtrodden, the under-privileged, the victims, and no matter what the cost I didn't want your child, your bright, good-looking child, to grow up down there in the dregs, the apathy and the vulgarity of the street, in the polluted air of a backyard. His gentle mouth should not learn the language of the gutter. His white skin should not know the rough, crumpled linen of the poor. Your child should have all the riches, all the comfort in the world; he should rise to your level, live in your world. For that reason, for that alone, my darling, I sold myself. It was no sacrifice for me, for what is generally called honour and dishonour meant nothing to me. You didn't love me, you, the only one to whom my body belonged. So I was indifferent to what happened to it. Men's caresses, even their deepest passion, didn't move me profoundly, although I had to respect some of them, and pity for their unrequited love often upset me when I thought of my own fate. They were all good to me, those I knew, they all pampered me, all respected me. There was one in particular, an elderly man, a titled widower, who loved me like a daughter. He was the one who used his influence to have the fatherless child, your child, accepted for the Theresianum. Three or four times he asked me to marry him—I could have been a countess today, mistress of an enchanting castle in the Tyrol, without a care in the world. For the boy would have had a kindly father who worshipped him and I would have had a peace-loving, distinguished and good man by my side. I didn't do it: however much he pressed me, however much I hurt him by my refusal. Perhaps I was foolish, for had I accepted I would now be living a quiet, secure life somewhere, my beloved son with me, but—why shouldn't I admit it to you—I didn't want to bind myself. I wanted to be free, free for you all the time. Deep down I unconsciously continued to cherish the old childish dream that you would perhaps call me to your side again, even if only for an hour. And I threw everything away for the possibility of that one hour—only to be free for you at your first call. Hadn't my whole life, from the time I was awakened from childhood, consisted of nothing but waiting; waiting for your pleasure?

'And that hour really came. But you didn't know it, you didn't suspect it, my darling! You didn't recognise me on that occasion either—never, never, never have you recognised me! I often used to meet you earlier, in theatres, at concerts, in the Prater, in the street—every time my heart jumped but you looked straight past me. I was certainly a different person outwardly; the shy child had become a woman, beautiful, they said, dressed in expensive clothes and surrounded by admirers. How could you recognise in me the shy girl in the subdued light of your bedroom? Sometimes one of the gentlemen I was accompanying would greet you. You would acknowledge him and look up at me, but your glance was that of a polite stranger, one of approval but never of recognition, distant, terribly distant. Once—I still remember it—I felt real anguish at this lack of recognition, although I was almost used to it by that time. I was sitting in a box at the opera with a friend and you were in the next box. The lights were lowered for the overture. I couldn't see your face any more, but I felt your breath as close to me as I did that night we were together. Your hand, your delicate, gentle hand, rested on the velvet division between our boxes. And I was overcome by an infinite longing to bend forward and humbly kiss the hand I loved so much, whose gentle caress I had once felt, but which belonged now to a stranger. The music swirled excitedly around me, the craving became ever more powerful, and so intensely were my lips drawn towards your beloved hand that I had to take a grip on myself, tear myself forcibly away. After the first act I asked my friend to take me away. I couldn't bear it any longer, having you so distant and so near in the darkness.

'But the time came, once more, one last time in my shambles of a life. It was almost a year ago, on the day after your birthday. Strange: I had been thinking of you all day, as I always celebrated your birthday as a feast day. I had gone out very early in the morning and bought the white roses I sent you every year in memory of an hour you had forgotten. In the afternoon I drove with the boy to the café Demel and in the evening we went to the theatre. I wanted him also to feel that this day was some kind of mysterious, youthful holiday without, of course, his knowing its significance. The next day I spent with my lover of that time, a wealthy young manufacturer from Brünn, with whom I had been living for the previous two years. He worshipped me and spoiled me, and also wanted to marry me, as the other men did. I refused him as I refused the others, without any apparent reason, although he showered me and the child with gifts and was himself a lovable man, in his slightly dull, submissive kindness.

'We went together to a concert where we met some high-spirited friends and we all had supper in a restaurant in the Ringstrasse. In the midst of the laughter and chatter there, I suggested we should go on to a dance hall, to the Tabarin. I usually loathed that kind of establishment, with its forced, alcohol-induced gaiety, like all 'gallivanting', and I normally always resisted such propositions. This time, however—it was as though some inexplicable magic power within me suddenly led me despite myself to throw out the suggestion in the midst of everyone's happy, agreeable excitement—I had, all at once, an unaccountable desire, as if I felt something special awaited me there. Everyone stood up quickly, as usual ready to please me, and we went over to the dance hall and drank champagne. Swiftly I was overcome with a frenzied, almost physically painful exhilaration, such as I have never known. I drank one glass after another, joined in the singing of bawdy songs, and felt almost compelled to dance or shout for joy. But abruptly—it was as though something icy cold or something burning hot at that instant touched my heart—I was torn apart: you were sitting at the next table with some friends, watching me with an admiring and covetous look: that look that always stirred me to my innermost depths. For the first time in ten years you looked at me again with all the unconsciously passionate power of your being. I trembled. I nearly dropped the glass I had in my hand. Fortunately my friends round the table didn't notice my confusion: they were lost in the noise of laughter and music.

'Your look became more and more ardent and set me on fire. I didn't know if you had finally recognised me at last; or did you desire me afresh as someone else, as a stranger? The blood rushed to my cheeks; I answered my friends absentmindedly. It must have been obvious to you how your gaze disturbed me. With an inconspicuous movement of your head that my friends wouldn't notice, you signalled to me to come out to the entrance hall for a moment. Then you paid the bill ostentatiously, took leave of your friends and departed; but not before you again gave a sign you would wait for me outside. I trembled as if I were cold, or in a fever. I couldn't speak, I couldn't control my quickened pulse. It so happened that two Negroes began at that moment an unusual new dance, clattering their heels and uttering shrill cries. Everyone turned to look at them and I took advantage of it. I stood up, told my friends I'd be back soon and went out to you.

'There you stood in the entrance hall, in front of the cloakroom, waiting for me. Your face lit up as I arrived. You hurried towards me with a smile. I saw immediately that you didn't recognise me, neither the child of long ago nor the young girl. Once again you approached me as a new, unknown person. "Have you an hour to spare for me too?" you asked me confidentially. I felt from the certainty of your manner you took me for one of those women who could be bought for an evening.

"Yes," I said, agreeing in the same tremulous and yet matter-of-course affirmative way as the young girl of more than a decade before in that darkened street.

"When could we meet, then?" you asked.

"Whenever you like," I replied—I was shameless where you were concerned. You looked at me a little surprised, with the same suspicious curiosity as on the earlier occasion when the promptness of my consent had astonished you.

"What about now?" you asked, a little hesitantly.

"Yes," I said, "all right."

'I was about to go to the cloakroom to fetch my coat when it struck me that my friend had the ticket for both our coats, which had been handed in together. It wasn't possible to go back and ask him for it without a proper excuse. On the other hand, I had no wish to sacrifice the hour with you that I had longed for for years. So I didn't hesitate for a second: I merely put my shawl over my evening dress and went out into the damp, misty night, without troubling about my coat, without considering the kind, well-meaning man who had been keeping me. I had made him look a ridiculous fool in front of his friends. After two years, his mistress ran off the first time a stranger whistled. Oh, I knew in my heart exactly how base, how ungrateful I was; what an infamy I was committing towards an honourable friend. I felt my behaviour was absurd and in my madness I had mortally offended a good man for ever. I felt I had torn my life in two—but what was friendship to me, what was my existence compared with my impatience to feel your lips on mine once again; to hear your words softly whispered in my ear. That's how much I loved you, I can tell you now, now everything is past and done with. And I believe if you were to call me from my deathbed I would suddenly find the strength to get up and go with you.

'There was a taxi at the door and we drove to your home. I heard your voice again, felt you amorously near me and was as dazzled, as childishly overjoyed, as overwhelmed as before. How I climbed those stairs again after more than ten years—no, no, I can't describe it. At that instant I felt everything twice over, the past and the present; and I was always conscious only of you. Little had changed in your room. There were a few more pictures and more books, here and there different furniture, but everything seemed really familiar. The vase with the roses stood on the writing-table—my roses I had sent you the day before on your birthday as a memento of a woman you didn't remember, didn't recognise even now, although she was beside you, holding hands with you and exchanging kisses. I was gratified, however, to see you had looked after the flowers. In that way you had a trace of my life, a breath of my love around you.

'You took me in your arms. Once again I spent a whole heavenly night with you. But you didn't even recognise my naked body. Overjoyed, I accepted your experienced caresses and saw that your passion made no distinction between a loved one and a whore; that you gave yourself wholly to your desire with all the unthinking, extravagant intensity of your being. You were so tender and gentle with me, the chance dance-hall encounter, so refined and so sincerely respectful, and at the same time so passionate in enjoying the woman. Dizzy from the old happiness, I sensed again the unique duality of your nature, the conscious, intellectual passion and the sensual, which had already enslaved me as a child. I have never known a man make love with such complete surrender to the moment, such a radiant outpouring of his deepest emotion—only to efface the memory in everlasting, almost inhuman forgetfulness. But I also forgot myself. Who was I, then, lying in the darkness beside you? Was I the eager child of days gone by; was I the mother of your child; was I the unknown woman? Oh, it was all so familiar; it had all been gone through before. Yet everything was ecstatically new that passionate night. And I prayed it would never end.

'But morning came. We got up late and you invited me to have breakfast with you. We chatted together and drank the tea which an unseen servant's hand had discreetly set out in the dining-room. Again you spoke with the entirely frank, cordial confidence natural to you. Again you asked no indiscreet questions, and showed no curiosity about what kind of person I was. You didn't ask my name, or where I lived. Once again I was only an affair for you, anonymous, an hour of passion that dissolves without trace in the haze of forgetfulness. You told me you now intended to go on a long journey—for two or three months to North Africa. I trembled in the midst of my happiness, for the words were already hammering in my ears: it's all over, all over and forgotten! I wanted to fall at your feet and cry out, "Take me with you, recognise me at last, finally, in the end, after so many years!" But I was still so shy, so cowardly, so like a slave, so weak in your presence. All I could say was, "I'm sorry."

'You looked at me with a smile. "Are you really sorry?"

'A sudden anger seized me. I stood up and looked at you, long and hard. Then I said, "The man I loved was always going away too." I looked at you straight between the eyes. "Now, now, he'll recognise me!" My whole being urged you, trembling.

'But you smiled at me and said by way of consolation, "But we always come back."

"Yes," I replied, "You come back. But by then you've forgotten."

'There must have been something unusual, something vehement in the way I spoke. For you stood up then, too, and looked at me in surprise and very affectionately. You put your arm round my shoulders. "One doesn't forget what is good. I shan't forget you," you said, and as you said it you looked at me searchingly, as if you wanted to imprint my image on your mind. And as I felt your penetrating look, searching, examining, taking in the whole of me, I believed at last, finally the spell of blindness was broken. "He will recognise me, he will recognise me!" My whole soul trembled at the thought.

'But you didn't recognise me. No, you didn't. Never had I been more of a stranger to you than I was at that moment, for otherwise—otherwise you could never have done what you did a few minutes later. You had kissed me, kissed me again passionately. My hair was disarranged and I had to put it right. And as I stood in front of the mirror I saw reflected in it—and I thought I would faint with shame and horror—I saw you push some large banknotes discreetly into my muff. I don't know how I managed to stop myself, then, from crying out, from slapping your face—I who had loved you since childhood and was the mother of your child—you were paying me for the night! To you I was a tart from the Tabarin, nothing more. You paid me, paid me! It wasn't enough that you had forgotten me. Now I had to be humiliated.

'I gathered up my belongings quickly. I wanted to leave at once. The pain was too great. I snatched up my hat. It was on the writing-table beside the vase with the white roses, my roses. Then I was seized with an utterly irresistible urge: I would try once more to make you remember. "Would you give me one of your white roses?"

"With pleasure," you said, immediately picking one out.

"But perhaps a woman gave them to you, a woman who loves you?" I said.

"Possibly," you answered. "I don't know. Someone gave them to me but I don't know who it was. That's why I like them so much."

'I looked at you. "Perhaps they're also from someone you've forgotten!"

'You looked astonished. I gazed at you fixedly. My expression begged you: "Recognise me, recognise me at last!" But your eyes smiled in a friendly way and had no recognition in them. You kissed me again. But you didn't recognise me.

'I hurried to the door for I was aware of the tears welling up in my eyes and I didn't want you to see them. I went out in such haste that I almost collided with your manservant, John, in the hall. Speedily and discreetly he stepped aside, opened the front door to let me out, and then—are you listening?—in that one, single second, as I looked at him, with tears streaming from my eyes, looked at the now elderly man, a light of recognition suddenly came into his eyes. In that one instant, do you hear me? In that one instant the old man knew who I was. He hadn't seen me since I was a child. I could have fallen on my knees before him and kissed his hands for that recognition. But I just quickly pulled from my muff the money you had scourged me with, and slipped it into his hands. He trembled and looked at me in alarm—at that moment he perhaps understood more about me than you did in your whole life. Everyone, everyone indulged me, everyone was good to me—only you, you alone forgot me. Only you, you alone, never recognised me!

'My child is dead, our child—now I have no one else in the world to love but you. But who are you to me, you who never, ever recognise me, who pass over me as though you were crossing a stream, and tread on me as though I were a stone? You go on and on and leave me to wait for ever. Once I thought I could hold on to you, ever elusive as you are, in the child. But he was your child. Overnight he has cruelly gone from me, on a journey; he has forgotten me and will never come back. I am alone again, more alone than ever. I have nothing, nothing of yours—no child any more, no word, no written line, no mementoes. And if anyone were to mention my name, it wouldn't mean anything to you. Why shouldn't I gladly die, since I am dead to you? Why not move on, since you are gone from me? No, darling, I am not reproaching you. I don't want to toss my misery into your cheerful home. Don't be afraid that I'll ever embarrass you again. Forgive me, but I must pour my soul out to you at this hour, when the child lies there dead and forlorn. I must speak to you just this once—then I'll go back silently into my obscurity, as I have always been silent where you are concerned. But you won't hear this cry as long as I am alive—you'll receive this testament from me only when I'm dead—from one who loved you more than anyone else and whom you didn't recognise; from one who always waited for you but for whom you never sent. Perhaps, perhaps you will call me then, and for the first time I shall be unfaithful to you; I shan't hear you any more, from the dead. I leave you no picture and no token, as you left nothing to me. You'll never recognise me, never. It was my fate in life; it will also be my fate in death. I won't send for you in my last hour. I am going without your knowing my name or what I look like. It will be easy for me to die since you won't feel it from afar. I couldn't die if my death were to cause you pain.

'I can't go on writing any longer. My head is so heavy . . . my limbs ache, I'm feverish. I think I must lie down now. Perhaps it will soon be over; perhaps fate will be kind to me for once and I won't have to see them take the child away . . . I can't write any more. Farewell, darling. Farewell. Thank you. It was good as it was, in spite of everything. I'll be grateful to you until my last breath. I'm all right: I've told you everything, you know now, no, you can only guess, how much I loved you. You have no encumbrance from that love. I won't fail you—that comforts me. Nothing will be changed in your splendid, pleasant life. My death will not affect you . . . that comforts me, my darling.

'But who . . . who will send you white roses now on your birthday? Oh, the vase will be empty, the little breath, the tiny trace of my life that once a year wafted around you will also be blown away! Darling, listen, I ask you—it's my first and last request to you—do it for my sake. Every birthday—it's a day after all when everyone thinks of himself—buy some roses and put them in the vase. Do it, darling, do it, as others have a mass said once a year in memory of a dead loved one. But I don't believe in God any more and don't want a mass. I believe only in you, I love you, and want to go on living only in you . . . Oh, only one day in the year, as I lived near you . . . completely, totally silent, I ask you to do it, darling. It's my first request and the last. Thank you . . . I love you, I love you. Farewell.'

His hands were shaking as he put the letter down. Then he meditated for a long time. Some confused recollection of a child next door, of a young girl, a woman in the nightclub, came to the surface, but it was a dim and muddled memory, like a stone sparkling and flickering without definition at the bottom of a running stream. Shadows flitted to and fro, yet no picture formed. He felt recollections of emotion, but still he didn't remember. It seemed to him that he had dreamt about all these figures, dreamt often and deeply, but even so only dreamt.

His glance fell on the blue vase in front of him on the writing-table. It was empty; the first time for years it had been empty on his birthday. He gave a start: it seemed to him as if a door had been flung open suddenly by an invisible hand, and a cold current of air from another world flowed into his peaceful room. He became conscious of a death and conscious of undying love. Something struck a chord in his innermost soul, and he strove ardently to reach out in spirit towards the unseen presence, as though he were hearing distant music.

I've had no will but yours... ever

...what I gave, I gave with all my heart... Yet you did not even remember my name!"

UNIVERSAL-INTERNATIONAL presents

JOAN FONTAINE
Unforgettably Matched for Love with

LOUIS JOURDAN
Romantic New Star of "The Paradine Case"

with MADY CHRISTIANS · MARCEL JOURNET · ART SMITH · CAROL YORKE
Screenplay by Howard Koch · From the Story by Stefan Zweig
Produced by JOHN HOUSEMAN · Directed by MAX OPULS

"Letter from an Unknown Woman"

A RAMPART PRODUCTION

LIFE   LIFE is published weekly by TIME Inc., 540 N. Michigan Ave., Chicago 11, Ill. Printed in U. S. A. Entered as second-class matter November 16, 1936 at the Postoffice at Chi-   Volume 24
May 17, 1948   cago, Ill. under the act of March 3, 1879. Authorized by Post Office Department, Ottawa, Canada, as second-class matter. Subscriptions $6.00 a year in U. S. A. and Canada.   Number 20

The Production

The production of *Letter from an Unknown Woman* was a happy one, involving a close-knit group who respected and sympathized with one another. In 1947 Joan Fontaine and her husband William Dozier, an executive at Universal Studios, chose Stefan Zweig's story about a woman who devotes her life to an unresponsive sybarite as the first film to be made by their independent company, Ramparts Productions. Dozier had been interested in the property for several years, and Fontaine had played a similar role in 1943 in *The Constant Nymph*. The couple brought in John Houseman, a friend of Dozier's and a past romantic interest of Fontaine's, to produce the film. As screenwriter, Houseman recommended Howard Koch, with whom he had worked in Orson Welles's radio theater. Koch, in turn, suggested the German expatriate Max Ophuls, who had directed *Liebelei*, a film with a similar subject and milieu, almost twenty years earlier.

The group possessed impressive credentials. *Liebelei* had won Ophuls the respect of movie cognescenti, and Houseman's stage work with Welles's Mercury Theater made him even more widely admired. Both Fontaine and Koch had won Academy Awards: Fontaine for *Suspicion* in 1941 and Koch for *Casablanca* in 1943. With this distinguished core group in place, the rest of the cast and production crew was quickly assembled, including cinematographer Franz Planer, who had previously served Ophuls as cameraman on *Liebelei*. Despite the usual last-minute rewriting and occasional friction on the set and during the editing, production proceeded smoothly. Upon completion, however, the film began to encounter difficulties. The executives at Universal judged it to have too European a flavor and gave it a poor release. The American reviews, by and large, were similarly unsympathetic, and no Academy Award nominations were forthcoming. However, the film was later discovered by a group of British critics who arranged for it to run in central London six months after the original British premiere in 1950. From that point on, its reputation among critics grew, and it eventually became a popular television offering. A detailed description of the film's production can be found in Lutz Bacher's unpublished dissertation "Max Ophul's Universal International Films: The Impact of Production Circumstances on a Visual Style" (Wayne State University, 1984).

Front and Center

John Houseman

An eminent producer, with impressive experience on Broadway and with Orson Welles's Mercury Theater as well as in movies, John Houseman brought considerable prestige to the production of *Letter from an Unknown Woman*. His cultivated and authoritative appreciation of Ophuls's aims and abilities undoubtedly contributed to the creation of what is now considered the most "Ophulsian" of all the films the director made in America.

At the same time, Houseman took an active role as producer, overruling Ophuls on such matters as the shooting style of the opera sequence. On other matters, such as the inability of the film's music director Daniele Amfitheatrof to realize Ophuls's ambitious conception of the musical score, Houseman's role appears to have extended only as far as sympathizing with the director's plight.

Houseman's assessment of the production as an "unmitigated commercial and critical disaster for us all" is born out by the film's early reviews, which show little understanding of its virtues.

Shooting was finished—a day under schedule—and we were still editing *Thieves like Us* when I began to make daily trips over the Cahuenga Pass to the old Universal studios in the Valley to discuss an altogether different project.

The Doziers—Bill and Joan—had reentered my life. They had set up a producing organization of their own at Universal Studio under the name of Rampart Films, of which Dozier would be the executive producer and Joan the star. For their first independent production Bill had chosen a story he had favored for some years—one I remembered he proposed to me when we were both at Paramount. This was Stefan Zweig's *Letter from an Unknown Woman*. I shared his enthusiasm for it as a vehicle for Joan and told him I'd be delighted to produce it for them.

To work on the screenplay I suggested Howard Koch, who was temporarily unemployed following a contractual dispute with Jack Warner. Dozier (who had

From *Front and Center* (New York: Simon and Schuster, 1979), pp. 210–218.

been Koch's agent when Howard first came out from New York) agreed. Koch read the story, liked it and signed up to work on it. And it was he who suggested a European emigré, Max Ophuls, as the perfect director for the picture. To convince us he showed us a French film Ophuls had made before the war, based on Schnitzler's *Liebelei*. It was a love story, but it was also a bitter comment on the prejudices of the Austrian military caste and the tragic stupidity of the dueling code. It was of the same Viennese period and milieu as Zweig's novella. We saw it and liked it and invited Ophuls to join us on the project.

Max Ophuls was a native of Alsace-Lorraine, from which my own father's family had come. He and I spoke French and, sometimes, German together, and he regarded me as a fellow European. He was a charming, sophisticated, enthusiastic but moody man who never quite adjusted to the Hollywood scene. After his shocking experience with Preston Sturges, who had taken him off a film (*Vendetta*) on his third day of shooting, he had lost an assignment (*Phantom Lady*) to his fellow expatriate Robert Siodmak before finally landing a directing job with Douglas Fairbanks, Jr., on a film that came to be called *The Exile*.

Dozier was a fast worker; within a week he had acquired Zweig's story and engaged Ophuls to work with Howard and myself in the preparation of the film. My contract with R.K.O. was nonexclusive; I had been so totally immersed in *Thieves like Us* that I found nothing to follow it. (Nick[1] and I had taken an option on David Garnett's *A Man in the Zoo* and prepared a treatment of it that had failed to enthuse Dore Schary.[2]) My thirty weeks at R.K.O. were almost over, and there were persistent rumors that the studio was about to be sold again—this time to the atrocious Howard Hughes. The Doziers' offer was an attractive one: I liked the property and the people with whom I'd be associated.

So for several weeks I worked sixteen hours a day, commuting between Burbank and Hollywood. I sat with Nick through the final editing and scoring and dubbing of *Thieves like Us*: we previewed it twice successfully and made only minor changes. In September we cut the negative, changed the title at Schary's request to *Your Red Wagon* (a blues number in the film, sung by Marie Wilson in the New Orleans nightclub) and started showing it to critics of the trade papers and national magazines. Iris Barry gave us a special running at the Museum of Modern Art in New York. Word was getting around that we had one of the sleepers of the year.

1. Director Nicholas Ray.
2. Dore Schary was then head of production at RKO.

Meantime, I was working every day with Howard and Max on their script. Dozier, as usual, was in a hurry; Joan had a starting date for a film at another studio. We were still working on the screenplay when we went into production. Though my personal commitment was not quite so deep as it had been to *Thieves like Us*, I found the making of *Letter from an Unknown Woman* an exhilarating experience. The entire production had a family atmosphere—a vaguely incestuous tone—which I did not find displeasing. Howard Koch and I were old collaborators, beginning with the Mercury radio shows (which I had engaged him to write in 1938 at a salary of $60 a week—increased, when we went commercial, to $125). We had worked together on the script of *The War of the Worlds*, then on his Woodrow Wilson play and more recently on the documentary material for *Tuesday in November*. With Max Ophuls I got on swimmingly in spite of his European-bred conviction—aggravated by his bad Hollywood experiences—that the producer and the director of a film were natural and deadly enemies.

Yet it took all my carefully cultivated elasticity to make the sudden transition from *Thieves like Us* to *Unknown Woman*. No two directors could have been more different in their cultural background and esthetic attitudes than Nick Ray and Max Ophuls. And no two films could have been more opposed in their mood and dramatic development than the two pictures on which I now found myself simultaneously involved. Both were love stories, but love among social outcasts in the Texas Panhandle during the Great Depression had little in common with the erotic romanticism prevalent in the Austro-Hungarian Empire at the turn of the century.

Letter from an Unknown Woman is bittersweet Viennese: it is the confession of a woman who has been in love for most of her life with a man to whom she has meant so little that—though they might have been intimate, in different ways, at three different times in their lives—he does not even remember her from one encounter to another. She loves him first as a child when he appears as a music student boarding in her mother's provincial home; again, after ten years, as a girl in her early twenties in Vienna when she goes to a concert he is giving as a successful performing artist, lets him pick her up outside the concert hall and enjoys one night of love with him that will last her a lifetime. Years later, as a married woman, the wife of a rich, successful government official, she meets him again; recklessly risking the ruin of the life she has finally built for herself, she once again gives herself to him. In the morning, when he goes, he leaves some bank notes on the night table—for services rendered.

The first two thirds of our picture were altogether romantic. They were a joy to work on and, later, to shoot. Joan Fontaine had proved in *Rebecca, Suspicion* and *Jane Eyre* that she was an expert at portraying the emotions of an adolescent girl in thrall to an older man. She had no difficulty at all in playing the teenage Lisa, crouched in the dark stairwell, listening to her idol playing Chopin upstairs in his room.[3] And she was charming and moving as the passionate young Viennese girl giving herself without regret in a romantic ecstasy to the man she has worshiped for half her life.

The third and last episode presented more serious hazards of writing and acting. The frame of Zweig's novella is a letter written by Lisa as she is dying; it is not a reproach but a profession of gratitude to the man who, without being aware of it, has given her all the love she has ever known. It is a tricky literary device that was valid in print but seemed less convincing when it was transferred to the more specific realism of film. And Joan, with her poignant immaturity, ran into problems of credibility when she was called upon to play a European *femme du monde* in her thirties.

Koch was a sincere, sober writer with a good sense of structure. The Vienna woods were not his territory, but he had Max by his side to guide him and to devise some of the script's freshest and most imaginative moments. For this was an atmosphere that Ophuls knew intimately and dearly loved: he used it in *Liebelei* and would use it again, years later, in *La Ronde*. During our weeks of preparation and all through production he was tireless and insatiable—to the point of exasperation—in his insistence upon authentic and imaginative detail. Many of the atmospheric points and physical actions that made the film memorable were created by him: the Sunday-morning band-concert in a small Austrian provincial town and the night sequence in the desolate, snow-covered Prater amusement park. Above all, I recall the deserted dance-hall with the ladies' string orchestra sawing away at their Strauss waltzes and the touching, entirely original scene of Lisa's seduction in the mock-up compartment of a European railroad carriage with the faded Alpine scenery moving by outside on a slowly rolling canvas cyclorama propelled by a little man furiously pedaling a stationary bicycle.

Once again I was busy casting; Mady Christians (Hesione Hushabye in the Mercury's *Heartbreak House*) was perfect for Lisa's mother; to play the lesser parts (though the war had been over for more than two years) the town was still

---

3. Actually, the pianist plays Liszt's Concert Étude in D-Flat Major.

filled with excellent middle-European character actors. We had one major casting problem: the object of Lisa's infatuation, who must begin as a struggling music student and turn convincingly into a sophisticated, world-renowned concert pianist. He must be European and (such was the stereotype created over the years by Charles Boyer) he should probably be a Frenchman. Boyer himself was neither available nor young enough for the early scenes of the film. Finally, Dozier discovered someone who seemed to have all the attributes for the part. Louis Jourdan was French, in his midtwenties, dark, slender, with regular features and flashing eyes. David Selznick had just starred him in *The Paradine Case* and had high hopes for him. He spoke good English (better than Boyer), he was classically trained and he was himself a passionate music lover: he seemed too good to be true. As it turned out he had everything, except sex—which for American audiences meant he lacked the combination of glandular and muscular attraction that makes for a sense of danger and therefore brings stardom.

Our production, one of Universal's few pretensions to quality that year, received scrupulous and expert treatment. We had Franz Planer, one of the world's great cameramen, and Golitzen, the studio's most distinguished designer. Between them, under Ophuls' direction, they gave the film its brilliant visual texture. Our source music was selected by Max with loving care. (I seem to remember that the recordings of our hero's piano playing were executed by José Iturbi?) All the elements seemed right—and yet, as the film moved into its final stages, I detected a disturbing tone of discouragement and diminishing energy. Some of this was inherent in the form of Zweig's novella, to which Koch had scrupulously—perhaps too scrupulously—adhered. Some had to do with our star's increasing self-doubt and Max's inability to assuage it. But finally it stemmed from Ophuls' own mercurial temperament.

One night, during the last week of shooting, I got a call from him long after midnight. I was asleep, but he begged me to drive out and meet him as soon as possible at an all-night joint in the Valley next to the studio. When I got there I found him plunged in raging gloom. We sat for two hours over drinks and coffee, then walked around the backlot, where the dawn was coming up over our Viennese Amusement Park. Max informed me that he had spent the previous evening running the rough cut of our film and it was his somber conclusion that our ending was downbeat, maudlin and wholly lacking in dramatic conviction. He blamed Zweig, Koch, Miss Fontaine, Jourdan, me and, most particularly, himself. This, he said, was his most important film—and he had failed! Once in a while he wept, blew his nose and went on talking. I knew there was truth in what he said—all the more since the censors in the Breen Office* had just insisted on changes that took much of the emotional shock out of Lisa's last moments with her lover. But at five in the morning, I found his attitude defeatist, self-indulgent and dangerous. I pointed out that it was too late in the day for him to be making these discoveries; that even if Howard were capable of it, it was impossible, at this stage of the film, to reshape the ending without losing the essential quality of Zweig's story. I assured him that the film was beautiful; I did all I could to send him back onto the set in a less calamitous frame of mind. Two hours later I watched him riding a boom with his usual enthusiasm and that night he called to tell me that the previous day's rushes were wonderful.

Except for occasional moments of blackness I found Max delightful to work with. As a director he was creative and resourceful, with a technical expertise such as I had never encountered and which he occasionally practiced for its own sake. During *Unknown Woman* we had only one serious falling-out. Ophuls was notorious, then and later, for his use of flashy, enormously long and elaborate camera moves. In the final section of our film, in the Vienna Opera House, where Lisa encounters her lover for the last time, Max saw an opportunity to surpass himself. For two days he rehearsed, laid tracks, made dry runs of a particularly convoluted traveling-shot that brought Lisa and her husband from their carriage into the main entrance, through the crowded lobby and the entire length of the foyer, which was filled with festive, elegantly dressed people, and up the grand staircase to the diamond horseshoe, where Lisa finally caught sight of her lover. Watching Max rehearse, I realized that he intended to do all this in one continuous spectacular shot: it meant an enormous amount of elaborately improvised business among members of the crowd; flying candelabra and moving scenery; continuous focus-changing for the camera and a running time, if we ever got the shot, of between two and three minutes. I was worried about it on two counts: first—the time and money spent rehearsing for many hours with a huge crew and several hundred dress-extras would be enormous; second—with the camera in constant motion and no chance to cut away, we would be irrevocably committed to a long, slow shot, which, for all its technical brilliance, might prove tedious in what we all regarded as the weakest part of our film.

*Formerly known as the Hays Office, after its founder, this was the industry-supported organization which, for more than forty years, administered the so-called Code that determined the moral and social content of Hollywood films. [Houseman's note.]

I had never interfered with Max on the set, but at the end of the first day's rehearsal for the scene I told him of my reserves. As he listened, the roll of fat on the back of his neck (which sometimes gave him a curiously Germanic look) grew thick and red. He muttered in French that he knew his business and that I should get off his back.

The next day he rehearsed again—obstinately, obsessively. When our eyes met on the set he looked through me. At noon we spoke again in French. I asked him to protect himself and our film, after he got his shot, with a couple of close-ups to which we could cut if his crane shot proved too long. It was elementary, routine protection, but Max eyed me suddenly with deadly hate: I had gone over to the enemy. I had sold out, I had joined the Front Office in its traditional practice of screwing the artist. He was the director, it was his film and he would have no part in sabotaging it. I told him that if he didn't make the close-ups I'd make them myself. I also gave him my word that I'd never use them without his consent.

The next day in midmorning Max got his crane shot. There was applause on the set. I was standing next to him, and when the applause died down I asked him if he was going to make the protection shots. Our eyes locked. After a long pause he ordered the camera moved in for two close-ups—one of Joan and one of Jourdan. They took less than two hours to make.

Max and I did not speak for two days. Then, during a noon break, I received an invitation to come down to the projection room and look at the assembly he had just completed of our last few days' work. The crane shot looked wonderful; by using the two close-ups it had been reduced, without loss of quality, to less than half its original length. As I was leaving the projection room I heard my name called in a thick Alsatian accent: "Tschon!" It was Max and he was smiling. "I'm glad ve got those close-ups, Tschon!" he said.

(We came out of *Letter from an Unknown Woman* with a warm, lasting friendship. We wrote to each other regularly after he returned to France, and we had a number of ideas for making another picture together, none of which worked out. Meantime Ophuls had turned out a series of successful, sophisticated films: *La Ronde*, *Le Plaisir*, *Madame De* . . . and, finally, the fine but ill-fated *Lola Montès*. Soon after that I went to Europe to make *Lust for Life*, and I called Max from Brussels, where we were preparing to shoot our mine scenes in the Borinage. He was in hospital still recovering from *Lola Montès* on which it was common knowledge that he had gone horribly over budget and later suffered a serious heart-attack. The first public reaction to that untidy, inspired, very personal film had been bitterly disappointing. I had difficulty getting through to his hospital room, and as soon as I heard his voice I recognized the blackness and the exhaustion. I said I'd try to come over and visit him as soon as I could. Max said not to come; he was seeing no one; *Lola Montès* was a calamity; he'd never make another film and he might as well be dead.)

Script to Screen with Max Ophuls

Howard Koch

A veteran screenwriter, who had credits such as *Casablanca*, *The Sea Hawk*, *Mission to Moscow*, and *The Letter* behind him when he began work on *Letter from an Unknown Woman*, Howard Koch brought a strong background in Hollywood production methods to his collaboration with Ophuls on the screenplay of *Letter from an Unknown Woman*. His contribution to this particular project appears to have primarily involved suggesting Ophuls as director and then providing Ophuls's ideas with a Hollywood polish.

In the following reminiscence, first published in *Film Comment* in 1970, Koch generously credits the film's director as the creator of many of the screenplay's bravura sequences. Koch, who was soon afterward to be blacklisted as a result of allegations made by the House Un-American Activities Committee, was never again to be involved with a project of this caliber.

During Hollywood's heyday most film productions were put together as haphazardly as the combinations that turn up on the roll of dice. Occasionally, but not often, the lucky number came up. I was one of the few American writers with the good fortune to have worked with the late Max Ophuls. Although few of his European films had reached America, he had already acquired a European reputation as a sensitive artist. Today, a decade and more after his death, he is one of the most revered directors by filmmakers and critics on both continents.

I met Max in the early forties at the home of a friend. With his wife and school-age son, he had escaped from occupied France to Switzerland one step ahead of the advancing Germans. After several months he and his family managed to obtain passage to this country, joining the swelling number of refugee artists centered in New York and Hollywood. In a burst of philanthropic zeal, the major movie studios opened their gates to these politically displaced writers, directors and actors, putting many of them on salary. But once having made the grand gesture, they did little to make use of their talents.

From *Film Comment* 6, no. 4 (Winter 1970–1971): 40–43.

At the time I was writing for Warner Brothers. Most of the refugees I met there were either idle or assigned to develop story properties the studio had no real intention of producing. As time passed, many of them became depressed as they realized that the production heads lacked confidence in their ability to adapt to the demands of the American movie market; to put it crassly, they were not considered "box office." There were exceptions, of course, but most of the refugees eventually found that they were being treated as charity subjects and, when the war ended and patriotic fervor dimmed, the charity was dispensed with increasing reluctance and finally not at all.

At the time I met Max he had neither work nor charity but was living precariously on the last of what funds he had been able to salvage from Europe. I remember my first impression of him as a baldish Peter Lorre, with the same heavy-lidded, wide-set eyes and the same impish sense of humor. Our rapport was immediate. I can't explain why in the first hour of our meeting I knew that I wanted to work with him on a film. It wasn't his reputation since I was hardly aware of his European career. Besides, by then I had learned that a large reputation based on a director's previous record is sometimes acquired by the accident of indestructible material and an invulnerable cast. Moreover, many well-known directors outgrow any humility they might have had when they were less successful, although humility seems a particularly desirable trait in a medium reliant on cooperative talents.

Max was not lacking in self-confidence but he didn't look upon film narcissistically as a public mirror to display his virtuosity. He had a deep respect for what other talents contributed and, particularly, for the film's basic content as expressed in the screenplay, a quality understandably endearing to a writer. This may come as a surprise to some critics who praise Max, and justly, as a superb stylist but, from my observation his style was invariably related to content, never at its expense.

One of his attributes that impressed me was his sensitivity to English words, since English was not his language and he spoke it brokenly with little regard for grammatical construction. Nevertheless, his ear was attuned to the most delicate nuances and he was never satisfied with a word or a line of dialogue until it expressed the precise shade of meaning needed to convey the idea or emotion.

At times I suspected that he clung to certain verbal eccentricities because they enhanced his special brand of humor. One day we were going to the studio in his old, battered car. Max was a terrible driver: he couldn't keep his mind—or his car—on the road. Fortunately he never went fast so his accidents, while numerous, were never serious. On this occasion he was tail-gating another car which slowed down without Max noticing and we collided with its rear end. Max was out of his seat in an instant and, after a brief survey of the other car, he doffed his little Tyrolean hat to its occupants and blithely announced, "It makes no never mind." The other driver was apparently so intrigued with Max's quaint manners and expression that he didn't climb out to look at his bent bumper—and off we went scot free of all the bothersome details of exchanging names, addresses and insurance agents.

Before long, Anne (my wife) and I became close friends with Max and his family: Hilde, his wife, a handsome woman in her forties who had been a leading German actress; Marcel, his talented teenage son; and his attractive young mistress, a refugee painter from Nazi Germany. Like other displaced Europeans, Max had transplanted his continental sexual habits to America, dividing his time equitably between the two menages. Since Americans are not adept at this sort of thing, Max undertook to instruct me on some of the finer points. One of his rules that I recall is that cut flowers are properly sent to one's mistress as they are perishable whereas a plant, being more durable and therefore more economical, is the correct choice for one's wife. Although delicacy required that his wife and mistress be kept separately, we were part of the intimate circle that included both.

However, two years passed before there was the opportunity I sought for a working relationship with Max. It came about by accident. John Houseman, an old friend from Martian days,* came to see me on the desert outside Palm Springs where we were then living. He brought with him a short story by Stefan Zweig entitled *Letter from an Unknown Woman* which he wanted me to dramatize for the screen. He had been engaged to produce the picture by Joan Fontaine and William Dozier, then husband and wife, who had formed their own company within the framework of Universal Studio. The tragic story, written in Zweig's lyrical prose, was in the form of a letter from a woman on her death bed to the *bon vivant* musician she had loved from girlhood and with whom she finally had a brief affair—only to discover in later years she was one of many and that he didn't even remember her name.

At first reading I was not impressed with the story as picture material. It was entirely subjective with only fragmentary incidents. Besides, it was in the highly charged romantic tradition of Vienna at the turn of the century—definitely not

---

*John Houseman and Howard Koch worked together on Orson Welles's famous radio drama about an invasion from Mars.

the kind of story Hollywood did well. Although I had respect for Houseman's taste, I foresaw the danger of sentimentality, a so-called "woman's picture" awash with tears. Then I thought of Max Ophuls. Possibly he could bring it off as he, like Zweig, was steeped in the romantic tradition. The upshot was that I agreed to write the screen play if the studio would accept Max as the director.

Fortunately, Houseman had seen *Liebelei*, Max's most admired European film, an exquisite piece of romantic nostalgia, also set in Vienna. He agreed that Max was ideal for *Letter* but he had to sell the idea of a foreign director they scarcely knew to Joan and Bill Dozier who, in turn, had to convince the Universal executives. Since Joan Fontaine was then their most important star, Dozier was able to obtain their somewhat reluctant consent.

At this point it was my function to plot a story line (continuity of scenes) that would carry the emotional progression of Zweig's story. Then followed the usual conferences with Max and Houseman and, after some revisions, with Joan and Bill Dozier. Everyone had criticisms and suggestions but, happily, no ego problems intruded so that each contribution could be accepted or rejected on its merits. At this stage, Joan's ideas in relation to the central character of Lisa were especially helpful, since she would be on the screen almost constantly and needed actable situations in which to convey her feelings for the musician at the three different periods in which he entered her life. It was a difficult role starting as the ardent, hero-worshipping girl of fourteen, then the young woman in her twenties when they had the affair, and finally the mature love-crossed woman of middle-age. Joan Fontaine was one of the few actresses capable of making the intensely romantic Lisa a credible character and I still regard the performance she eventually gave as one of the most brilliant I've ever seen on film.

Up to now Max had made a few suggestions but stayed mostly in the background as he believed the creative process of constructing a dramatic story was in the writer's province. But once I had the first draft screenplay written, he became deeply involved, testing every line of dialogue and every image for period validity and nuances of character. Out of his own memories of Vienna came ideas for new scenes such as the one in which the lovers appear to be traveling together in a train compartment, gazing out the window at the exotic, foreign scenery which turns out later to be merely a rotating backdrop in one of the amusement concessions in Vienna's Prada [Prater].

In recent years I've read with some bewilderment statements of French film directors, such as Truffaut, identifying their methods with those of Max Ophuls whom they apparently regard as a sort of mentor and precursor of the New Wave.

Yet these directors are among the chief exponents of the auteur theory, popularized by *Cahiers du Cinema* and *Sight and Sound*, which holds that a director "authors" a film on the set and later in the cutting rooms with some small assist from a "dialogue writer."

Since this practically dispenses with the screenplay as a basic ingredient in the creative process, it could hardly be further from Max's approach to picture making. No one could be more meticulous in the preparation of a script for its transition to the screen. I don't mean to suggest a slavish rigidity to what was written since, naturally, Max often improvised on the set, but these improvisations were in the nature of refinements, not basic changes in the story line or characterizations.

For the final polishing we went over to Catalina Island off the California coast. Max had a phobia about flying and this was his first flight. For the half hour in the air, he sat hunched over in one of the seats, refusing to talk or look out the window, resigned to imminent death in a fiery crash. When the plane landed safely, I'm sure to Max it was like a last-minute, unexpected reprieve.

During our stay in Catalina, I recall that Max kept repeating, "This script needs more air." At first I wasn't sure what he meant but in due course I came to realize that "air" referred to atmosphere, but in the broadest sense—that each scene must have a life of its own apart from its dramatic function in the story. And in this area Max was the acknowledged master. No scene that he directed ever existed in a vacuum and, in the case of *Letter* the detail of Viennese life in that period saturated the screen.

One example comes to mind. In the lyrical Prada sequence, the lovers are dancing in a deserted ballroom, oblivious to everything but each other. Since music was an obvious necessity, I had written in shots of a conventional, male orchestra playing while Lisa (Joan) and her lover (Louis Jourdan) waltzed. Max, recalling that women musicians were often employed in Viennese amusement parks, cast an all-female band. The scene was late at night and the women were desperately tired and the music they played between swigs of beer was equally tired. The humor of these frowsy women scraping their violins and wishing to God that these moon-calf lovers would stop dancing so they could go home, counterpointed the lyrical mood and added period flavor (air).

Under the supervision of Max and an Austrian technical advisor the sets were so authentically Viennese that few people who saw the film could believe they were built on a Hollywood stage. The shooting under Max's assured direction went ahead smoothly, with all of us—Max, Joan, Dozier, Houseman and myself—very happy with the daily rushes. Only one incident that took place near the end of the shooting schedule marred the working relationship between the star and the director.

Max was born in Alsace-Lorraine whicn is either French or German depending on which side won the last war. His temperament reflected both national backgrounds. Generally, he seemed much more French than German but on occasion a Prussian trait was exposed—mostly in regard to women. While shooting one scene Joan objected to some direction he gave her and Max made the mistake of accusing her of "behaving like a star." Joan walked off the set and stayed off for two days. It took all Houseman's diplomacy to bring her back to finish the picture.

The shooting ended on schedule, a rough cut was made, then a final cut or one we thought was final. We all felt good about the result and a vacation was in order. Anne and I went East; Max and his family stayed in our house on the desert.

Our departure was a mistake. While we were away, the studio executives came into the projection room with their sharp knives and slashed away at the film to "make it move faster." Since they are mostly occupied with the business end of picture making, this is their one opportunity to be "creative" and also to exercise their authority over the film's real creators.

When Max and I returned to the studio, we were told that twenty minutes had been taken out of the film's running time. We ran the re-edited print in shocked silence until it was over and then we exploded. Instead of "moving faster" the picture now seemed interminable.

Something we learn from experience is that clock time and screen time have little to do with each other. As long as his interest is held, clock time doesn't exist for the viewer. Two hours in a movie house may seem short while twenty minutes may seem to drag on forever, depending on the extent to which the audience is involved in what is happening on the screen.

Letter from an Unknown Woman, by its nature, required slow pacing and minute attention to evocative detail. What the studio heads had done was to strip much of the flesh from the bones of the story. Since the film had very little plot in the usual sense, and since its highly romantic premise was difficult to sustain, it would only work if the audience were so caught up in its spell that they were willing to suspend their disbelief for the duration of the show.

I have a theory, perhaps debatable, that any story, however slight, will hold an audience so long as the motivations and actions of its characters are credible in relation to the circumstances surrounding their fictional lives. In its abbreviated version *Letter* had preserved the story incidents but had lost the ambience which gave credible life to its characters. As a result, the film was shorter in actual minutes but, in failing to convince the viewer and hold his interest, it seemed much longer.

Houseman agreed with our objections but it took all his powers of persuasion to keep Max from invading the inner sanctum of Universal's top brass and telling them exactly what he thought of them—which, of course, would only have made them more obdurate. When the Doziers finally threw their weight on our side, we were able to replace the cut footage and reinstate the original version.

However, a film is never safe from tampering until it's "in the can," meaning ready for distribution and, even then, it can be so mishandled that it never reaches its intended audience. The sales department of Universal regarded *Letter* as a foreign film, which in those days meant art but no box office. It was tossed out on the market with almost no advance advertising and no attempt to publicize its special qualities. Even with good reviews it didn't survive long enough to find its American audience and the studio wrote it off as a complete loss of the eight hundred thousand it cost to produce.

By the sheerest accident it was resurrected in Europe. Universal had sold the British rights to a third-rate English distribution chain that didn't even have a releasing outlet in London. It happened that one of the editors of the prestigious *Sight and Sound* was visiting a small town where *Letter* was playing.* Since the film had not been shown in London and he had never heard of it, he thought it must be one of Hollywood's "B" pictures. But he had great respect for Joan Fontaine and decided to see it anyway. Apparently he was so impressed by the film and shocked by its treatment that he began a one-man crusade on its behalf. *Sight and Sound* took up the cause and soon it was playing long runs in London and the other European capitols. Since then it has become one of the standard revivals at Britain's National Film Theatre.

---

*This was Simon Harcourt-Smith, who subsequently published an appreciation of the film in *Sight and Sound*.

Interview with Max Ophuls

Jacques Rivette and François Truffaut

U nhappily, these brief comments, part of a 1957 interview by Jacques Rivette and François Truffaut in *Cahiers du Cinema*, represent the only substantive remarks Ophuls made about *Letter from an Unknown Woman* following its release. His frustration with the American film industry and his joy at having won himself a position directing a film so well suited to his talents are evident in his comments.

Ophuls: It was largely thanks to a writer, whose name I'm sure you know, Howard Koch, who was a friend of mine, that the doors of the office of Bill Dozier opened for me. He was the husband of Joan Fontaine and vice-president of the studio, and I discussed the project with him. Before the work could really get under way, we had to win the approval of the company president, Bill Goetz. The president, not just the vice-president. Ah! heirarchies . . . I knew how difficult it was to arrange to meet him, and to be able to speak to him in absolute peace and quiet—the telephone always interrupts a conversation. But there was a turkish bath at the studio and I arranged to take a steam bath at the same time as he did. Naked, in the showers, I tackled him about *Letter from an Unknown Woman*. I told him that I was the only director in the world who could make this film and, shaking his head, he replied simply: 'Why not?' And that was that.

Rivette/Truffaut: Were you given absolute freedom?

Ophuls: Absolutely. There was a script in existence already, but I got permission to rework it completely, together with Howard Koch, to make it the way I saw it. Since the studio chiefs were very apprehensive, they arranged for a preview. Do you know about previews? The spectators fill in cards which can prove decisive for the film's release. The screening was held in Pasadena, a town near Hollywood. We were terribly eager to know the results, so we waited just by the cinema, under the neon sign of a men's outfitters. Finally, we got the first bundle of cards. One of us read aloud. One card: 'Did you like the film? . . . Not at all. Was the story clear? . . . No.'

From "Interview with Max Ophuls," trans. Jennifer Batchelor, in *Ophuls*, ed. Paul Willemen (London: British Film Institute, 1978), pp. 21–22.

The head of the studio drew out the cards one by one. At each 'yes' or 'no', he looked at me, pleased or annoyed, approving or very reproachful. These cards were very detailed, as you will see:
'How did you find the film? . . . Terrific.
Was the story clear? . . . Crystal clear.
And the casting? . . . Brilliant.
The music? . . . Beautiful.
What changes in the cast would you suggest? . . . It was perfect.
What do you think of the theme? . . . Marvellous.
Could you identify with the characters? . . . Absolutely.
Will you recommend this film to your friends? . . . Certainly.
Sex? . . . Male.
Age? . . . 9 years.'

It was a very happy production. I had further proof of that only recently. A fortnight ago, Bill Dozier, who hadn't been to Europe for ages, came to Paris and telephoned me here. Like all Americans in transit, he was in bed, a victim of the good food and he hadn't set foot outside his hotel. He told me that the film was having a second career on television. On its release in America, its career had been fairly insignificant; I trembled lest the producers—who had become real friends—would never get their money back. But receipts in Europe were very good and now, it's one of the most popular films on American television. It's a very interesting phenomenon: certain rather intimate films fail when shown in the cinema, but do very well on television.

Letter to John Houseman

Max Ophuls

The following letter documents some of the difficulties involved in the production of *Letter from an* *Unknown Woman* and suggests the special importance Ophuls attached to the music in the film.

January 30, 1948.

Dear John:

I am in the midst of dubbing, and as you can well imagine, in the midst of trouble. Consequently, I cannot answer your very nice letter with as much warmth and detail as I should like. Your splendid cooperation, despite any worrisome differences, has made me feel your absence keenly. I miss you very, very much.

Absorbed in your New York business, your voice sounded a bit worried, so I hasten to advise you that the score is not as bad as we thought it would be—but it is by far not as good as we had hoped for. You know, John, when you go to an Italian restaurant, whenever you turn away the waiter invariably throws some cheese on your food. You have to watch the guy. So with the score. Whenever I turn away, they take the great masters out and put some original music in. These poor people are bored to death with me. I harrass them day and night. And I'm all alone. You're not here to defend me. Yet, politely, I continue to voice my objections. I'm so damn polite, sometimes the cause gets lost! My only ally is Bill Dozier. My opponents, gentlemen whose names you know.

Imagine, John, the following: Lisa leaves the box in the opera. (By the way, the added scenes are beautiful.) She is outside the opera house waiting for her carriage. Stefan comes out. Presto! The music from inside the opera house changes in [the] Amfitheatrof score [to a] love motif! It took me two days to let them allow Mozart only to be heard during this scene. I won my point finally with a nasty remark. I said, "Probably the conductor of the opera knew about the problem between Lisa and Stefa[n] outside, so inside switched his tune!" This gives you an inkling how things are. My sense of humor still works.

You neglected to give me your telephone number. I need it to call you after the preview.

Thanks again for all your nice thoughts and "Merde" for your new play.

Lots of love,
Max Ophuls

Reviews and Commentaries

Reviews and Commentaries

Letter from an Unknown Woman has generated an impressive body of commentary, serving as a rich source of inspiration for critics of various methodological persuasions. Because the recent articles on the film are so substantial and the initial reviews so vapid, we have included only reviews from the *New York Times* and *Variety* to represent the early reaction, concentrating instead on the scholarly responses that came later.

Initially, critical interest centered on the way *Letter from an Unknown Woman* constituted part of the oeuvre of an acknowledged auteur by reiterating themes and motifs of other Ophuls films. *Letter* lends itself especially well to auteurist analysis because, despite its genesis within the Hollywood system (with all the institutional constraints and collab-orative input that mode of production implies), the film shares many of the distinctive motifs of Ophuls's other work: long, lyrical camera movements; rhythmical pacing, emphasizing graceful flow and rhyming repetitions; opulent, nostalgic settings; expressive iconographic motifs, including staircases, railway stations, and places of public amusement; and a romantic yet gently ironic tone.

In England, Ophuls's work was recognized by critics such as Gavin Lambert, Karel Reisz, and Lindsay Anderson, writing in the journals *Sequence* and *Sight and Sound*. In 1958 Britain's National Film Theater mounted a retrospective of his films, and the British Film Institute published *Ophuls: An Index* by Richard Roud. In the same year, in France, Claude Beylie also published a book on Ophuls, capping a burgeoning interest in the director's work among the auteurist group centered around the journal *Cahiers du Cinéma*. In the United States interest in Ophuls as an auteur first became widespread in 1968 when, in his landmark book *The American Cinema*, Andrew Sarris canonized the director by including him in his pantheon of cinematic masters. In 1971 *Film Comment* published a special section on Ophuls, including an introduction by Sarris and an essay on *Letter from an Unknown Woman*. Sarris and others continued to write on the director for *Film Comment* throughout the 1970s.

In recent years discussions of *Letter from an Unknown Woman* have shifted ground, focusing not on the film's authorship but on its generic roots in the woman's film. The 1973 publication of Molly Haskell's *From Reverence to Rape: The Treatment of Women in the Movies* initially drew the attention of feminist critics to this formerly maligned genre. Subsequent interest on both sides of the Atlantic focused on how *Letter from an Unknown Woman*, as a film about a woman directed to a female audience, exemplified a number of the concerns of feminist film theory. The most central of these concerns has been the position of the female as an object of voyeuristic display, the implications of voice-over narration by a woman, the use of music in women's melodrama, the inscription of class issues in such films, and the construction of temporal modes associated with the rhythms of women's lives.

New York Times

Bosley Crowther

Bosley Crowther's review of *Letter from an Unknown Woman*, while certainly among the most uninformed of those published on the film's initial release, provides a good indication of how little respect most contemporary critics had for the woman's film and how unknown Ophuls was to most of them.

Let your imagination picture a beautiful, sad-eyed Joan Fontaine standing outside in a snowstorm, with her nose pressed against a window-pane, yearning with lonely ardor toward the warmth of a never-to-be romance, and you'll have a fair-sized notion of the nature and atmosphere of "Letter From an Unknown Woman," which came to the Rivoli yesterday.

For this handsomely put-together picture about the unrequited love of a girl for a dashing young concert pianist, based on a story by Stefan Zweig, is as obvious an onslaught on the heart-strings as that old-fashioned tear-jerker tableau, glimpsed between velvet pull-curtains and scented with scattered rose leaves. Indeed, it has all the accessories of that brand of moist-handkerchief romance, including sad music played on violins and the death of an illegitimate child.

Apparently that's how Miss Fontaine wished it, for not only is she the picture's star, but she and her husband, William Dozier, produced it with John Houseman's aid. And apparently, too, as producer she was b[i]ased toward herself as star, for it cannot be stated too strongly that the picture is largely Miss Fontaine's.

From the moment she gapes in girlish wonder at the arriving furniture of the new tenant in her Viennese neighborhood, she is utterly to the fore. And from the moment she looks upon that tenant, the young pianist, she's in love with him. Through girlhood, maidenhood and modeling for a slim but respectable livelihood, she worships the ground this glamorous fellow melodically treads upon. Even when he deserts her after a night of mechanical bliss, she continues to feel most kindly toward him and happily bears his child. And finally, when married and wealthy, she once again meets him in a crowd, she gladly forgets her kindly husband and goes chasing after her dream.

From *New York Times*, April 29, 1948.

That's all right, if all you are after is an hour and a half of wistfulness, of lingering love-lorn expressions and pseudo-Viennese "schmaltz." And if that is all you are after, you will find plenty of it in this film—a little heavy, perhaps, in its expression, but wistful and "schmaltzy," none the less. As the lady of deathless adoration, Miss Fontaine virtually wrings herself dry, and as the darling but fickle concert pianist, Louis Jourdan saturates the air with charm. Together they make a pleasant unit for conditioning the romantic atmosphere. No one else in the picture gets much of a chance—or counts.

But if you are looking for sensibility and reasonable emotion in a film, beware of this overwritten "Letter." It will choke you with rhetoric and tommy-rot.

Variety

Writing for the more knowledgeable and self-interested audience within the film industry itself, the *Variety* reviewer comments on various aspects of the production and the quality of its personnel, noting especially Ophuls's expert direction.

"Letter From An Unknown Woman" is a first for the new Rampart Productions, independent company organized by Joan Fontaine and William Dozier. Debut film is a distinguished offering, production-wise, giving Rampart a strong woman's picture for Universal distribution. If backed with exploitation playing up femme appeal and high production qualities b.o. returns should be gratifying.

Picture teams Miss Fontaine and Louis Jourdan, French actor, as co-stars and they prove to be a solid combination. Both turn in splendid performances in difficult parts that could easily have been overplayed.

Story follows a familiar pattern but the taste with which the film has been put together in all departments under John Houseman's production supervision makes it a valid and interest-holding drama. The mounting has an artistic flavor that captures the atmosphere of early-day Vienna and has been beautifully photographed.

Story unfolds in flashback, a device that makes plot a bit difficult to follow at times, but Max Ophuls' direction holds it together. He doesn't rush his direction, adopting a leisurely pace that permits best use of the story. Film is endowed with little touches that give it warmth and heart while the tragic tale is being unfolded. It concerns a young girl who falls in love with a neighbor, a concert pianist. She follows his career from the sidelines until one night they meet on the eve of his departure for a concert tour. His promise to return isn't kept and later she marries another man to give her son a name and home. Years later she again meets her only love but he fails to remember. Story is told as he reads a letter from the girl, written after the second meeting and just before she dies of typhus.

Supporting roles are brief but effectively handled in keeping with high

From *Variety*, April 10, 1948.

quality of the entire picture. Mady Christians, Marcel Journet, Art Smith, Carol Yorke, Howard Freeman, John Good and others creditably supply the backing performances.

The ace lensing is by Frank Planer. Daniele Amfitheatrof's music score is topnotch and art direction, settings, costumes and other contributions earn the same rating.

Baxt.

Max Ophuls

Andrew Sarris

The most influential auteur study published in English, Andrew Sarris's 1968 *The American Cinema*, was not least remarkable for its high valuation of Ophuls's work. Sarris placed Ophuls in his pantheon of "directors who have transcended their technical problems with a personal vision of the world." Ophuls's conspicu- ously idiosyncratic cinematography is analyzed by Sarris as evidence of such a personal vision—a vision which, for most auteurists, transcends other filmic elements such as acting and dialogue that had formerly been considered the primary attributes of good filmmaking.

The cinema of Max Ophuls translates tracking into walking. His fluid camera follows his characters without controlling them, and it is this stylistic expression of free will that finally sets Ophuls apart from Murnau and Hitchcock. However, the track is such a conspicuous element of film technique that Ophuls has never been sufficiently appreciated for his other merits. Even when he is most bitter, he never descends to caricature. His humor is never malicious, his irony never de- structive. Like Renoir, he was one of the first genuinely international directors, the kind of artist who did not slur over national differences in the name of a spurious universality, but who defined national differences as functions of a larger unity. Consequently, Ophuls's American films, particularly *Caught* and *The Reckless Moment*, express a perceptive vision of America's glamorous fan- tasies (*Caught*) and the obsessive absorption with family at the expense of so- ciety (*The Reckless Moment*). Conversely, his treatment of European subjects in *The Exile* and *Letter from an Unknown Woman* lent grace and sensibility to the American cinema at a time when it was reeling from its false realism.

We claim Max as our own only to the extent that he happened to pass in our midst during his long voyage to sublimity. His influence was not so decisive as Murnau's or so pervasive as Renoir's. In the final analysis, Ophuls is, like all great directors, inimitable, and if all the dollies and cranes in the world snap to attention when his name is mentioned, it is because he gave camera movement its

From *The American Cinema* (New York: Dutton, 1968), pp. 70–72.

finest hours in the history of the cinema. When Joan Fontaine mounts the staircase to her lover's apartment for the last time, Ophuls's camera slowly turns from its vantage point on a higher landing to record the definitive memory-image of love. For a moment we enter the privileged sanctuary of remembrance, and *Letter from an Unknown Woman* reverberates forever after with this intimation of mortality. Love, the memory of love, the mortality of love comprise the Ophulsian heritage. If Ophuls seemed inordinately devoted to baroque opulence, his devotion was nevertheless strong-minded enough to contemplate an underlying human vanity tinged with sadness at its impending doom. The sensuous fabrics and surfaces of the Ophulsian world never completely obscure the grinning skeletons in the closets, and luxury never muffles tragedy.

The main point is that Ophuls is much more than the sum of all his camera movements. What elementary aestheticians overlook in Ophuls is the preciseness of his sensibility. His women may dominate subjectively, but his men are never degraded objectively. James Mason in *Caught* does not know what Barbara Bel Geddes is feeling when he proposes to her, but Ophuls conveys through the acting sensibility of Mason that a man need not understand what a woman feels to be capable of providing love. The Bergman-Antonioni problem of communication between the sexes does not arise in Ophuls simply because the director recognizes the two separate spheres of men and women. The Ophulsian view is never feminist, like Mizoguchi's, or feminine, like Bergman's and Antonioni's. No Ophulsian male, for example, is ever caught with his pants down like Gunnar Bjornstrand in *Smiles of a Summer Night* or Gabriele Ferzetti in *L'Avventura*, and no Ophulsian female ever displays the smug complacency toward her own moral superiority evidenced in the superior expressions of Eva Dahlbeck and Monica Vitti. We have instead the desperate effort of Wolfgang Liebeneiner in *Liebelei* to recapture his lost innocence with Magda Schneider on a sleigh ride that is mystically reprised by the camera after they both have died. It is not merely the moving camera that expresses the tragedy of lost illusions, but the preciseness of the playing. There is a direct link between Leibeneiner and Gérard Philipe's jaded count in *La Ronde* looking deep into Simon Signoret's eyes to find something he has forgotten forever. There is the same delicacy of regret nearly twenty years apart.

Some critics, particularly in England, have objected to the softening of Schnitzler's cynicism in the Ophuls version of *Liebelei* and *La Ronde*, not to mention the Ophulsian rendering of De Maupassant in *Le Plaisir*. Ophuls himself once observed that Schnitzler wrote *Liebelei* after *Reigen*, and not before.

The implication is clear. It is cynicism, and not idealism, that is generally the mark of youthful immaturity, or rather it is the cynic who is generally the most foolish romantic. A cynic delights in the trivial deceptions lovers practice on each other, and his attitude is particularly fashionable in a culture dedicated to the happy ending. There is a time in every film critic's life when he thinks that Billy Wilder is more profound than John Ford, and that nastiness is more profound than nobility. However, the acquiring of moral wisdom comes with mortal awareness, and vice begins paying back all its youthful debts to virtue. At such a moment, Ophuls becomes more profound than Schnitzler and De Maupassant, and *Madame de* becomes infinitely more tragic than *The Bicycle Thief*. By showing man in his direst material straits, De Sica and Zavattini imply a solution to his problems. Ophuls offers no such comforting consolation. His elegant characters lack nothing and lose everything. There is no escape from the trap of time. Not even the deepest and sincerest love can deter the now from its rendezvous with the then, and no amount of self-sacrifice can prevent desire from becoming embalmed in memory. *"Quelle heure est-il?"* ask the characters in *La Ronde*, but it is always too late, and the moment has always passed.

This is the ultimate meaning of Ophulsian camera movement: time has no stop. Montage tends to suspend time in the limbo of abstract images, but the moving camera records inexorably the passage of time, moment by moment. As we follow the Ophulsian characters, step by step, up and down stairs, up and down streets, and round and round the ballroom, we realize their imprisonment in time. We know that they can never escape, but we know also that they will never lose their poise and grace for the sake of futile desperation. They will dance beautifully, they will walk purposively, they will love deeply, and they will die gallantly, and they will never whine or whimper or even discard their vanity. It will all end in a circus with Lola Montès selling her presence to the multitudes, redeeming all men both as a woman and as an artistic creation, expressing in one long receding shot, the cumulative explosion of the romantic ego for the past two centuries.

Ewig hin der Liebe Glück

Robin Wood

Robin Wood, one of the British critics associated with the auteurist journal *Movie*, published this analysis of *Letter from an Unknown Woman* in 1976 as part of a book-length collection of essays entitled *Personal Views*. Wood's auteurist perspective is apparent in his enumeration of typical Ophulsian themes and motifs, his concern with defining the Ophulsian style by comparing Ophuls to other directors, and his preoccupation with visual effects as a key to the film's deepest meanings. The *Movie* critics have been especially preoccupied with directors whose personal style is expressed within the confines of the Hollywood industry, and for this reason they have paid special attention to Ophuls's American films. Following this tradition, Wood ranks *Letter from an Unknown Woman* as Ophuls's most perfectly realized work.

The foyer of the Vienna Opera; close-up of the placard announcing a performance of Mozart's *The Magic Flute*—an opera that sets beside the 'absolute' love of Tamino and Pamina, and their progress through perfect union towards spiritual transcendence, the very earthly and relative desires of Papageno, who wants 'Ein Mädchen oder Weibchen' and it does not much matter which or who. The camera tracks right, revealing the spectators during the interval between the two acts, moving about, talking. It picks up first one pair, now another, moving with each a little way then transferring to the next as if its attention had been distracted. The effect is dual, arising, one might say, out of a tension between content and style: the movement looks arbitrary, as if it did not matter which group or person the camera focused on (and none is a character with whom the fiction is concerned) or where it moved next; yet the movement (both of people and of camera) is so meticulously choreographed, so graceful and fluent, that we cannot but feel (even if subconsciously) that everything in the shot has been predetermined. Meanwhile, the off-screen voice of Lisa (Joan Fontaine) speaks of Chance and Destiny, telling us that nothing happens by chance, that our every

From *Personal Views* (London: Gordon Fraser, 1976), pp. 116–132.

step is counted. As she finishes, the camera in its peregrinations has arrived at the foot of the left-hand staircase that rises with its twin to unite on the level of the dress circle. Lisa and her husband come into view; as they mount, the camera cranes gracefully up to disclose the whole stairway, an ornate chandelier entering the frame, interposed between us and the characters. Lisa hears people talking about Stefan Brand, the man she has always loved and (unknown to him) the father of her son. A moment later she will see him at the foot of the right-hand stairway and the course of her life will be abruptly changed.

It would be an exaggeration to say that the whole of Ophuls (or even of *Letter from an Unknown Woman*) is contained in that shot: Ophuls's art at its best achieves a degree of refinement and complexity that demands that virtually every statement we might make about it be delicately qualified. It provides, none the less, in the centrality of its concerns and motifs, a valuable starting-point.*

During Ophuls's career (which spans three decades in four countries), he evolved one of the most striking and instantly identifiable visual styles in the cinema: a style which, like Ozu's or Mizoguchi's, is inextricably linked with certain recurrent motifs, and which in itself embodies a view of existence. In that evolution, *Letter from an Unknown Woman* is poised stylistically midway between two films to which it is so closely related in theme and narrative movement that one might regard the three (though they are in different languages) as an Ophuls trilogy. In comparison, *Liebelei* (1932) appears less refined and less complex though it has a freshness of incidental invention that, while certainly not absent from the later works, is there more subordinated to structural precision; while *Madame de . . .* (1953), a great film and a masterpiece, appears just a trifle overblown. I had better add here, parenthetically, that the film most of Ophuls's champions single out as his greatest, *Lola Montes*, seems to me a failure, albeit a brilliant and distinguished one. It is easy to see why it has been valued so highly: it has many of the marks of a final testament, a definitive statement. But no other film of consequence has suffered so disastrously from a central error of casting: the empty, doll-like figure presented by Martine Carol, in a role demanding the Dietrich of the 'thirties, the Dietrich of von Sternberg,

*One of British television's only unequivocal services to the cinema (apart from showing a lot of movies) was a series of BBC schools programmes devised and written by Victor Perkins. Perkins gave me a transcript of the programme on *Letter from an Unknown Woman*, and I am indebted to it for several specific ideas in the present essay. The debt is, however, more general: Perkins's script generated all my subsequent thinking about Ophuls, whom I had previously not valued highly.

leaves the film without a heart, and the humanity and passion of Ophuls's vision are at last overwhelmed by the proliferations of décor.

Though the method is somewhat artificial—a style being more than the elements that go to compose it, its essence created indeed by the interaction of those elements—it seems reasonable to approach Ophuls by listing some of the most striking stylistic features and recurrent motifs of his work. The list is not intended as exhaustive; far less are the examples offered as illustration, a complete catalogue of which would fill a book.

1: The tracking-shot (often with crane) and long take. It has become a commonplace that to discuss Ophuls is to discuss the meaning of his tracking-shots, and I shall return to this later. The tracking-shot is already established as a central stylistic strategy in the pre-World War II movies; it reaches its extreme (some would say excessive) elaboration in the post-Hollywood French films of the 'fifties. *Letter from an Unknown Woman* again represents a perfect mid-point in this evolution, the stylistic practice developed to a point of total expressive mastery but not yet to the point of domination it has reached by *Madame de . . .*

2: Staircases; movement up or down them, encounters on them, frequently accompanied by a crane movement. This is an important motif even in the Hollywood films on contemporary American subjects (*Caught* and, especially, *The Reckless Moment*) from which many Ophulsian 'trademarks' are of necessity excluded.

3: Other places of transition; doorways, thresholds, entrances.

4: Bedrooms. Rarely the scene of passionate embraces (Lisa's willing surrender to Stefan is exceptional); more often the setting for the expression of separateness (the conjugal bedroom scenes of *La Ronde* and *Madame de . . .*, the isolation of Lucia in *The Reckless Moment*, the imprisonment and delirium of the heroine of *Caught*).

5: Stations, trains, scenes of arrival and departure. There are obvious examples in *Letter* (three) and *Madame de . . .* (two); a particularly touching, almost wordless one in *Liebelei* (the errant wife seen off by her brother-in-law), where everything essential is communicated through the movements of hands; an important scene in *The Reckless Moment* is set in a bus station departure-room.

6: Carriages. Against the sterility of the husband/wife bedroom scene of *Madame de . . .* is set the passionate reunion of the lovers in a carriage; there are important carriage duologues in *Letter* and *Lola Montes*; the Lucia/Donnelly relationship in *The Reckless Moment* begins to develop in a car on a moving ferry.

7: Dances; the logical extension (in privileged cases, the perfect expression) of the 'life-as-constant-movement' theme which the previous motifs combine to suggest. The supreme example is in *Madame de . . .* : the growth of the lovers' mutual passion shown through an unbroken succession of dances, the only circumstances in which they can touch. The dance as meeting-place also figures in films as diverse as *Letter* and *Caught*. (One wants also to acknowledge the potency in Ophuls's films of the *negation* of these recurrent motifs: the staircase in *Caught* which the heroine *does not* ascend, the ball in *De Mayerling à Sarajevo* from which Sophie and Franz-Ferdinand are—in effect—excluded.)

8: Music, especially Mozart, the Viennese tradition, the waltz. Paralleling the use of *The Magic Flute* in *Letter*, *Liebelei* opens at a performance of *Il Seraglio*; the pattern of relationships in the film (the 'ideal' love of the principals set off by the frivolous affair of Theo and Mitzi) corresponds fairly clearly to the Belmonte-Constanza/Pedrillo-Blonde opposition in Mozart's opera. Gluck's *Orfeo ed Eurydice* figures in *Madame de . . .* , the heroine's feigned discovery of the 'loss' of the ear-rings she has pawned to pay debts being accompanied by Orpheus's lament for irrecoverably lost love ('Che faro senza Eurydice?'), the effect at once ironic and anticipatory. Ophuls made a film version of *The Bartered Bride*; waltz themes by Oscar Strauss run through *La Ronde* and *Madame de . . .* as Liszt's 'Farewell' waltz does through *Lola Montes*; even in *Caught* a character plays *Tales from the Vienna Woods* on the piano. Beyond such specifics, Ophuls's films can be regarded as possessing a metaphorical musical flow, as if the lilt and fluency of the Viennese waltz tradition and the simultaneous/ambivalent gaiety and pathos of Mozart were caught up in the movement of the films.

9: 'Old Vienna' itself; a state of mind as much as a location. Ophuls made films in four countries and four languages but he returns repeatedly to his reconstruction of Vienna—*Liebelei*, *Letter*, *La Ronde*. The 'feel' of *Madame de . . .* is so Viennese that one keeps forgetting it is ostensibly set in Paris. 'Vienna, 1900' reads the caption that opens *Letter*, and at the beginning of *La Ronde* Anton Walbrook (in his capacity as *metteur-en-scène*) creates 'Vienna, 1900' before our eyes, at the same time acknowledging his preference for the past, with neither the turbulence of the present nor the uncertainty of the future.

10: Theatres, opera-houses, places of entertainment. *Divine* is centred on the theatre; *Liebelei*, *De Mayerling à Sarajevo*, *Letter* and *Madame de . . .* all contain key scenes set in opera-houses; Lola Montès dances in an opera-house taken over for that purpose by her royal patron, and ends her career in the circus-ring. As well as relating to the motifs of constant transition (Ophuls's characters often seeming most 'at home' in an opera box or foyer) this also points to Ophuls's concern with role-playing, with the ambiguities of appearance-and-reality. The distinction between stage and box becomes blurred: both are stages, where actors are on view and must give performances. The dance-floors of *Madame de . . .* , the recurrent ceremonials and tours of inspection of *De Mayerling à Sarajevo*, are other related manifestations; so is Charles II's final entrapment in the royal role in *The Exile*.

11: Soldiers. Military men figure prominently among Ophuls's characters: *Liebelei*, *Sarajevo*, *The Exile*, *Letter*, *La Ronde*, *Madame de . . .* all contain important examples. The sympathy extended to them varies, but the stress is always on ceremony and performance, on the army as an extension of the 'theatre', the humanity of older and more high-ranking soldiers (*Madame de . . .*'s husband) in danger of becoming atrophied beneath their role.

12: Duels. Necessarily less frequent than most of the other components in my list; but it is worth noting that *Liebelei*, *Letter* and *Madame de . . .* all culminate in fatal duels (implicitly in the case of *Letter*, but there, too, unambiguously) in which lover is shot by offended husband, the deaths (off-screen) in the first and third both established by the fact that there is no second shot fired. One might see the significance of the duel as the point where theatre and life fatally coincide, where one of the actors, at least, cannot get up to take a bow at the end of the performance.

13: Ornate and elaborate, often cluttered décor, at once opulent and suffocating; chandeliers, glass, mirrors, lights, glitter.

14: Objects intervening between characters and camera, especially during tracking-shots; bars, trellis-work, nets, foliage, pillars.

15: A fondness for framing the characters—in mirrors, in doorways, between pillars, in windows. We first see the face of Madame de . . . framed in a small, ornate mirror on her dressing-table, after she has been indirectly characterized through her material possessions and her attachment to them; in *Sarajevo*, Sophie is caught motionless between two pillars at the moment when, in her role as governess, the secret mutual attachment between her and Franz-Ferdinand is discovered; examples could be multiplied indefinitely. Most typically, these arrests are momentary, occurring in the course of a tracking-shot, a point of brief stasis during a character's progress from room to room, from stage to stage, on the road to destiny.

16: Echoes and near-repetitions. Sometimes these take the form of refrains running through the whole film ('Who is it?'—'Brandt'—'Good evening, Mr. Brandt'; or the 'Quelle heure est-il?' of *La Ronde*), a part of its 'musical' rhythm, acquiring overtones of irony and poignance. More striking are specific echoes of scenes, situations, dialogue, that recapitulate the past in order to underline the distance the characters have travelled. Both *Letter* and *Madame de . . .* are largely constructed on 'paired' scenes: in the latter, for example, two visits to the church, two visits to the jeweller, two scenes of farewell at the station, in each case the details of *mise-en-scène* (camera-movement, disposition of the actors) underlining the parallel.

17: Flashbacks. The sleigh-ride of *Liebelei* is recapitulated at the end after both the lovers are dead; *Letter* and *Lola Montes* (and *La Signora di Tutti*, reputedly one of Ophuls's greatest films) are structured in flashbacks; the repetitions in the latter part of *Madame de . . .* have the function of continually calling the past to our minds, evoking ghostly flashbacks as it were. The flashback structures of *Letter* and *Lola Montes* are not ingenious, decorative complications, nor are they merely nostalgic, but are essential to the film's meaning. One might say that the flashback or its equivalent is as central to Ophuls as it is alien to Hawks.

18: Circles; the merry-go-round of *La Ronde*, the circus-ring of *Lola Montes*, the recurrent foreign countries of the fairground 'railway' in *Letter*. *Madame de . . .* opens with the camera moving in a semi-circle around the room as the heroine tries to decide what to pawn, finally returning (without a cut) to the earrings on to which it first directed our attention. The image of the circle—the return to the point of departure—is closely connected to the use of repetition and flashback as structural devices.

19: Chance, Fate, Predestination (according to taste); Ophuls's characters call it Fate, his style and method seeming partly to endorse them. Anton Walbrook in *La Ronde* unites various functions whose combination suggests a connection between style and theme, *mise-en-scène* and destiny. He is, he tells us, 'anyone'—he is we, the audience, and can fulfil our desire to know everything; associated during the long opening tracking-shot with both stage and studio, he is also the *metteur-en-scène*, choosing the décor, positioning and directing the actors; and in so far as he is assimilated into the film's fiction, he is a 'Fate' figure, controlling and helping to execute the characters' destinies. In this last function he carries the suggestion that Fate for Ophuls is not quite absolute: at several points, characters *almost* miss crucial appointments, the 'ronde de l'amour' *almost* breaks down, it is not certain that the circle will be completed.

20: Time, clocks, watches. In their state of perpetual transition, Ophuls's characters are the prisoners of time and its passing. In the first half of *Sarajevo*, a watch becomes itself the instrument of Fate; in *La Ronde* (where this motif is most explicit and insistent), the characters are forever asking the time, and it is always later than they wish to believe; the husband/wife episode is dominated by the image of the clock, its pendulum ticking in the centre foreground of the screen, the couple in their separate beds disposed symmetrically to right and left.

21: The extinction of lights; a motif often unobtrusive, and only rarely raised to the level of overt symbolism, but remarkably consistent. The most striking and expressive instance is at the end of the suite of ball-scenes in *Madame de . . .* where, at the last dance, on a deserted floor, with the musicians packing up to leave, the lovers waltz with their coats on, Louise tells Donati that her husband returns tomorrow, and a servant walks round extinguishing the lights one by one, the single take (the camera seeming to dance with the actors in a continual suspension) ending on the harp as a black cover is placed over it. The darkening and deepening of tone at the end of *La Ronde* is subtly intensified by the extinction of a street-lamp as the Count comes out of the prostitute's house into the cold dawn.

22: Women. One cannot conclude such a list without noting the degree to which Ophuls's cinema is woman-centred: it is as unusual for one of his films to have a man as central consciousness as for one of Hawks's to be centred on a woman (the obvious Hawks exception, *Gentlemen Prefer Blondes*, in its characteristic presentation of women as aggressors confirms rather than qualifies the generalization). Traditionally, the female principle has been regarded as passive, the male active, and, without wishing to suggest that Ophuls's films endorse any simplistic opposition of male and female roles, one cannot but feel a connection between the emphasis on fatality in his movies and his gravitation to woman-centred subjects. In *Liebelei*, *Sarajevo* and *La Ronde* interest is divided more or less equally between the sexes, though even here (especially in *Sarajevo*) one may feel an emotional gravitation to the female characters pulling against the scenario. The only Ophuls film I know which has a man as central figure is his first Hollywood movie *The Exile*, which was written and produced by its star, Douglas Fairbanks Jnr., who clearly saw it as a vehicle for his own disputable talents. Ophuls decorates the occasionally risible masculine acrobatics with some beautiful camera-movements, but one senses him wishing he could tell the story from the point of view of the Dutch girl (Paule Croset); and the most intimately Ophulsian sequence is undoubtedly that centered on Maria Montez. On the other side, the tally is imposing both in quantity and quality: of the films I have seen, *Divine, Letter, Caught, The Reckless Moment, Madame de . . .* , *Lola Montes* are all firmly centred on a female consciousness.

It is easy to relate all these components (grouping them accordingly) to certain basic assumptions (themselves interdependent) about existence: reality and illusion, life as dream, transcience, destiny. But the recognition of the philosophical basis of an artist's work should never become an ultimate end: usually, reduced to this level of abstraction, the philosophy will be merely banal. In art, the underlying assumptions that make up an artist's 'view of life' gain their validity from the precision, intensity and sensitivity with which they are concretely embodied in actual works, not *vice versa*. From the perception of an Ophulsian world-view, then, one returns to the realized detail of the films. No mere catalogue of motifs can do justice to the delicacy of tone and effect to which a conjunction of such motifs may contribute. Before focusing finally on *Letter from an Unknown Woman*, I offer one last example from *De Mayerling à Sarajevo*, at once one of the finest and most underestimated of all Ophuls's films.

The Countess Sophie Chotek, in love with the Archduke Franz-Ferdinand but unable to marry him, becomes governess to an aristocratic Austrian family. Franz-Ferdinand establishes himself as a regular visitor, letting it be assumed that he is courting one or other of the older daughters but actually using this as a cover for meetings with Sophie. In one scene we see a family group being posed for a photograph on the lawn of the chateau; Franz-Ferdinand is among them. Ophuls shows us this from a high angle in long-shot: we have the tableau posed as on a stage for the photographer (with Franz-Ferdinand, in particular, acting a role), and our own distance from this includes the photographer as part of the performance. The camera then moves back to 'place' this group within the frame of an upstairs window, turning it already into a picture, and as the track backwards continues we suddenly have Sophie within the frame, looking down on the scene as a spectator. Our response is subtly modified with the change in perspective: we realize that we have been watching the scene on the lawn from her viewpoint, and at once the tone is coloured by deeper emotional resonances, the sense of distance separating the lovers, the pretence they must maintain in public, the contrast between private emotion and public performance. Ophuls thereupon cuts to a long-shot of Sophie from the other side of the room, emphasizing her aloneness and changing our perspective once again: it is *she*, framed in the décor, who now becomes a figure in a picture at which we are looking. Emotionally the sequence is central to Ophuls's world: the poignance of separation, or 'ideal' love thwarted. What I want to stress here—to take up again in discussing *Letter*—is the delicacy with which Ophuls determines our relation to the action, and the shifts in that relation, the way in which our passing tendency to identify with Sophie, her mood, her actual viewpoint, is qualified by a cut that detaches us from her, making her appear as trapped and helpless from *our* vantage-point as Franz-Ferdinand appeared from hers. One might not consciously register the effect here as 'ironic', but the pervasive possibility of irony is as essential to the Ophuls tone as his romanticism.

More must be said about Ophuls's tracking-shots. The Linz sequence in *Letter* can be taken as fairly representative: a relatively relaxed scene at a lower pitch of emotional intensity than those directly involving Stefan, hence exemplary of Ophuls's habitual practice. The first part of the scene consists of two long track-ing-shots: One, Lisa, her mother and stepfather meet (by prior arrangement) a general and his handsome young nephew (a lieutenant), who it is hoped will become Lisa's suitor. They walk through the streets, the lieutenant questioning Lisa about Linz, slightly disapproving of her attachment to Vienna, attributing it to a fondness for music, and telling her they have good music in Linz too. The camera accompanies them through most of the shot, pausing to show the hopeful faces of the watching parents. Two, a shot that reverses the movement of the first, starting outside the church (the point the young couple had reached) where a military band is now playing in the square. The camera accompanies Lisa and the lieutenant as they walk past the band, pausing finally on the parents who are at the table of a sidewalk café expecting to celebrate the announcement of an engagement.

Apart from their unusual length in time and distance (but increasingly *usual* in Ophuls's later, post-Hollywood, films), the shots display a number of representa-tive characteristics. Firstly, grace and elegance: the point at which traditional Anglo-Saxon criticism of Ophuls (represented, for example, by Karel Reisz, Lindsay Anderson, and by Richard Roud in an early monograph it is charitable to assume he would prefer to forget) begins and ends; the tendency was to regard Ophuls's film as sentimental novelettes overdecorated with frills. One should not, I think, overreact by denying the gracefulness importance in its own right: the delight in sensuous movement, the pleasure of creating beautiful and fluid im-ages, is clearly a major factor in Ophuls's creative impulse. Secondly, connection: naturally inherent in a style based on camera-movement (see artists as different from each other as Renoir and Welles). In both shots we are led from group to group without a cut; the suggestion is of the interconnectedness of lives, the simultaneity of actions that impinge on each other. Thirdly, camera-distance. The characters are placed in an environment and in relation to each other, not isolated by cutting or by close-up. Further, the distance between camera and characters fluctuates during the take, so that our spatial relationship to them is not constant. Fourthly, the use of foreground objects intervening between camera and characters. Occasionally the effect is ironic (the workers' cart that rudely interrupts the pompous formalities of introduction); more usually the effect is of a graceful ornamentation and a subtle distancing, our view of the characters temporarily interrupted. Fifthly, 'musical' form: the two shots are variations on each other, part repetition, part inversion. Sixthly, symmetry and circularity: the characters are brought back to where they started. But we are aware at once that time has elapsed and the situation changed: the lieutenant is about to propose.

The function of style in a work of art is not simply that of embodying the artist's vision; an important aspect of style is the defining of a relationship between the work and its audience: in the cinema, between the spectator and the characters and action on the screen. One can define the function and meaning of the Ophuls tracking-shot further by juxtaposing it with the camera-movements of Hitchcock and Preminger. Since *Rebecca* (his first American film), one of the instantly identifiable characteristics of Hitchcock's *mise-en-scène* has been the *subjective* tracking-shot, that places us in the actor's position and gives us the sensation of moving with him; this usually alternating with backward tracking-shots of the actor moving. The device is a logical extension of the Hitchcockian principle of audience-identification, an expression of his desire to 'put the audience through it'. In the 'classical' Preminger films of the 'forties and 'fifties, camera-movement has an opposite function, which can be briefly illustrated from *Laura*. Consider the famous sequence leading up to Laura's return—Mark McPherson's obsessive exploration of her apartment and personal belongings, his growing infatuation with a woman who is supposed to be dead. Here a subject that might well have attracted Hitchcock (think of *Vertigo*) is treated in a manner very different: instead of the fragmentation of Hitchcockian montage, Preminger uses as few takes as possible; at no point are we placed in McPherson's position or asked to see things from his (physical or mental) viewpoint; the only close-ups occur in the middle of takes, the character moving into close-up then out again into medium- or long-shot.

Subjective shots are very rare in Ophuls, and I can think of no subjective tracking-shots outside the scene in *The Reckless Moment* where Lucia Harper disposes of Ted Darby's body—a sequence that looks deliberately shot *à la* Hitchcock. In *Letter* there is a brief moving subjective shot from Lisa's position on the swing as she listens to Stefan's music; and there are the shots of Lisa from Stefan's viewpoint, notably as he turns at the gate to see her behind the glass of the door she has opened for him. The *Reckless Moment* sequence is interesting because of the ways (apparent *hommage* as it seems) that it is *not* Hitchcock: interspersed with the alternating shots of 'person looking' and 'what she sees' are shots that distance her from us, shots that use décor (the boathouse steps and struts) in a characteristically Ophulsian way, as a framing device.

Yet neither are Ophuls's tracking-shots really like Preminger's. For one thing, Preminger's, though polished and smooth, lack the actively expressive, 'musical' dimension of Ophuls's: their main ambition is to be unobtrusive. If the subjective shot is infrequent in Ophuls, it is almost totally alien to Preminger. The camera in *Laura* moves to *watch* the character rather than to implicate us in his movements; having followed McPherson's tour of the living-room it not only stops to survey his progress to the next room in detached long-shot, it drops slightly so that a chair-back intrudes into the foreground of the frame. That chairback has nothing of the gracefully ornamental function of intervening objects in Ophuls; it is there simply to keep us at our distance. Ophuls's camera has a much stronger tendency to move *with* the characters, beside them and at their pace (in *Madame de . . .* , to waltz with them); though this is continually offset by intrusions into the frame, by the variability of camera-distance, by the (less frequent, but not uncommon) transference of attention to other characters, other groups. Equally removed from the audience-participation techniques of Hitchcock and the clinical objectivity and detachment of Preminger, Ophuls's camera-work achieves a perfect balance—in terms of the spectator's involvement—between sympathy and detachment. The sense of closeness without identification is essential to Ophuls's cinema: it is an aspect of that constant delicate intermingling of tenderness and irony that characterizes the Ophuls 'tone'. It relates similarly to a common structural feature of Ophuls's films: our intimate involvement with the characters is continually balanced by the fact that we always know more than they do. Our knowledge of historical facts in *Sarajevo* and *The Exile*, the flashback structures of *Letter* and *Lola Montes*, the merry-go-round symbolism of *La Ronde*, the obstinately recurrent ear-rings of *Madame de . . .* , all in their different ways place the spectator in a position of superior awareness.

The point can be further developed by reference to a crucial structural feature of *Letter*: the pervasive tension between subjective narrative and objective presentation. One can exemplify this most obviously by indicating the moments where Ophuls patently 'cheats'. The main body of the film is offered as a visualization of Lisa's letter; the question is, *Whose* visualization? Hardly Stefan's: the minor characters (Lisa's mother and stepfather, the lieutenant, etc.) whom Stefan does not know, are obviously not presented merely as he imagines them. The conventions of the first person narrative in the cinema encourage us to accept the visualization as 'how Lisa experienced it'; a moment's reflection will show us that much of the time Ophuls is taking great liberties with such an assumption. Consider the Prada [Prater] sequence, where Lisa and Stefan, during their first evening together, visit a 'world tour' railway in the funfair (the 'train' remains stationary while backdrops of exotic countries move past the window), then dance together in a café. Throughout the sequence, we see that Lisa is completely enclosed in the world of her dream, aware of nothing except Stefan and the apparent realization of her fantasies. Ophuls, however, shows us a lot that is outside that world: the old man who works the levers that operate the backdrops, the old woman Stefan pays for the entertainment. While Lisa and Stefan dance together, Ophuls cuts in a bit of dialogue between the singularly unromantic women of the ladies' orchestra, who drink beer, chew sausage and complain of being kept late ('I like to play for *married* people—they've got homes'). All this, clearly, is outside Lisa's consciousness, and could not have been described in the letter. Despite the subjective narrative, Ophuls does not restrict us to Lisa's viewpoint. The tendency of the film to draw us into her vision is balanced and counterpointed throughout by a conflicting tendency to detach us from the 'dream' and comment on it ironically, hinting at a prosaic reality that Lisa excludes, exposing some of the very unromantic mechanisms on which the dream depends. Ophuls's choice of music for the opera scene is very precise: as Lisa leaves her box, disturbed by Stefan's presence in the auditorium, and on her way to her fatal reunion with him outside on the steps, Act Two of *The Magic Flute* begins (incorrectly) with *'Ein Mädchen oder Weibchen'*. The irony is clearly lost on Lisa; neither is it exactly simple. Papageno's desire for *any* girl or woman relates to Stefan's amorous pursuits and contrasts with Lisa's single-minded dedication to one man; yet, as the film reveals, Stefan's philandering has masked a search for the woman who might save him, the 'unknown goddess' whom he failed (but, there are hints, only *just* failed) to recognize in Lisa.

Ophuls's love of near-repetition or echo itself becomes a distancing device even as it intensifies the poignancy of the action: again, we always know more than the characters. Sometimes, the discrepancy between their awareness and ours is slight. When Stefan Jnr. leaves by train and repeats the words ('Two weeks. . . .') his father called to Lisa just after his conception, we see Lisa herself react to the 'echo.' Yet we have more grounds for premonition than she: we know there is something amiss with the first compartment Stefan was put in, and as Lisa walks away we learn that there was a typhus case on the train. Ophuls's delicacy of effect might be represented by the shot of Lisa leaving the platform, the foreground of the image dominated by the spikes on the railings that form a barrier. Their harshness and gleaming coldness communicate a sense of the pain experienced by Lisa at that point, but the ominousness of the image conveys more than a subjective impression: we know from the beginning of her letter that she 'may be dead', and we see her here as a trapped woman.

One might make a similar point with the two scenes involving white roses. In the earlier, during their first evening together, Stefan buys Lisa a single white rose from a friendly old lady; in the later, Lisa, visiting Stefan for what is to prove the last time, after she has broken her marriage and seen her son off at the station, buys a whole bunch from an old man who is 'just closing up', but has 'still a few flowers left'. Again, the foreboding is experienced by Lisa but more precisely defined for the audience: the sense of 'too late' associates itself with overtones of death—the anticipated death of Lisa, Stefan's impending duel, the typhus on the train.

Ophuls's fondness for 'echoes' is not restricted to the 'twinning' of scenes or incidents: it is expressed equally through the minutiae of *mise-en-scène*, the positioning of the camera, its angles, its distance, its movements. Occasionally, Ophuls creates a delicate irony solely through the use of the camera: about to leave for Linz, Lisa runs from the station at the last moment, intending to offer herself to Stefan. Finding him out, she awaits him on the stairs just above the door to his apartment. (The location has already accumulated certain emotional associations: it is where Lisa earlier crept during the night to listen to Stefan playing the piano.) Stefan comes home, but with another woman. We watch their entrance into the hallway (accompanied by the already familiar exchange with the hall porter: 'Who is it?', etc.) almost from Lisa's position, the camera just behind her, looking down at them, panning right as they come up the stairs and disappear into the apartment. The effect is close to that of a subjective shot, encouraging us to share Lisa's disillusionment very directly: she leaves for Linz. Some years (though only about ten minutes of screen time) later, we have the sequence of Lisa's evening with Stefan: the visit to a café frequented by musicians, the gift of the white rose, the lobster dinner, the enchanted visit to the deserted, out-of-season Prada [Prater], the dance. Finally, Stefan takes her home with him: it is the ideal culmination and fulfilment of Lisa's romantic fantasy. Ophuls comments on it—and distances us again from Lisa's enchantment—by recapitulating the earlier shot's *mise-en-scène*: again we look down on the lovers from the stairs, again the camera pans to show them entering the apartment, and Lisa becomes but one woman in a never-ending succession—to Stefan, the suggestion is, scarcely distinguishable from the others, though the suggestion is qualified by other details in the preceding sequence.

I have so much stressed the delicacy of balance between identification with Lisa and detachment from her viewpoint because the film has so often been perceived (even by many of its professed admirers) as a sort of glorified 'women's novelette' redeemed by Ophuls's taste and sensitivity. Such a distinction between subject-matter and treatment (besides doing grave injustice to Howard Koch's screenplay) is totally belied by the film. Its meaning is created by, and inseparable from, the detail of the *mise-en-scène* and the structure of the scenario, and it is there that one must look to account for the complexity of its total effect.

The fascination of certain films depends on our (often uncomfortable) awareness of the suppressed, ghostly presence of an alternative film saying almost precisely the opposite, lurking just beneath the surface. In some cases (Bergman's *Winter Light* and Chabrol's *Juste Avant la Nuit* are prime examples) this tension becomes so great, the suppression of the 'alternative' film so precarious, that the conclusion can only be enigmatic, open to the most contradictory interpretations, the tensions left unresolved. This is not quite true of *Letter*: the ending, while complex in tone, ambivalent in its balancing of the tragic and the affirmative, represents a genuine, and deeply satisfying, resolution. Yet the more times one sees the film, the more one has the sense—it is a mark of its greatness—of the possibility of a film *against* Lisa: it would require only a shift of emphasis for this other film to emerge. It is not simply that Ophuls makes it possible for us to blame Lisa for destroying her eminently civilized marriage to a kind (if unpassionate) man, and the familial security he has given her and her son; it is also *almost* possible to blame Lisa, and her refusal to compromise, for Stefan's ruin. If the 'echo' shot from the top of the staircase suggests that his night with Lisa is like all the others, this is qualified by other pieces of evidence: he *does* seem to recognize Lisa's difference (though fleetingly and never quite unequivocally), he *does* appear impressed by her perception that his playing reveals a man who has not found what he is looking for, he *does* go to the trouble of finding out where she works (and *after* she has spent the night with him, so this is not merely the compulsion of an obsessive seducer). One can admire the 'absoluteness' of her refusal to have him notified of the birth of their child; one can equally (given the reflective distance from the fiction that Ophuls's style permits us) condemn the perversity with which she denies him his one chance to 'realize' the glimpse of possibilities he has had, to confront responsibilities, to acknowledge the child who will die before Stefan knows he ever existed. Later, we see the Stefan who confronts Lisa on the opera-house steps as a desperate and haunted man—an image that his subsequent 'cynical seducer' routine obliterates more completely for Lisa, perhaps, than for us. When she leaves his apartment, he has just declared that something she said the night before has been haunting him all day; she leaves without waiting to hear what it was, but Ophuls—as the camera lingers on the white roses and guttering candle—allows us to consider the possibility that a woman less devoted to an ideal might even at this late stage have been able to do something for a man not entirely beyond reach. The old flower-seller's remark (to which that last lingering shot of the roses might be felt to refer us back), for all its ominous overtones, can be taken as epitomizing this sense of fragile possibilities amid the encroaching, darkness: there are '*still* a few flowers left'. Lisa is in the mainstream of Ophuls's heroines and there is little doubt that the film is ultimately with her; yet its moral and emotional tensions can be suggested by saying that Stefan, on the other hand, has something about him of a male Lola Montes.

Ophuls's fondness for formal repetition and symmetry underlines the sense of destiny the films express: history repeats itself with variations, characters are returned to their starting-point that they may see how far they have travelled. I want to return, similarly, to mine: Fate, and the tracking-shot. One further comparison may give further definition to the significance of Ophuls's camera-movements. Like them, Renoir's tracking-shots, and his fondness for foreground/background counterpoint, suggest a view of life as constant flux, perpetual motion. The essential difference lies in the sense that in Renoir the camera is habitually at the service of the actors. One would not wish quite to declare the opposite of Ophuls—one never feels that the actors' movements are subordinated to an independently ('aesthetically') conceived camera-movement. But in Renoir the actors are free: one's impression is that the action is worked out in collaboration with them and the camera-movements (which rarely have the conscious elegance of Ophuls's) are determined accordingly. An Ophuls shot is a perfect unity of actor-movement and camera-movement. His people are in constant transition with little chance of standing still and taking stock: hence the importance in his work of staircases, doorways, stations, dance-floors. But at the same time they are trapped within the carefully predetermined movement, just as they are trapped within the clutter of décor: they must move from *here* to *here* via *there*. Perpetually in motion, they are perpetually imprisoned—even as a piece of music, once it has begun, must move to its predetermined close. Ultimately, Ophuls's tracking-shots signify both Time and Destiny. In *Letter*, our sense of the inexorability of time is intensified by the flashback structure, which allows Ophuls to counterpoint the passing of the years in Lisa's narrative with the passing of the hours as Stefan reads her letter—the two time-schemes at last converging and uniting in the closing minutes, as Stefan finishes the letter and the carriages arrive to bear him to the duel with Lisa's husband. The moment of bitterest irony in the film—given its force by the whole context of style and structure—is Stefan's remark to Lisa during their last meeting that 'For us, all the clocks in the world have stopped'.

The only escape from entrapment in time that Ophuls envisages is achieved through doubling back, re-living the past in order to transcend it. Hence the significance of flashback structures in his work. The ending of *Letter* is surely among the most poignant in the history of the cinema, at once desolating and exalting, tragic and affirmative. When Stefan, on his way to the duel, pauses and turns at the gate to see Lisa as she was the very first time he noticed her—but a Lisa, now, who fades, leaving only emptiness—we are intensely aware of the waste and loss: the loss not only of both their lives and of all Lisa has sacrificed for an impossible ideal, but of the relationship that might have been. At the same time it is a moment of supreme triumph: at the moment of recognition and remembrance, both the leading characters triumph over time, though one is already dead and the other on his way to die. Stefan's departure for the duel is at once suicide and redemption, the vindication of Lisa's romantic devotion, his acknowledgment of her vision. Should one finally talk of Fate or of Predestination? In France, Ophuls has had his Catholic interpreters (notably Claude Beylie), and *Letter* certainly permits a Catholic reading, with the first meeting of Stefan and Lisa presided over by a statuette of the Virgin, the crucifix dominating the room where Lisa's son has died and where she writes the letter, the appended note (the last thing Stefan reads) praying that God may have mercy on them both. Ophuls, I think, permits such a reading but does not demand it: the film is not inconsistent with the much more obvious ambiguity of *Madame de . . .* , where the similar religious motifs can be taken straight or read ironically.

Ophuls is ultimately (and because of, rather than despite, the pervasive irony) one of the cinema's great Romantics. The word has become so debased and simplified that it demands immediate qualification: there is, I have tried to insist, nothing simple or simplifying about Ophuls's commitment to Lisa's commitment, and it is never a matter of blind or uncritical identification. Lisa retains a yearning for a perfection unrealizable in life, yet the yearning confers upon life (even if posthumously) its highest dignity and value, and this Ophuls profoundly respects. The word 'romantic' has many uses: one talks of a 'romantic schoolgirl', and one talks of Keats as a 'Romantic poet'. The two usages have come to seem so distinct that it is worth remembering what they basically have in common: the romantic schoolgirl's yearning after an idol stems from the same urge as the Romantic poet's after the nightingale. So it is not impossible for Ophuls, dealing apparently with the former, to raise it through his art to the stature and significance of the latter.

The Ophuls Text:
A Thesis

Paul Willemen

As part of the editorial collective that founded the British journal *Screen*, Paul Willemen is committed to an ideological perspective that grows out of a synthesis of semiotics, Althusserian Marxism, Lacanian psychoanalysis, and feminism. Willemen's characterization of the Ophuls oeuvre as a "text" suggests the radical formalism that marks this group of critics. Willemen's anthology on Ophuls, published by the British Film Institute in 1978 following a retrospective of his films at the Edinburgh Film Festival, marked an important milestone in film scholarship. Though the anthology is entitled *Ophuls*, Willemen's ambivalence toward the notion of Ophuls as author (as he suggests in the book's introduction) is a resistance toward "the charting of a consecration of a 'great artist.'" Of greater interest to Willemen is the way Ophuls's films enact scenarios of repression, the issues of which are rooted in the institutions of commercial cinema, in particular in the strategies of voyeurism and exhibitionism as they relate to a politics of gender difference.

The few reviewers and critics that have attempted to deal with Ophuls' films all revert regular as clockwork to a handful of terms such as baroque, style, camera virtuosity, rhythm, formalist, fascination, romantic, nihilist, etc. As Alan Williams pointed out in his thesis on Ophuls[1], the traditional film theories have

From *Ophuls* (London: British Film Institute, 1978), pp. 70–74.
1. Alan Williams wrote: 'Roy Armes, in a formulation which is representative of those critics who dismiss Ophuls, has called the director " . . . virtually a test case of one's approach to the cinema. For those whose concern is purely visual and whose ideal is an abstract symphony of images, Ophuls has the status of one of the very great directors. For spectators and critics who demand in addition to the images the sort of human insight and moral depth that a play or a novel can give, he is merely a minor master, a maker of exquisite but rather empty films."' (*The French Cinema since 1946*, Vol.1.)

'An entire monograph could be written examining the critical presuppositions which structure these few sentences. We would wholeheartedly agree that Ophuls is a "test case" of thinking about film, but the "test" is not demonstrated with the help of the style/content dichotomy invoked here, but by the very fact that the dichotomy arises at all. Here, in a particularly superficial case, style

been unable to cope with the work of Ophuls: starting with the idea that he must
be an author as opposed to a mere director, his work is then reduced to empty
formalisms, or 'pure style', praised by the so-called *mise en scène* critics such as
Jacques Rivette, or dismissed by moralists fixated on forms of content such as
'characters' and themes. Accepting this crude form/content opposition, a few
others sought for profound statements about the human condition in selected
combinations of 'style' and 'story'. The most productive and intelligent approaches have concentrated on the specific combinations in Ophuls' work of the
sequence-shot and montage (Brian Henderson, Victor Perkins and Andrew
Sarris), thus to some extent demonstrating why neither montage critics nor
sequence-shots critics such as André Bazin were able to find a way of reading the
peculiar 'in between' strategies deployed in the films.

A second set of terms that surfaces regularly in writing about Ophuls is that
his films all focus on women, even if the original source material for the plot, no

---

equals image and content equals "human insight and moral depth". These two are taken, implicitly,
as wholly independent. (. . .) The subjects of many Ophuls films are pretexts for the films themselves as spectacles in their own right. "Content analysis" is not appropriate, for the films are not
"about" their subjects in any direct manner (and, furthermore, these subjects are borrowed from
other works). For this reason, the present study has eschewed filmic "content" except as it is inflected
by modes of presentation. A "subject" summary by Richard Roud (in *Max Ophuls–An Index*) demonstrates the problems of content analysis as applied to Ophuls: "What are Ophuls's subjects? The
simplest answer is: women. More specifically: women in love. Most often, women who are unhappily
in love, or to whom love brings misfortune of one kind or another. The surroundings in which they
live are usually luxurious, in any event, they generally manage at least one performance at the opera
and one ball during the course of the film. They usually live between 1880–1900. . . . The setting is
usually "Vienna": sometimes it is actually Vienna. Either way it is not the real *fin-de-siècle* Vienna—
but rather an ideal Vienna—the city of operetta and Strauss waltzes.'
'This passage exemplifies one of the most typical strategies of contemporary film criticism as
applied to directors—the attempt to construct an "ideal film", of which the actual works are mere
manifestations. (. . .) The problem is that Sarris and the other auteurists merely changed the emphasis of the *politique des auteurs* without discarding (in practice, if not in theory) two of its more
suspect premises. First, the notion of an all-powerful and consistent creative force is still invoked
to valorise minor films of favoured directors at the expense of notable works by otherwise undis-
tinguished ones. (. . .) The auteurists' second, more damaging premise is the implicit retention
of the notion of an "ideal film" only imperfectly expressed in an *auteur's* actual works. *Madame de
. . .* and *Letter from an Unknown Woman* are the auteurists' favoured Ophuls films; they are also the
most "typical" in terms of their subjects (they share all of the features cited by Roud, above). *Auteur*
criticism does not seem interested in *La Ronde*, for example, except in that it relates to these two
films.' A. L. Williams, *Max Ophuls and the Cinema of Desire—Style and Spectacle in Four Films,
1948–1955*, Univ. of New York at Buffalo, 1977 (unpublished).

matter how classic or prestigious a piece of literature it may be, has to be pulled rather violently in that direction. The best examples are perhaps *Liebelei* and *Werther*, where in each case a female character somehow gets to be dramatically privileged over the male protagonist. This notion relates, as will be argued later, to the fact that in these films, as in the rest of Ophuls' work, women tend to be produced as pivots within intricate and elaborate narrative structures and as privileged objects of the look, that of the audience as well as that of intra-diegetic characters.

A third set of terms, produced mainly by content oriented critics, relates to a contradiction between the filmed and the filming. For instance, Karel Reisz remarked in an essay in *Sequence* (No. 14, 1952): 'Ophuls is clearly fascinated by the world he depicts, but never allows its surface charm to obscure the price that has to be paid for its preservation. The social conventions, so pleasant to observe from a distance, conceal a rigid and merciless discipline.'

This rigidity, this rigorous Order, transgression of which can bring death, is then depicted in the most fluid and flexible of ways. As if what was repressed by the Law, the rigorous social order, re-emerges as excess in the *mise en scène*. The most striking example here is perhaps the literalism, i.e. the literal production in the filmic text of a verbal metaphor in *Le Plaisir*. As a joke, and it is interesting that he should have chosen to say it in this way, Ophuls explained that the reason for the convoluted crane movement along the walls of the brothel in the *Maison Tellier* episode, peering through windows but never cutting to the inside of the house, was because the Maison Tellier was precisely a *maison close*, a closed house. Behind its doors and windows is locked away what a rigorous social morality excludes from its legal order. So the camera is on the side of the Law, but it is the repressed (here the repression of the verbal term combined with the inscription of socio-sexual repression) which moves it along, obsessively circling its object of fascination, describing in its movement the outlines of the gaps in the social fabric, catching glimpses of the forbidden areas, but from the outside. The tracks, dollies and crane movements constantly holding out the promise that in passing, or in the shift from one look to another as, e.g., in the transition via the spyglass in *The Exile*, the look may find its object of desire. But never shall it be offered too detailed and close up a scrutiny by a fixed gaze. It is also interesting to note that Ophuls appeared to be aware of the sexual implications of isolating a person for the look, the sexual implications of cutting to close-ups offering, e.g., the body of a woman for access to the look. In *Le Plaisir*, he shoots the five prostitutes in the train in mid- and long-shots, always attempting to keep as many of them as possible in frame at the same time. The reason for this, Ophuls explained, referring to another literalism, was that Maupassant described the women as 'a bunch of flowers' and that he was reluctant to 'pick' one of them! The film that turns entirely on this inscription of the look and the desired scene is of course *Lola Montes*, where the woman is explicitly and directly put on show, offered to the fixed and fixing gaze of viewer (in the film and of the film) and camera. But what the look finds is a mask, the woman as masquerade, as screen. The film's narrative and diegesis fragment under the pressure of the desire of penetrating beyond that mask, with the look as mark of desire to possess what always escapes. Every new scene/seen promising to satisfy what the previous one provoked. But as the 'real' object is never that which the look finds, always landing on a stand-in, the look is offered (moves to) scene after scene, each constituting a trap for it, something in which it can loose itself, something to 'fill' the eye and capture it, but nevertheless always lacking what it is looking for, and thus forever re-launching the wish to look again or to look elsewhere. It is in this sense that Ophuls' films engage with the cinema as spectacle, or, to put it in the words of Stephen Heath, 'with the relations sustained in cinema, as cinema.' In Ophuls, cinema becomes a machine for the entrapment of the look. It is also in this sense that the function of the soundtrack of the films can begin to be understood: the inscription of signifiers off screen, emphasising the unseen, what has been withheld from the eye. Alan Williams remarked[2] that often the soundtrack refers to represented spectacles such as theatre or opera performances, i.e. precisely what is socially given to and for the look, while the cinema thus comes to stand under the sign of the look at that which is socially withheld, reactivating as an institution specifically designed for this, the nexus look/desire and scene/seen.

2. In each case, the apparent contradiction between interpolated representation (opera) and narrative (the supposed lived experience of the characters) results from a temporarily restricted spectator knowledge of the latter. *Letter From An Unknown Woman*, *Madame de . . .* , and *Lola Montes* all share the curious trait of never actually showing the spectator the performance that is heard. In each case, visual information remains within the narrative universe while aural information (the arias, the sound of Lola's feet on the stage) refers to the performance. In this way the spectator is required to actively integrate (perceive simultaneously) levels of the filmic universe which are, for the purposes of understanding, resolutely separate . . . Again, the final result of this structure is not to suggest that 'art falsifies life', even though this reading is suggested at particular points. Rather, it is the relation of 'life' to the spectacle which is called into question. The societies and characters presented in the films are themselves suggested to be works of representation. In this context, the opera, theater, and dance performances strewn through the films are representations of representations. Alan Williams, *op. cit.*

According to the rules of patriarchy, it is at this intersection that the figure of woman is produced as image. At the juncture of order, the Law and the repressed, the unconscious, woman is produced as the signifier of desire. Moreover, a signifier which represents the subject for that other signifier, the look, thus instituting and producing the cinema spectator, that specific subject produced by/for the cinematic institution.

The ceaseless metonymy set in motion by the look, the ceaseless inscription of difference (the scene is never quite what is to be seen), in order for the film to remain within a certain formula of narrative, indeed for it to end at all, it must be circumscribed, contained in some way. Interestingly, for a cinematic practice turning on the look, a number of the films end by the inscription of a full stop on the sound track (see, e.g. *Liebelei, Letter From An Unknown Woman, Madame de . . .*): the duel marked by the pistol shot (or expected shot) off-screen, present only as sound, in the same way that the social spectacles referred to above are marked as sounds only. In the duel scenes, it is the sound that ends the film, not the image track which often spills over into an epilogue extendable ad infinitum, signifying not so much a coming to rest as a freezing of a particular scene, as with the couple on the beach, one in an invalid's chair, frozen as a specific relationship for the rest of their lives and gradually letting the image track run out. It isn't that there is no more to be seen, merely that, from then on, everything is endless repetition or rather, sameness, marked by the signifier of total loss, death. What the sound track puts an end to is the difference, the desire which drove the look from one stand-in to another, by as it were filling with a sound that gap between what was looked for and what was available to be looked at. It isn't surprising that such a sound should simultaneously signify death.

The dialectic of order and excess turning on the pivot of the look at the female also finds its mark on three different levels in the films, one related to the narrative structure, the other two to the *mise en scène*. Firstly, as suggested earlier, the impact of the scopic drive on the narrative fragments and distorts it. The linear, orderly telling of the story from beginning to end breaks open, turns back on itself, regresses (flashes back) on the trace of the memory of plentitude. The expectation of the look satisfied produces a movement backwards into the future, the expected recovery in the future (of the unreeling of the film, scene after scene) of the memory of the look satisfied. A variant on this: the perpetual recommencing of the story, the renewal of the trajectory, the repetition or doubling of scenes (see, e.g. *La Ronde, Le Plaisir, La Tendre Ennemie* for the recommencing of stories, while *La Ronde, Madame de . . .* and *Letter From An Un-*

known Woman offer startling examples of doubled scenes). Once more the complex inscription of this aspect of the dialectic is to be found, not surprisingly, in the very same film that most directly and explicitly engages with the cinematic representation of the look: *Lola Montes.*

Secondly, the dialectic of balance, symmetry on the one hand and excess on the other, is also to be found on the level of the arrangement of the profilmic event: characters will be placed in symmetric or harmoniously balanced relations to each other, with figures on the left/right of the screen, or objects balancing a figure on the other side of the frame, or threesomes with the side figures looking at the central one, etc. Even the sets reproduce this sense of symmetry via double stairways, the shape of a circus tent, the entrance to a house, mirrors reflecting a figure, etc. Simultaneously, however, there is a proliferation of excessive detail, filling up the image with impediments to the look, obstacles between scene and seen, as well as the proliferation of objects in the sets themselves, literally filling the image to overflowing, offering an endless series of objects for the gaze. In this sense, the look is invited to wander through the scene resting now on one object, then on another, while on the other hand the overall composition offers the spectacle of fixed proportions harmoniously balanced in the most classical manner, guiding and captivating the look, directing it to the focus of the frame. The result is that the look is simultaneously subjected to two forces, pulling it in different directions.

Thirdly, there is the conduct of the camera: the combination of restlessness, ceaseless movement, the function of which was indicated earlier, with repetitions of movements at different times, although often accompanying a doubled scene on the level of the narrative, as, e.g., the movements and camera positions in the station and church scenes in *Madame de . . .* (a film in which nearly every element is doubled, replayed, echoed or inverted, either simultaneously via mirrors or at a later moment in the film) and the repeated tracking shots in *Letter From An Unknown Woman.* A second aspect of the camerawork in relation to the pro-filmic event reproducing the stasis/process dialectic, to use Julia Kristeva's terminology, is the use of a moving camera in relation to a moving figure, both remaining equidistant and thus in a fixed, static relation to each other, while the process, the excess is displaced onto the background objects (furniture, walls, trees, etc.) moving through the image. The clearest example of this occurs towards the beginning of *Madame de . . .* where she moves through her apartment at a frantic pace but at a fixed distance from the camera accompanying her movements, the furniture and decors providing the movement in the frame, in a way echoing the revolving landscapes in the amusement park in *Letter From An Unknown Woman*.

Each of these registers of text construction inscribes simultaneously a breakthrough of excess, the transgression of a 'rigid and merciless discipline' as Karel Reisz put it, and the strategies to contain and recover, to neutralise through reinscription or repetition what the Law had to expell, to repress in order for it to come into existence. In that sense, Ophuls's cinema can be seen as the dramatisation of repression, where the repressed returns and imprints its mark on the representation, undermining and at times overwhelming that manifestation of secondary elaboration called 'a coherent scenario'.

The Question Oshima

Stephen Heath

Another member of the *Screen* group, Stephen Heath shares Paul Willemen's theoretical grounding, moving still further away from a consideration of Ophuls's film as an expression of the unique sensibility of a single author. Instead, Heath analyzes *Letter from an Unknown Woman* as a representative artifact embodying cultural tensions and contradictions centering on the female body and its relation to a male spectator, a critical approach most influentially articulated by Laura Mulvey, another *Screen* critic, in a 1975 essay entitled "Visual Pleasure and Narrative Cinema." Heath uses Ophuls's film to contrast to Nagisa Oshima's *In the Realm of the Senses* (English release title, *Empire of the Senses*), which he sees as a work that breaks the Hollywood codes of representation followed in *Letter*.

Consider a film such as *Letter from an Unknown Woman* (Max Ophuls, 1948), a film of which from one perspective—that of the question to cinema—*Empire of the Senses* is the direct and ruinous remake. At the centre of *Letter from*, a classic Hollywood narrative film with genre specificities (the 'woman's film') and stylistic markings ('Ophuls' as the name for 'extensive use of music, long elaborate takes with flowing camera movement', etc.), is the full image, sexuality as look, the *looked-for image*. Lisa (Joan Fontaine) models and is *the model*: radiantly dressed and lit, she circles for the gaze of prospective clients at the fashionable dress shop where she earns her living and at the same time for that of the spectator who has paid to *see* the film. Twice, as she does so, men, spectators in the film, respond to the perfection of the flawless—*whole*—body, to the image of a female beauty, of the female *as beauty*, which holds the sexual cinematically as just that: the desired and untouchable image, an endless *vision*. As always, however, the centered image mirrors a structure that is in excess of its effect of containment, that bears the traces of the heterogeneity—the trouble—it is produced to contain: sexuality here is also the 'more' that the look elides, that is elided from the look, and that returns, constantly in the

From *Questions of Cinema* (Bloomington: Indiana University Press, 1981), pp. 145–164.

figures of its absence. After the first modelling scenes, Lisa spends one night
with Stefan (Louis Jourdan), the man she has loved and worshipped in silence
since childhood; as they begin to kiss, the image fades, the screen is left black
with nothing to see. Evidently, this is convention, its context the Hays Code,
the awareness of what can and cannot be shown. But convention is never simply
a fact outside a film: what can and cannot be shown, the determining confines
of image and look, is in *Letter from*, is part of its film action and meaning. The
fade, the image absent, is *Letter from*'s momentary and fundamental figure,
comprising in its elision the time of acknowledgement and consequent guilt
(Lisa is caught up in the more than the image, the one night makes her preg-
nant, detailing her suffering the film details her punishment for transgression)
and of denial and consequent innocence (the unshown leaves Lisa pure, intact
as image, still perfect; she is only ever daughter or sister and then mother to
Stefan, never—the exact function of the fade, the meaning of the convention in
the film—a sexual lover). Immediately afterwards, the film goes back to the
image of Lisa modelling, now for Stefan, and continues with its drama of
vision, the image that Stefan has lost and the images that he remembers as Lisa
remembers in her letter, as we remember through the narrative which orders
our memory of the film, *our* vision.

Centered image, drama of vision, space of the look, towards a coherence of
vision of us: classically, narrative cinema operates on a very powerful apparatus of 'looks' which join, cross through, and relay one another. Thus: 1) the
camera looks (a metaphor assumed by this cinema) . . . at someone, something: the profilmic; 2) the spectator looks . . . at, or on, the film; 3) each
of the characters in the film looks . . . at other characters, things: the intra-
diegetic. This series possesses a certain reversibility: on the one hand, the
camera looks, the spectator looks at what the camera looks at and thereby sees
characters in the film looking; on the other, and equally, the spectator sees
characters in the film looking, which is to look at the film, which is to find the
camera's looking, its 'having looked' (the mode of presence in absence on
which cinema is here founded). The first and second looks, moreover, are in a
perpetual interchange of 'priority', of 'origination': the camera's look is found
only by looking at the film but the former is the condition—one of the condi-
tions—of the latter. The series of looks is then the basis in turn for a pattern
of multiply relaying identifications (a term that would need to be carefully
specified in each case): the turn between the first and second looks sets up the
spectator's identification with the camera (rigorously constructed, with heavy
constraints on, for example, camera movement); the look at the film is involved

in identifying relations of the spectator to the photographic image and its movement, to the human figure presented in image, to the narrative which gives the
sense of the flow of images, acts as guide-line; the looks of the characters allow
for the establishment of the various 'point-of-view' identifications.

The power of such an apparatus is in the play it both proposes and controls:
a certain mobility is given but followed out—relayed—as the possibility of a
constant hold on the spectator, as the bind of a coherence of vision, of, exactly,
a vision. Remembering Bazin's fascination with the shot of Yvonne de Bray in
Cocteau's (and Jean-Pierre Melville's) *Les Enfants terribles* (1950): 'the object
of the shot is not what she is looking at, not even her look; it is *looking at her
looking*'. The apparatus is the machinery for the fiction of such a position,
for the totalizing security of 'looking at looking'—and at 'her'. No surprise,
therefore, that the achievement of that security, the institution of cinema in
film, becomes the actual narrative of so many films, their relentless concern.
Years after her single night of love, Lisa encounters Stefan once more at a performance of *The Magic Flute*: as Papageno sings 'A maiden or a woman' ('if a
feminine mouth will kiss me, I'll soon be well again'), Stefan turns in his seat
trying to seek out Lisa's face, the face of the woman who now—as always—is
gone; an extreme close-up, pulling free in its extremeness from any simple
assignation of a time and place in the diegesis, as much an index of the film's
organizing activity, shows the seeking eyes, with Lisa commenting in her voice-
over letter-narration that 'somewhere out there were your eyes and I knew I
couldn't escape them'; he follows her down into the foyer, 'I've seen you somewhere, I know'; and so it goes on, the entire film a problem of seeing and
knowing, of the image glimpsed and lost and remembered—as of *the* woman,
the mother (Lisa is always in Stefan's past, the time of his—and the film's—
desire), the goddess ('the Greeks built a statue to a god they didn't know but
hoped some day would come to them; mine happens to be a goddess'). . . .

It is not by chance that, after years of the history of the 'theatrical cinema'
Vertov foresaw and loathed, the Brakhage film, like the Oshima, should be
involved directly with death; the 'quasi-obscenity of seeing' is a profound
connection of death and the sexual (the latter equally directly marked in *The
Act of Seeing*, the fragmented male body). That connection is known in classic
cinema but exactly as a violence and dispersion which apparatus and narrative
are there to contain, and to contain on the image: the image, finally, of the
women: 'looking at her looking'. Think again of *Letter from an Unknown
Woman* and its arresting gaze on the illuminated body of Lisa/Joan Fontaine,

the film the theatre of that. The image for such a gaze is the center and determination of the suspended scenario of narrative film, its constantly desired primal scene. With the apparatus securing its ground, the narrative plays, that is, on castration known and denied, a movement of difference and the symbolic, the object lost, and the conversion of that movement into the terms of a fixed memory, an invulnerable imaginary, the object—and with it the mastery, the unity of the subject—regained. Like fetishism, narrative film is the structure of a *memory-spectacle*, the perpetual story of a 'one-time', a discovery perpetually remade with safe fictions.

This is the context of the particular economy of repetition in classic cinema where narrative is in fact the order of a *bearable* repetition. The coherence of any text depends on a sustained equilibrium of new informations, points of advance and anaphoric recalls, ties that make fast, hold together. One part of the particularity of classic cinema is its exploitation of narrative in the interests of an extreme tendency towards coalescence, an economic tightness of totalization; the film is gathered up in a whole series of rhymes in which elements—of both 'form' and 'content'—are found, shifted, and turned back symmetrically, as in a mirror; the most simply obvious instances in *Letter from* include the café scenes (Stefan entering with Lisa to cancel a previous rendezvous/Lisa entering alone to look for Stefan), the train departures (Lisa bidding farewell to Stefan, her one-night lover, for 'two weeks'/Lisa bidding farewell to Stefan, her son from that night, for 'two weeks'), the views from the staircase (as Stefan brings up first one of his many women-friends and then Lisa), and, of course, the carriage scenes which open and close the film, looping it round on itself. . . .

In its films, classic cinema is a certain balance of repetition: a movement of difference and the achievement in that movement of recurring images—for example, the woman as 'the same', a unity constantly refound. Narrativization, the process of the production of the film as narrative, is the operation of the balance, tying up the multiple elements—the whole festival of potential affects, rhythms, intensities, times, differences—into a line of coherence (advance and recall), a finality for the repetition.

The realized narrative, the term of the process, is historically specific, is a mapping of the *novelistic* for the reproduction of which the cinematic institution is developed and exploited; the novelistic, that is, is the category of the specification of narrative in film, as in the novel to which cinema is made to furnish a successor. The title of the novelistic is *Family Romance* (or, a recent avatar, *Family Plot*); the problem it addresses is that of the definition of forms

of individual meaning within the limits of existing social representations and
their determining social relations, the provision and maintenance of fictions of
the individual; the reality it encounters a permanent crisis of identity that must
be permanently resolved by remembering the history of the individual-subject.
Narrative lays out—lays down as law—a memory in film from the novelistic as
the reimaging of the individual as subject, the very representation of identity
as the coherence of a past safely negotiated and reappropriated—the past 'in'
the film (*Letter from an Unknown Woman* with its overall theme of remembering within which a whole family romance can be carried along in fragmentary mnemic traces of a sexual history known and denied by its knowledge
in these representations) and 'of' the film (*Letter from* with its direction, its
rhymes, its constant images, its positioning of view for viewer, its unifying
relations of the subject watching).

Time and Desire in the Woman's Film

Tania Modleski

Much recent work in feminist film criticism has attempted to open up a space within mainstream cinema to allow for more positive analyses of female characters and female spectators. Tania Modleski's essay, first published in *Cinema Journal* in 1984, is a good example of this trend, which builds on recent film and feminist theory to construct a model that emphasizes generic considerations. Modleski's 1981 book, *Loving with a Vengeance: Mass Produced Fantasies for Women*, was a seminal study of this kind, discussing several women's genres in the context of women's lives. Modleski's essay on *Letter from an Unknown Woman* uses similar methods to analyze the woman's film, arguing that movies of this kind, designated for a female rather than a male audience, may demonstrate a psychic economy discernibly different from that of other films.

Max Ophuls's 1948 film, *Letter from an Unknown Woman*, which is set in turn-of-the-century Vienna, begins late at night with the hero of the story, Stefan, returning by coach to his home and promising to fight a duel at dawn. That his attitude toward the situation is utterly frivolous is obvious from his remark as he steps out of the coach: "Gentlemen, I don't so much mind being killed, but you know how I hate to get up in the morning." Reaching his home, he tells his mute servant, John, that they should prepare for immediate departure since he does not intend to fight the duel. At stake here is a man's word. "A man's word is his honor," and, as Adrienne Rich observes, this notion of honor usually has "something to do with killing."[1] The terms of the drama seem already to have been posed with utter clarity. Stefan lives a life of ease, indulgence, and irresponsibility, unwilling to accept the values of duty and sacrifice espoused by his patriarchal society.

From *Cinema Journal* 23, No. 3 (Spring 1984): 19–30.

1. Adrienne Rich, *On Lies, Secrets, and Silence: Selected Prose 1966–1978* (New York: Norton, 1979), p. 186.

We might suspect, then, that the film's movement will involve Stefan's coming to repudiate the former childishness of his ways and to acknowledge the sway of patriarchal law. And indeed the final sequence of the film shows Stefan bravely setting off to keep his word and get himself killed. Thus, though the body of the film concerns the story of Lisa, the woman referred to in the title, it would appear that her story is really a story of and for the man, and, looked at this way, the film seems to provide exceptionally strong support for those critics who contend that there *is* no such thing as a woman's film, that Hollywood films are always dramas of and for the male.

When Stefan enters the house, he is given a letter which begins, "By the time you read this, I may be dead." It is the letter from the unknown woman who has indeed lived her life in and for Stefan, has even had a child by him, and yet has remained silent about her life-long devotion until her words, written in death's shadow, can no longer possibly bring her any benefit. At stake, then, is not only a man's word, but a woman's silence. At one point in the film, Lisa explains her radical refusal to speak about her own and their son's existence; "I wanted to be the one woman you had known who never asked you for anything." As Lisa perceives it, to speak as a woman would mean losing herself and becoming an object like the many other women in Stefan's life. However, when her own impending death releases her from her vow of silence, she only reveals how little of herself there is to know, so thoroughly has she become one with the man. Lisa's is the classic dilemma of what psychoanalysis calls the hysterical woman, caught between two equally alienating alternatives: either identifying with the man or being an object of his desire.

"Silence is the mark of hysteria," writes Hélène Cixous. "The great hysterics have lost speech, they are aphonic, and at times they have lost more than speech. They are pushed to the point of choking, nothing gets through." [2] It seems fair to say that many of the classic film melodramas from the 30s through the 50s are peopled by great, or near-great, hysterics—women possessed by an overwhelming desire to express themselves, to make themselves known, but continually confronting the difficulty, if not the impossibility of realizing this desire. In the various film versions of *Madame X* (another title signalling the woman's anonymity), the heroine's son is defending her from criminal charges, unaware that the woman is his mother. Though she longs to reveal herself to her son, she

2. Hélène Cixous, "Castration or Decapitation?" trans. Annette Kuhn, *Signs: Journal of Women in Culture and Society* 7, no. 1 (Autumn 1981):49.

refuses to speak, for fear of ruining his status and career. In *The Old Maid*, Bette Davis's character, who has had a child out of wedlock, masquerades as the old maid aunt to her own daughter so that the daughter may marry a suitable—rich, upper-class—man. And Stella Dallas, on becoming aware of her hopelessly lower-class life style, pretends to be interested in having a sexual affair in order to provoke her daughter to leave her. The central truth about Stella's feelings— that she loves her daughter to the exclusion of all else—remains unexpressed to the end.

In a short but illuminating article on film melodrama, Geoffrey Nowell-Smith has theorized a close connection between melodrama and conversion hysteria. He claims that castration is always at issue in Hollywood melodrama because "melodrama is fundamentally concerned with the child's problems of growing up into a sexual identity within the family, under the aegis of a symbolic law which the Father incarnates."[3] Now this applies to all the aforementioned films, and perhaps most obviously to *Letter from an Unknown Woman*, in which the duel may be understood as the castration Stefan finally comes to accept. But, Nowell-Smith argues, acceptance of castration never occurs without repression, and in melodrama, what is repressed at the level of the *story* often returns through the music or the mise-en-scène. Hence melodrama's resemblance to conversion hysteria, in which "the energy attached to an idea that has been repressed returns converted into a bodily symptom."[4] Although Nowell-Smith's argument is persuasive, he never notes that traditionally medical science and psychoanalysis have labelled *women* hysterics.[5] Yet surely we find here a clue as to why for a large period of film history melodrama and the "woman's film" have been virtually synonymous terms. If women are hysterics in patriarchal culture because, according to the feminist argument, their voice has been silenced or repressed, and if melodrama deals with the return of the repressed through a kind of conversion hysteria, perhaps women have been attached to the genre because it provides an outlet for the repressed feminine voice.

Peter Brooks argues in his book on nineteenth-century stage melodrama that melodrama may even be *defined* as a genre which works to overcome all repression in order to achieve full expressivity. In the nineteenth century, it was the

3. Geoffrey Nowell-Smith, "Minnelli and Melodrama," *Screen* 18 (Summer 1977):116.
4. Ibid., p. 117.
5. A point made in passing by Griselda Pollock in her "Report on the Weekend School," which appears in the same issue of *Screen*, p. 109.

beauty of moral virtue that continually sought expression over whatever attempted to silence, bury, or negate it. Often this beauty would be conveyed in *visual* terms, in the form, say, of a tableau. Nevertheless, melodrama is *not* primarily about the problems of sight and insight–the problems, that is, of tragedy. Brooks makes this point nicely in his discussion of the special place of the mute in many melodramatic plays:

> One is tempted to speculate that the different kinds of drama have their corresponding sense deprivations: for tragedy, blindness, since tragedy is about insight and illumination; for comedy, deafness, since comedy is concerned with problems in communication, misunderstandings and their consequences; and for melodrama, muteness, since melodrama is about expression.[6]

One need only point to the importance of the mute servant John in *Letter from an Unknown Woman* to demonstrate the force of Brooks's remarks. John is melodrama's equivalent to the figure of blind Tiresias in tragedy. He is, finally, the only character who is able to recognize Lisa and to name her, filling in the signature she herself has not been able to complete at the end of her letter.

It is this essentially melodramatic preoccupation with expression and muteness that Stephen Heath misses when he characterizes the entire problem of *Letter from an Unknown Woman* and of narrative cinema in general as one of "*seeing* and *knowing.*"[7] In effect, Heath is collapsing all genres into one quintessentially masculine genre: tragedy, the paradigmatic example of which is *Oedipus*, with its privileging of sight and insight. For Heath, the project of the film is to present the woman "as a desired and untouchable image, an endless vision."[8] And indeed a crucial moment of the drama occurs when Stefan, on his way to fight the duel, glances back over his shoulder and sees Lisa standing behind the glass door where he first saw her years ago. The image of the woman, forever silenced, is presented as the lost object whom Stefan may mourn and incorporate, thereby successfully taking up castration. He can now assume his place in patriarchal culture, and Lisa's image disappears from the screen.

But though Heath deplores the repression of the woman effected by turning her

6. Peter Brooks, *The Melodramatic Imagination: Balzac, Henry James, Melodrama, and the Mode of Excess* (New Haven: Yale Univ. Press, 1976), pp. 56–57.
7. Stephen Heath, "The Question Oshima," in *Questions of Cinema* (Bloomington: Indiana University Press, 1981), p. 148.
8. Ibid., p. 146.

into a sight whose only meaning is the insight it offers the man into his life, he himself may be said to maintain this repression. As Brooks points out, melodrama cannot be fully grasped by analyzing it solely in terms of seeing and knowing. To continue relying on these terms is to obliterate what may be seeking expression through the women in the films; and it is also to contribute to the hystericization of the female *spectator*, who is offered the limited choice between identifying with the man in his active desire or identifying with the passive, apparently mute object of that desire.

But how are we to begin attempting to locate a feminine voice in texts which repress it and which, as we saw in *Letter from an Unknown Woman*, grant possession of the Word only to men? Nowell-Smith, we have seen, suggests that the repressed aspects of the script reside in the mise-en-scène. Thomas Elsaesser, in an essay on film melodrama and its historical antecedents, argues that melodrama may best be understood in terms of "spatial and musical categories" rather than "intellectual or literary ones."[9] Melodrama is, after all, a hybrid form which traditionally combines music and drama. In a brief discussion of the use of fairgrounds and carousels in film melodrama, Elsaesser claims that these motifs "underscore the main action" and at the same time take on an independent significance. "What such devices point to," Elsaesser concludes, "is that in melodrama the *rhythm* of experience often establishes itself against its value (moral, intellectual)."[10] As wide-ranging as Elsaesser's essay is, tracing the development of melodrama cross-culturally through many centuries, he does not address himself to women's particular attraction to the genre. However, it is possible to appropriate his insight for our purposes, and so we will begin by looking at melodrama's rhythm for meanings which are opposed to the male Word.

In *Letter from an Unknown Woman*, Lisa and Stefan enjoy one night together, and this episode occurs in the middle of the film. They dine, dance, ride in a coach, and visit an amusement park where they sit in a stationary train while on a painted backdrop the scenery of the world revolves around them. Carousel music plays as they discuss the pleasures of travel. When they run out of countries to visit, Stefan pays the attendant to begin again, saying, "We will revisit the scenes of our youth." For Lisa these words are prophetic: after losing Stefan for many years and finding him again, she revisits the scenes of their youth in her quest to

9. Thomas Elsaesser, "Tales of Sound and Fury: Observations on the Family Melodrama," *Monogram* 4 (1973):6.
10. Ibid., p. 3.

be reunited with him—returning to the place where they had dinner, buying flowers from a vendor as they had years ago, and going back to his apartments where they once made love. Most painful of all, she revisits the train station where Stefan departed from her so many years before, and this time sends her son away from her—to his death, as it turns out. This excessive repetition characterizes many film melodramas, and perhaps reaches its apotheosis in the 1932 film *Back Street*. At the end of this film the heroine, about to die, revisits in fantasy the scene of her youth when she missed meeting her lover and his mother in the park. As a result of this lost opportunity, she was not able to marry the hero and instead became his mistress, forced to reside in the back street of his life. Her final thoughts materialize on the screen as she pictures herself walking in the dazzling sunlight of the park towards the mother and son who welcome her into their family.

Unlike most Hollywood narratives, which give the impression of a progressive movement toward an end that is significantly different from the beginning, much melodrama gives the impression of a ceaseless returning to a prior state. Perhaps the effect may be compared to sitting in a train watching the world move by, and each time you reach a destination, you discover that it is the place you never really left. In this respect melodrama appears to be quite closely linked to an hysterical experience of time and place. The hysteric, in Freud's famous formulation, suffers from reminiscences. In melodrama, the important moments of the narrative are often felt as eruptions of involuntary memory, to the point where sometimes the *only* major events are repetitions of former ones. In *The Old Maid*, for example, four weddings occurring among two generations comprise the large units of the film, huge gaps in time separating some of these units. Melodrama, then, tends to be concerned with what Julia Kristeva calls the "anterior temporal modalities," these modalities being stereotypically linked with female subjectivity in general (with the "cycles, gestation, the eternal recurrence of a biological rhythm which conforms to that of nature")[11] As Kristeva notes, this conception of time is indissociable from space and is opposed to the idea of time most commonly recognized in Western thought: "time as project, teleology, linear and prospective, unfolding; time as departure, progression, and arrival—in other words, the time of history."[12] The train which first carries Stefan away from Lisa and then takes her son to his death is a train that departs, progresses,

11. Julia Kristeva, "Women's Time," trans. Alice Jardine and Harry Blake, *Signs: Journal of Women in Culture and Society* 7, no. 1 (Autumn 1981): 16.
12. Ibid., p. 17.

and arrives, whereas the train on which Lisa prefers to travel is one which, like the woman, always stays in its place. And as the world turns, visiting inevitably becomes a revisiting.

Two conceptions of time here seem unalterably opposed: the time of repetition, which for Lisa means never entering history, but forever remaining child-like, fixated on the scenes of her youth. And the time of history which Stefan definitively enters at the end of the film when he takes his journey by coach to meet Lisa's husband and his own death. For Stefan this means, as we have already observed, that he must put away childish things and repudiate the self-indulgent life he has been leading in order to become a responsible adult. It is no mere coincidence that Stefan's entry into historical time and adulthood occurs simultaneously with his coming to accept the binding power of the word and the sway of death. For to quote Kristeva, this "linear time is that of language considered as the enunciation of sentences . . . and . . . this time rests on its own stumbling block, which is also the stumbling block of that enunciation—death." [13] And with the entry into historical time and language occurs the birth of desire: Stefan looks back at Lisa with recognition and longing only when the possibility of possessing her is forever lost. In accepting his place in language and history, he must assume a certain relation to desire: one based on an expectation destined to remain eternally unfulfilled.

But I have been a bit disingenuous in considering the antinomy between "hysterical time" and what Kristeva calls "obsessional time" to be based on sexual difference. Superficially it appears that in the film woman's time is hysterical time and man's time is obsessional time. Closer analysis, however, reveals that Stefan is the hysteric until the last few moments of the film, whereas Lisa adopts an altogether different relationship to time and desire which points beyond this deadly antinomy. For Stefan is the one who truly suffers from reminiscences. He cannot remember the name or the face of the woman who is the mother of his child and who is also, as the film implies, his muse. In a way, he has had a family, a career, and an entire life and never known it: the woman has lived it for him. When he sees Lisa, he struggles to overcome his forgetting and, in anguish, speaks of something which lies just over the edge of his memory. Unable to remember the woman who alone gives his life significance, Stefan is doomed to an existence of meaningless repetition, especially in relation to women, who become virtually indistinguishable to him. Moreover, it might plausibly be argued that insofar as Lisa is forced to keep repeating events, she is to a certain

13. Ibid., p. 17.

extent enacting *his* compulsion, for she herself has not forgotten a single moment with him.

That men may be hysterics too is an important point for feminism. Perhaps we have too quickly and unreservedly accepted theories of feminine hysteria. For if it can be said, as Lisa herself does say, that she has had no life apart from the moments with Stefan and his son, it is equally true that Stefan has had no life except the one Lisa has lived on his behalf. She has undergone all the joys and sorrow attendant on loving, possessing and losing a family while he, the father of that family, has remained oblivious. The woman and her emotional life is what Stefan has repressed and, like John Marcher in Henry James's "The Beast in the Jungle," he is doomed to keep suffering his fate without ever having known it.

Intuitively, of course, we ally melodrama with the feminine insofar as it is a genre quintessentially concerned with emotional expression. Women in melodrama almost always suffer the pains of love and even death (as in *Dark Victory*) while husbands, lovers, and children remain partly or totally unaware of their experience. Women carry the burden of feeling for everyone. *Letter from an Unknown Woman* simply takes this situation to its furthest extreme and shows that though women are hysterics with respect to male desire, men may be hysterics with respect to feminine "emotion"; unable to experience it directly, they gain access to it only at second hand.

Lisa's letter might be said to perform the "talking cure" for Stefan. If women are traditionally considered hysterics because, in Catherine Clément's concise formulation, they feel in the body what comes from outside the body, we can again see how Stefan is placed in the position of hysteric, as throughout the long night it takes to read the letter the disembodied feminine voice is repeatedly shown to be speaking through the mute Stefan.[14] And just as Freud said that the hysteric is a visual type of person whose cure consists in making a " 'picture' vanish 'like a ghost that has been laid to rest,' . . . getting rid of it by turning it into words," so too is Stefan cured when after reading Lisa's letter, he looks back at her image behind the glass door, and looks back again to find that the picture has vanished.[15] The ghost of femininity—that spectre that haunts cinema—has been laid to rest.

Stefan's trajectory represents an interesting variant on that which Laura

14. Catherine Clément, "Enslaved Enclave," in *New French Feminisms*, ed. Elaine Marks and Isabelle de Courtivron (Amherst: University of Massachusetts Press, 1980), p. 134.
15. Quoted in Joan Copjec, "*Flavit et Dissipati Sunt.*" *October*, 18 (Fall 1981):21.

Mulvey claims is typical of one strain of melodrama. In her "Afterthoughts on 'Visual Pleasure and Narrative Cinema,'" she suggests that there is a kind of film in which "a woman central protagonist is shown to be unable to achieve a stable sexual identity, torn between the deep blue sea of passive femininity and the devil of regressive masculinity." [16] Mulvey points to Freud's theories of femininity, according to which the young girl first goes through an active masculine phase before attaining the "correct" feminine position. In *Letter from an Unknown Woman*, it is the man who first goes through a feminine phase before reaching the active, phallic phase and thus achieving a stable sexual identity. It is possible that Stefan's experience is analogous to that undergone by the male spectator of melodrama. For it may be that insofar as films like this are appealing to men (and there is plenty of evidence to suggest that *Letter from an Unknown Woman* strongly appeals to male critics), it is because these films provide them with a vicarious, hysterical, experience of femininity which can be more definitively laid to rest for having been "worked through."

And it may be that one of the appeals of such a film for women is precisely its tendency to feminize the man, to complicate and destabilize his identity. There is a moment in *Letter from an Unknown Woman* when confusion in sexual identity reigns supreme—the moment when after years of separation Lisa sees Stefan again at the opera. Briefly we see a close-up of Stefan through a soft focus filter, the device typically used in filming beautiful women. The image appears against a gray background which renders its diegetic status uncertain. The cutting from Lisa to Stefan further enhances this uncertainty, as it is unclear how each is placed in relation to the other and who is looking at whom. Finally, ambiguity reaches almost vertiginous extremes when over the image of Stefan, which is strongly coded to connote what Mulvey calls "to-be-looked-at-ness," Lisa's voice says in some panic, "Somewhere out there were your eyes and I knew I couldn't escape them." [17] Nowell-Smith argues that often the "'hysterical' moment of a text [that is, the moment when the repressed element returns to find expression in a bodily symptom] can be identified as the point at which the realist representative convention breaks down." [18] Here we find a classic example of an hysterical

16. Laura Mulvey, "Afterthoughts on 'Visual Pleasure and Narrative Cinema' Inspired by 'Duel in the Sun,'" *Framework*, nos. 15/16/17 (1981): 12.
17. Laura Mulvey, "Visual Pleasure and Narrative Cinema," in *Women and the Cinema* ed. Karyn Kay and Gerald Peary (New York: Dutton, 1977), p. 418.
18. Nowell-Smith, "Minnelli and Melodrama," p. 117.

moment in which the possibility of feminine desire being actively aimed at the passive, eroticized male is briefly glimpsed while being explicitly denied at the verbal level. Interestingly, in Heath's discussion of this scene, he for once listens only to the words, which articulate woman's traditional position as object of the look, and completely misses the subversive element of feminine desire which is struggling for expression in the body of the text.[19]

Partly because the erotic is conventionally equated with the feminine, it is paradoxically not the virile, masculinized male, the so-called "man's man," who elicits woman's desire in many of these films, but the feminine man: the attractive, cosmopolitan type (John Boles in *Stella Dallas*, *Only Yesterday*, and the first version of *Back Street*) or the well-bred, charming foreigner (Charles Boyer in the second version of *Back Street*; Louis Jourdan in *Letter from an Unknown Woman*). Moreover, the man with "feminine" attributes frequently functions as a figure upon whom feminine desires for freedom from patriarchal authority may be projected. Here I disagree with Mulvey who claims that in classic women's films like *Stella Dallas* the masculine figure enables the heroine to postpone the power of patriarchy.[20] *Stella Dallas*, in fact, provides a clear example to the contrary.

At the beginning of the film, Stephen Dallas, played by John Boles, is the son of a failed patriarch. His father, having gone bankrupt, has committed suicide, and Stephen has retreated from the world to take a management position in a rural factory. He is frequently figured as the rather lovely though unwitting object of Stella's desirous gaze as she watches him from behind her white picket fence or stares at his photograph in a newspaper clipping. He seems to be in all ways the antithesis of Stella's harsh and repressive father, and on him Stella pins her hope of escape from this patriarch. In a stunning sequence which ends the opening section of the film, Stella's father discovers that Stella has not been home all night. He sits with his back to the camera in the foreground of the picture and bangs his fist on the table shouting that Stella must never come home again. The mother cowers in the background and Stella's brother stands arguing with his father in the middle ground. This is a scene straight out of a nineteenth-century melodrama in which the stern patriarch prepares to exile his fallen daughter into the cold, cruel world. The sound of Stella's voice interrupts the argument, and the brother opens the door to Stella and Stephen who are coming up the porch stairs announcing their marriage. As the son runs back into the house, the screen door

---

19. Heath, *Questions of Cinema*, p. 148.
20. Mulvey, "Afterthoughts," p. 15.

bangs shut on the couple, still outside, and the image fades. Patriarchy and its cruelties and excesses seem to be abruptly left behind, and the next scene shows Stella, now living in the city, returning from the hospital with her new-born daughter. However, the power of patriarchy has merely been postponed, since Stephen proves to be more domineering than Stella can bear. So she relinquishes her desire for men altogether and transfers it exclusively to her daughter.

The feminized man is attractive, then, because of the freedom he seems to offer the woman: freedom to get in touch with and to act upon her own desire and freedom to reject patriarchal power. The latter point is made forcefully in *Letter from an Unknown Woman*, whose family romance involves two sets of fathers: the true fathers and the false fathers.[21] The false fathers—representative of patriarchal values and attitudes—are, firstly, Lisa's stepfather, a man attached to the military who takes Lisa away from Vienna and attempts to marry her off to a stiff, boring young lieutenant; and, secondly, the stepfather of Lisa's son, a military man always prating about duty, sacrifice, and responsibility. This is the man with whom Stefan is destined to fight the duel. Stefan, the father of Lisa's child, is one of the true fathers. Although he is a womanizer, this activity paradoxically womanizes *him*, for it immerses him in a sensuous existence stereotypically associated with the feminine and running counter to the life of self-denial espoused by Lisa's husband. And then there is Lisa's real father, who, though dead, is very much alive in Lisa's imagination. On the train in the amusement park Lisa tells Stefan of all the make-believe journeys she and her father took when she was a little girl, vividly evoking the pleasures and pains encountered in various climates. Lisa's father strikingly resembles the pre-oedipal, imaginary father Julia Kristeva has theorized.[22] He is the spokesman for creativity and play and as such he represents a potential escape from the two neurotic modes of existence in which Stefan is successively trapped: the hysterical and the obsessional. If Stefan, who could be a great pianist, were to heed the message given him by Lisa through the imaginary father, he would no longer be forced to choose between a sensuous but meaningless and repetitive existence and a life given over to duty and sacrifice.

The "pre-oedipal" father is, I would argue, another manifestation of the femi-

21. Nowell-Smith discusses the way melodrama "enacts, often with uncanny literalness, the 'family romance' described by Freud—that is to say the imaginary scenario played out by children in relation to their paternity, the asking and answering of the question: whose child am I (or would I like to be)?" See p. 116.
22. Julia Kristeva, "Woes of Love," lecture given at the Center for Twentieth Century Studies, University of Wisconsin-Milwaukee, Milwaukee, Wisconsin, November 2, 1982.

nized male who helps the woman reject the repressive father by authorizing her own desire. For while Lisa appears here to be doubly an hysteric, invoking the words and activities of one man for the benefit of another, she is actually articulating a relation to the world that in the film is uniquely her own. On the train and elsewhere Lisa demonstrates an allegiance to the imagination which she considers superior to lived experience.[23] Clearly this applies to her entire existence, since she has had only one brief interlude with Stefan in a lifetime of desiring him. Like the voyages she took with her father, her journey with Stefan has gone nowhere, has been an adventure mainly of consciousness.

But that it has *been* conscious makes all the difference. We have seen that *Letter from an Unknown Woman* enacts a process of mourning for the man. Stefan has forgotten everything he has had and never realized what he could have had, and therefore in reading the letter he must work through the pain of loss and nonfulfillment in order to "lay the ghost to rest." Lisa, however, has remained fully aware of what was and what might have been; and having buried nothing she has no need to mourn. Hélène Cixous finds in the question of mourning a difference between men and women. I would like to quote her at length because her words open up the possibility of a new way of thinking about women's experience in melodrama and women's response *to* melodrama:

> Man cannot live without resigning himself to loss. He has to mourn. It's his way of withstanding castration. He goes through castration, that is, and by sublimation incorporates the lost object. Mourning, a resigning oneself to loss, means not losing. When you've lost something and the loss is a dangerous one, you refuse to admit that something of yourself might be lost in the lost object. So you "mourn," you make haste to recover the investment made in the lost object. But I believe women *do not mourn*, and this is where the pain lies. When you've mourned it's all over after a year, there's no more suffering. Woman, though, does not mourn, does not resign herself to loss. She basically *takes up the challenge of loss . . .* , seizing it, living it. Leaping. This goes with not withholding; she does not withhold. She does not withhold, hence the impression of constant return evoked by this lack of withholding. It's like a kind of open memory that ceaselessly makes way.

23. For example, on the way to the amusement park, Stefan remarks that he only visits it in the winter, never in the spring when it is so much more beautiful. Lisa replies that perhaps he prefers to imagine its beauties rather than to experience them.

And in the end, she will write this not withholding, this not writing: she writes of not writing, not happening.[24]

On the train which goes nowhere, Lisa describes journeys which did not happen, and the exquisite enjoyment they occasioned. In doing so, she articulates one of the basic pleasures of melodrama, which is also fundamentally about events that do not happen: the wedding that did not occur; the meeting in the park that was missed; and, above all, the word that was not spoken. Not speaking is very different from *keeping* one's word—the very phrase suggests the withholding and the resistance to loss which Cixous attributes to masculinity. Lisa resists speech not out of a need to hoard the word and not only because she wants to be different from Stefan's other women. Rather, she refuses to hold on to a man who has forgotten her, and what's more important, refuses to *hold him to* an obligation. Not seeing the relationship in terms of an investment or debt—that is, in terms of the property relations which, according to Cixous, structure masculine sexuality—she will not make him pay. So she takes up the challenge of loss and lives it. And from one point of view this challenge is more radical than the one Stefan takes up at the end of the film, resigning himself to his loss and the fate which consequently awaits him.

Cixous's words invite us to look deeper into the experience of loss which is at the heart of melodrama. After all, what lingers on in our memories long after the films have ended are just those moments when the heroine relinquishes all that has mattered in her life: Lisa saying goodbye to her son at the train station, where he promises, like his father before him, to see her in two weeks; Stella Dallas standing behind an iron fence watching her daughter's wedding through the window; Bette Davis's heroine in *Dark Victory* waiting in a darkened room for death to overtake her, having cheerfully sent her husband off to a medical convention. Cixous, in a rather poetic manner, suggests that in order to understand woman's experience of loss, we must go beyond the traditional psychoanalytic model based on the male's castration anxiety and his relation to the lost object. Nor do we gain in understanding by relegating woman to the position of hysteric, where film critics and theorists have been eager to place her. For though I began this paper by indicating that Lisa, the archetypal melodramatic heroine, seems to fit neatly into the psychoanalytic category of hysteric, I would now like to point to

24. Cixous, "Castration or Decapitation?," p. 54.

the inadequacy of this model for understanding the position of woman in the woman's film.

The experience Lisa attempts to articulate on the train to nowhere is neither obsessional nor hysterical. It is not obsessional, for it does not entail moving forward through time and space towards an ever-receding goal until one reaches the stumbling block of death. She shows that one can *be moved* without moving. And it is only superficially the experience of an hysteric. According to Freud, the hysteric, who suffers from reminiscences, is "linked to place." [25] Now, this would seem accurately to characterize Lisa as she sits in a train that stays in place and reminisces about past journeys with her father. But the point is that Lisa does not *suffer* from reminiscences, as Stefan does. She voluntarily and even joyfully evokes them, here as elsewhere ceaselessly gives way to them, demonstrating the possession of the "open memory" Cixous describes. Hence the impression of constant return, which in her case has nothing compulsive about it. In his discussion of the film, Stephen Heath remarks, "Repetition is the return to the same in order to abolish the difficult time of desire, and the resurgence in that very moment of inescapable difference." [26] This is only partly true: it is true of Stefan, who, because he does not recognize the object of his desire, makes his experience with Lisa a mere repetition of those he has had with other women. For Lisa, however, and perhaps for all the women in melodrama constantly revisiting the scenes of their youth, repetition and return are manifestations of *another* relationship to time and space, desire and memory, and it is of this difference that the text speaks to me. [27]

25. Quoted in Kristeva, "Women's Time," p. 15.
26. Heath, *Questions of Cinema*, p. 156.
27. I would like to thank Kathleen Woodward and the Center for Twentieth Century Studies for generously providing me with a fellowship which enabled me to research and write this essay.

Filmography and Bibliography

Ophuls Filmography, 1930–1955

The following filmography, based on those previously published in Richard Roud's *Max Ophuls: An Introduction*, Andrew Sarris's introduction to the director's work in *Film Comment*, and Paul Willemen's *Ophuls*, represents all of the known projects Ophuls was involved in as a director that advanced as far as the shooting stage. Because of the often confusing and contradictory nomenclature in the various sources involving terms such as "script," "scenario," "story," "adaptation," "dialogue," and the like, we have here listed under the heading "Script" all writers who have been credited with having contributed to a given screenplay in any way.

1930 *Dann schon lieber Lebertran* (*I'd Rather Take Cod Liver Oil*). Germany.
Script: Emeric Pressburger, Erich Kästner, and Max Ophuls. Based on the story by Erich Kästner.

1931 *Die verliebte Firma* (*The Company is in Love*). Germany.
Script: Hubert Marischka, Ernst Marischka, Fritz Zeckendorf, Bruno Granschtädten, and Max Ophuls.

1932 *Die verkaufte Braut* (*The Bartered Bride*). Germany.
Script: Max Ophuls, Curt Alexander, and Jaroslav Kvapil. Based on the comic opera *Prodana nevesta* by Freidrich Smetana.

1932 *Die lachende Erben* (*The Happy Heirs*). Germany.
Script: Trude Herka, Felix Joachimson, and Max Ophuls. Based on the story by Trude Herka.

1932 *Liebelei*. Germany.
Script: Curt Alexander, Hans
Wilhelm and Max Ophuls. Based
on the play by Arthur Schnitzler.

1933 *Une Histoire d'amour*
(French version of *Liebelei*).
Germany.
Dialogue: André Doderet.

1934 *On a volé un homme*
(*A Man Has Been Stolen*).
France.
Script: René Pujol and Hans Wilhelm.

1934 *La Signora di Tutti*
(*Everybody's Lady*). Italy.
Script: Curt Alexander, Hans
Wilhelm, and Max Ophuls. Based
on the novel by Salvator Gotta.

1935 *Divine*. France.
Script: Colette, Jean-Georges Auriol,
and Max Ophuls. Based on the book
L'Envers du music hall by Colette.
Adapted by J. G. Auriol and Max
Ophuls.

1936 *Valse brillante de Chopin*.
France. (Six minute short.)

1936 *Ave Maria de Schubert*
France (Five minute short.)

1936 *La Tendre ennemie*
(*The Tender Enemy*). France.
Script: André-Paul Antoine, Curt
Alexander, and Max Ophuls. Based
on the play *L'Ennemie* by André-Paul
Antoine.

1936 *Komödie am Geld*.
(*The Trouble with Money*).
Germany.
Script: Max Ophuls, Walter Schlee,
and Alex de Haas.

1937 *Yoshiwara*. France.
Script: Maurice Dekobra, Arnold
Lipp (Lippschultz), Wolfgang
Wilhelm, Jacques Companeez, and
Max Ophuls. Based on the novel
by Maurice Dekobra.

1938 *Werther*. France.
Script: Hans Wilhelm, Fernand
Crommelynck, and Max Ophuls.
Based on Goethe's novel *The Sorrows
of Young Werther*.

1939 *Sans lendemain*
(*With No Tomorrow*). France.
Script: Jean Villème (Hans Wilhelm),
Jean Jacot (Hans Jacobi), André-Paul
Antoine, and Max Ophuls.

1940 *De Mayerling à Sarajevo*.
France.
Script: Curt Alexander, Max Ophuls,
Marcelle Maurette, Jacques Natanson,
Carl Zuckmayer, and André-Paul
Antoine.

1940 *L'Ecole des femmes*.
(*School for Wives*). Switzerland.
Unfinished.

1946 *Vendetta*. USA.
(Ophuls replaced by Preston Sturges,
Stuart Heisler, and Mel Ferrer.)

Script: W. R. Burnett. Based on the novel *Columba* by Prosper Mérimée.

1947 *The Exile*. USA.
Script: Douglas Fairbanks, Jr. Based on the novel *His Majesty the King* by Cosmo Hamilton.

1948 *Letter from an Unknown Woman*. USA.
Script: Howard Koch. Based on the novella by Stefan Zweig.

1949 *Caught*. USA.
Script: Arthur Laurents. Based on the novel *Wild Calendar* by Libby Block.

1949 *The Reckless Moment*. USA.
Script: Henry Garson, R. W. Soderberg, Mel Direlli, and Robert E. Kent. Based on the story "The Blank Wall" by Elizabeth Sanaxay Holding.

1950 *La Ronde*. France.
Script: Jacques Natanson and Max Ophuls. Base on the play *Reigen* by Arthur Schnitzler.

1952 *Le Plaisir*. France.
Script: Jacques Natanson and Max Ophuls. Based on the stories "La Masque," "La Maison Tellier," and "Le Modèle" by Guy de Maupassant.

1953 *Madame de . . .*
(a.k.a. *The Earrings of Madame de . . .*).
France/Italy.
Script: Marcel Achard, Annette Wademant, and Max Ophuls. Based on the novel by Louise de Vilmorin.

1955 *Lola Montès*.
France/Germany.
Script: Jacques Natanson, Annette Wademant, Franz Geiger, and Max Ophuls. Based on the novel *La Vie extraordinaire de Lola Montès* by Cécil Saint-Laurent.

Selected Bibliography

All English language sources that deal substantively with *Letter from an Unknown Woman* are included here, along with the most important foreign language material.

Affron, Charles. *Cinema and Sentiment*. Chicago: The University of Chicago Press, 1982, pp. 46–47, 97–103.

Annenkov, Georges. *Max Ophuls*. Paris: Le Terrain Vague, 1962.

Archer, Eugene. "Max Ophuls and the Romantic Tradition." *Yale French Studies* 17 (1956):3–5.

Bacher, Lutz. "Max Ophuls's Universal International Films: The Impact of Production Circumstances on a Visual Style." Unpublished dissertation. Wayne State University, 1984.

Beylie, Claude. *Max Ophuls*. Paris: Editions Seguers, 1963.

Camper, Fred. "Distance and Style: The Visual Rhetoric of Max Ophuls: *Letter from an Unknown Woman*," *Monogram*, no. 5 (1974):21–24.

Corliss, Richard. "Howard Koch." In *Talking Pictures: Screenwriters in the American Cinema 1927–73*. Woodstock, New York: Overlook Press, 1974, pp. 102–122.

Greenspun, Roger. "Corrections: Roger Greenspun on *Letter from an Unknown Woman*." *Film Comment* 11, no. 1 (January-February 1975):89–92.

Haskell, Molly. "The Woman's Film." In *From Reverence to Rape: The Treatment of Women in the Movies*. New York: Penguin, 1974, pp. 153–188.

Heath, Stephen. "The Question Oshima." *Wide Angle* 2, no. 1 (1978):48–57. Reprinted in *Ques-*

tions of Cinema. Bloomington: Indiana University Press, 1981, pp. 145–164.

Harcourt-Smith, Simon. "A Strange Suppression." *Sight and Sound* 19 no. 1 (March 1950): 34–36.

Henderson, Brian. "The Long Take." *Film Comment* 7, no. 2 (Summer 1971): 6–11. Reprinted in *A Critique of Film Theory.* New York: Dutton, 1980, pp. 48–61; and in *Movies and Methods.* Ed. Bill Nichols. Berkeley, Los Angeles, and London: University of California Press, 1976, pp. 314–324.

Houseman, John. *Front and Center.* New York: Simon and Schuster, 1979.

Hughes, William. "Howard Koch." In *Dictionary of Literary Biography, Volume 26: American Screenwriters.* Ed. Robert E. Morsberger, Stephen O. Lesser, and Randall Clark. Detroit: Gale Research Company, 1984, pp. 178–185.

Kerbal, Michael. *"Letter from an Unknown Woman." Film Comment* 7, no. 2 (Summer 1971): 60–61.

Koch, Howard. "From Script to Screen with Max Ophuls." *Film Comment* 6, no. 4 (Winter 1970–1971): 40–43. Reprinted in *Hollywood Screenwriters.* Ed. Richard Corliss. New York: Avon, 1970, pp. 125–132.

Mancini, Michéle. *Max Ophuls* 55–56. Il Costoro Cinema. Firenze: La Nuova Italia, 1978, pp. 79–85.

Masson, Alain. "Le gravité du frivole." *Positif*, nos. 232–233 (July-August 1980): 39–51.

McVay, Douglas. *"Letter from an Unknown Woman." Focus on Film* 35 (April 1980): 20–30.

Modleski, Tania. "Time and Desire in the Woman's Film." *Cinema Journal* 23, no. 3 (Spring 1984): 19–30.

Perkins, V. F. *"Letter from an Unknown Woman." Movie*, nos. 29–30 (Summer 1982): 61–72.

Pipolo, Tony. "The Aptness of Terminology: Point of View, Consciousness and *Letter from an Unknown Woman." Film Reader* 4 (1979): 166–179.

Reisz, Karel. "Ophuls and *La Ronde." Sequence* (January 1952): 33–35.

Rivette, Jacques, and François Truffaut. "Entretien avec Max Ophuls." *Cahiers du Cinéma*, no. 72 (June 1957): 7–25.

Roud, Richard. *Max Ophuls: An Index.* London: British Film Institute, 1958.

Sarris, Andrew. "Max Ophuls." *The American Cinema.* New York: Dutton, 1968, pp. 70–72.

Sarris, Andrew. "Max Ophuls." *Moviegoer*, no. 3 (1966). Reprinted in *Interviews with Film Directors.* New York: Bobbs-Merrill, 1969, pp. 350–356.

Sarris, Andrew. "Max Ophuls: An Introduction." *Film Comment* 7, no. 2 (Summer 1971): 57–59.

Silverman, Kaja. "Dis-Embodying the Female Voice." In *Re-Vision: Essays in Feminist Film Criticism.* Ed. Mary Ann Doane, Patricia Mellencamp, and Linda Williams. Los Angeles: The American Film Institute and University Publications of America, 1984, pp. 131–149.

Walker, Michael. "Ophuls in Hollywood." *Movie*, nos. 29–30 (Summer 1982):39–48.

Williams, Alan Larson. *Max Ophuls and the Cinema of Desire: Style and Spectacle in Four Films, 1948–55.* New York: Arno Press, 1980.

Williams, Forrest. "The Mastery of Movement: An Appreciation of Max Ophuls." *Film Comment* 5, no. 4 (Winter 1969):71–74.

Willemen, Paul, ed. *Ophuls.* London: British Film Institute, 1978.

Wilson, George. "Max Ophuls' *Letter from an Unknown Woman.*" *MLN* 98, no. 5 (December 1983):1121–1193.

Wood, Robin. "Ewig hin der Liebe Glück," *Personal Views.* London: Gordon Fraser, 1976, pp. 116–132.

Zweig, Stefan. "Letter from an Unknown Woman." Trans. Jill Sutcliffe. *The Royal Game and Other Stories.* New York: Harmony Books, 1981, pp. 216–250.